NEW TOUCHSTONES First

Michael & Peter Benton

Hodder & Stoughton
A MEMBER OF THE HODDER HEADLINE GROUP

Orders: please contact Bookpoint Ltd, 130 Milton Park, Abingdon, Oxon OX14 4SB. Telephone: (44) 01235 827720, Fax: (44) 01235 400454. Lines are open from 9.00–6.00, Monday to Saturday, with a 24 hour message answering service.

British Library Cataloguing in Publication Data
A catalogue record for this title is available from The British Library

ISBN 0 340 77147 X
First published 2000
Impression number   10 9 8 7 6 5 4 3 2
Year   2005 2004 2003 2002

Cover photo 'Allee des Alyscamps in Arles' Vincent van Gogh, 1888. © The Bridgeman Art Library/Private Collection.
Typeset by Multiplex Techniques Ltd, Kent.
Printed in Great Britain for Hodder & Stoughton Educational, a division of Hodder Headline Plc, 338 Euston Road, London NW1 3BH by J. W. Arrowsmith Ltd., Bristol.

Contents

PART C: TEN POETS

Key Points in the National Literacy Strategy KS2 and where to find appropriate material

Note that certain requirements, such as comparing and contrasting poems on similar themes, performing poems, writing poems based on real and imagined experience and so on, appear in many places throughout this book. The references given are to those parts of the book in which examples of these aspects of poetry will most readily be found. They are not exhaustive. A short form of each relevant requirement is given in column 2 below: the precise details will be found in the NLS under the numbers given in brackets.

Year & Term	Short form of NLS requirement and precise location in NLS	Relevant material in *New Touchstones First*
Y4 Term 1	Compare and contrast poems on similar themes (7)	Part B
	Find out more about popular poets etc. & read further (8)	Part C
	Write poems based on personal and imagined experience (14)	Part B, Activities
Y4 Term 2	Understand use of figurative language … locate similes (5)	Part A, Comparisons
	Identify older poetry (language use, vocabulary, archaisms (6)	Part C, Shakespeare. Poems by Herbert, Marlowe, Jonson, Blake
	Patterns of rhyme (chorus, couplet, alternate rhymes) (7)	Part A, Unit 5 couplets. Also Unit 7 and Part B, Ballads
	Writing poems based on structure and/or style of poems read (11)	Many examples throughout, e.g. Activities in Part B, Seasons
Y4 Term 3	Understand terms: verse, chorus, couplet, stanza, rhyme, rhythm, alliteration (4)	Many examples, e.g. Part A, Unit 5 and Unit 1 (alliteration)
	Clapping/beating out rhythms & syllables (5)	Part A, Unit 7
	Use of rhyme, e.g. couplets, no rhyme, alternate rhyme (6)	Many examples, e.g. Part B, Seasons and Ballads section
	Forms (7)	Part A, Unit 1, Unit 5, Unit 7. Part B, Stories, Ballads
	Read further (stories or) poems by a favourite writer (9)	Part C (Ten Poets. NB introductions and workshop)
	Experiment with different styles and structures of poems (14)	Many opportunities, e.g. Part A, Unit 1, Unit 5, etc.
Y5 Term 1	Read a number of poems by significant poets and understand what is distinctive about their poems (6)	Part C (Ten Poets)
	Analyse & compare style and themes of significant poets; justify personal taste; impact of rhymes, etc. (7)	Part C
	Convey feelings, reflections or moods in a poem (16)	Part A, Unit 10
	Metaphors and similes (17)	Part A, Unit 4
Y5 Term 2	Read a range of narrative poems (4)	Part A, Unit 7; Part B, Stories, Ballads and 'Pied Piper' sections
	Perform poems in a variety of ways (5)	Very many opportunities, e.g. Part A, Unit 6 but also Units 1, 2, 3, 7, and Part B, Love, Ghosts, Stories, Ballads sections, etc.

	Understand terms and identify features of different kinds of poem, e.g. ballad, sonnet, rap, elegy, narrative (6)	Part A, Unit 1, Unit 5 Part B, Stories, Ballads and Narrative sections. Jonson's elegy 'On My first Sonne' in Family; in Part C, Grace Nichols' 'Baby-K Rap Rhyme'
	Differences between literal and figurative language (10)	Part A, Comparisons
	Write extensions, e.g. additional verses (12)	Part B, Seasons; Nonsense…many more
Y5 Term 3	Read, rehearse and modify performance of poetry (4)	Part A, Units 1, 6, 7; Part B, Love, Nonsense, Ghosts, Stories, Ballads and 'Pied Piper' sections
	Explore appeal of older literature through reading accessible poems…(6)	Throughout, but perhaps particularly Part C
	Use performance poems as models for polished writing (11)	Many opportunities throughout. See Y5 Term 3 (4) above
Y6 Term 1	Articulate personal response to a poem (3)	Throughout, but esp. Part A, Unit 8, Looking and Seeing, Units 9, 10 and Part C poets
	Familiarity with work of some established authors (4)	Part C (Ten Poets)
	Write poems using active verbs, personification…(10)	Part A, Unit 2, active verbs in 'Lodore'; Unit 1 'Riddle' and Unit 3 'Windy Nights' as examples of personification
Y6 Term 2	How poets manipulate words through sound, rhythm, rhyme, assonance, connotations, figurative language, ambiguity (3)	Throughout, but perhaps esp. Part A, Units 1, 2, 3, 8
	Investigate humorous verse: how poets play with meanings; nonsense words; the appeal of humorous verse (4)	Part A, Unit 1; Part B, Nonsense verse. Some of Part A, Unit 7 Storytelling and Part B, Stories
	How messages, moods and feelings are conveyed in poetry	Throughout
	Read and interpret poems where meanings are implied or multi-layered; discuss, interpret and challenge (6)	Many opportunities, but perhaps esp. Unit 8, Rossetti, Herbert, Bible Unit 9, 'Amo Ergo Sum'; Unit 10; Part B, 'Children' in Love section; Part C, Duffy
Y6 Term 3	How linked poems relate to one another by theme, format repetition (2)	Part B e.g. 'Seasons' section
	Describe and evaluate the style of an individual poet (3)	Part C (Ten Poets)
	Write a sequence of poems linked by theme or form, e.g. Haiku Calendar (13)	Part A, Unit 9

Where to find information on/examples of:

Please note that this is not an exhaustive list. There are many more examples of a number of key terms throughout the book.

To The Teacher

The *Touchstones* anthologies have undergone several revisions since their beginnings in the 1960s, the last of which was just prior to the advent of the National Curriculum in the late 1980s. *New Touchstones* brings the anthologies up-to-date in a thorough-going reappraisal of the series in the light of the National Curriculum requirements at the different Key Stages. In particular, *New Touchstones First* focuses upon the development of pupils' knowledge and skills at Key Stages 2 and 3 as outlined in *The National Literacy Strategy* (see summary of key points, p. vi). Just as Matthew Arnold's original idea of a 'touchstone' needs reinterpretation in successive generations, so the principles upon which the series is based, while remaining constant, simultaneously reflect the changing cultural conditions in which poetry teaching operates. These principles have proved both popular and durable. They are:

(i)   that an anthology of poetry for pupils should have a generous inclusiveness which acknowledges that the poems pupils may enjoy, feel provoked by, remember and, maybe, find valuable are as likely to come from a jokey performance script by Michael Rosen as they are from a song by Shakespeare. Pupils should be offered a wide variety of voices; their poetry experience should neither be restricted by narrowness of vision nor limited to specifically targeted purposes. We abrogate our responsibilities as literature teachers if we allow the boundaries of poetry in school to be set solely by that which is officially examined.

(ii)   that a mix of old and new poetry is important. It is as misguided to think that what is 'relevant' to pupils in the new millennium can only be poems written in the late twentieth century as it is to promote the study of pre-twentieth century poetry merely on the grounds of its 'heritage' status. Poems by Keats or Blake can have a good deal more relevance to life today than contemporary poems that foreground the ephemeral preoccupations of the present. Yet one of the advantages of poetry is its power to interpret the present for us. To set the work of recent writers in the context of that of their predecessors helps to illuminate the complementary qualities of both.

(iii)   that the concept of a 'teaching anthology' remains fundamental. The romantic notion that all teachers need to do is to read a lot of poetry to their classes so that its virtues, by some mysterious osmosis, will create a life-long love affair has long been discredited. Conversely, and far more apparent, there is the dislike that is generated in pupils by teachers who insist on line-by-line analysis, which, in most cases, leads to the imposition of the teacher's views and the neglect of the pupils' responses. The approaches to teaching that we advocate are based on the premise that pupils' activities in reading and responding are the necessary preludes to their critical understanding of poetry.

(iv) that 'creative' and 'critical' writing complement each other. Learning by doing is a natural process with poems. All pupils have something to say: by channelling their ideas and feelings into making their own poems as well as into commentary upon those of published poets, each informs the other. Pupils' criticisms gain the confidence of being written by 'practitioners' who have tried writing poems themselves; their imaginative writing gains from their developing knowledge of different forms and techniques.

New Touchstones First has been composed with these principles in mind. It is constructed in three parts.

PART A: TEN UNITS

The purposes of this part of the book are to help pupils to enjoy and understand poems and to develop their knowledge of how they work.

Each of the ten units aims to do three things:

(i) to concentrate upon a main aspect of how poetry works, such as word sounds, imagery, or how feelings and ideas are expressed in different forms;

(ii) to give examples of these aspects at work in particular poems; and

(iii) to suggest ways in which pupils can talk and write about poetry and become more confident in expressing their views.

The units can be studied in any order. However, they have been arranged so that the first five have a more technical emphasis upon playing with words within the discipline of form, upon sound and rhythm, metaphor and simile; whereas the second five introduce more general aspects such as how narrative works, creating word-pictures, or the expression of feelings and ideas in verse. None of these items can be separated out as neatly as this organisation into units suggests, but it is a convenient way of drawing attention to different aspects of how poems are written. It may also help to explain why some poems appeal to us more than others.

PART B: TEN THEMES

Most poems are, by nature, 'solo performances' – responses to experience which stand on their own. Yet, similarities abound in subject matter, tone of voice, expressions of feelings and thoughts, formal qualities and so on. While there will always be some sense of arbitrariness in thematic arrangements, nonetheless, it is clearly valuable to explore these similarities when they present themselves. The themes we have chosen are deliberately varied. Some focus upon familiar surroundings and interpret aspects of home, family, friends and childhood ('Me', 'Family' and 'Love'); others, conversely, deal with the unfamiliar, the fantastic, or the nonsensical, where the rules of normal living are turned upside down ('Nonsense' and 'Ghosts and Ghouls'). There are three different groups of stories ('Ballads', 'Stories' and 'The Pied Piper of Hamelin') offering various aspects of narrative, a range of traditional and modern tales, and providing a long poem around which a whole class project can be developed. There are also selections under the headings 'Creatures' and 'Seasons' since these themes have a perennial appeal to this age group. The suggestions indicated by this icon for classroom activities at the

 end of each theme reflect both the autonomy of the individual poems and the advantages of comparative work. Talking, reading, writing, sketching, improvisation – all have a part to play in the study of poetry.

PART C: TEN POETS

The main criterion in this part of the book is to give a representative sample of each poet's work of sufficient substance for pupils to gain a clear sense of the writer's style, subject matter and way of looking at the world. The selection of poets was governed by the wish to include pre-twentieth century as well as contemporary writing and to indicate that poetry in English reflects a variety of cultural backgrounds. We are aware that any list raises questions of exclusions as well as inclusions. We should make clear, therefore, that for this particular age group we have naturally drawn upon some of the major figures in the canon of children's literature, for example Lear, Carroll, Stevenson, de la Mare and Farjeon. In selecting the more recent writers, we did not want to duplicate material already published in our other volumes; and, with some reluctance, we decided not to feature Roger McGough and Michael Rosen, whose work is so widely known and easily accessible. Charles Causley is arguably the best modern writer of poetry for children and, together with the markedly different voices of Elizabeth Jennings, Grace Nichols and Carol Ann Duffy (whose five poems were specially commissioned for this volume), there is a challenging and diverse selection of modern writing. The pages entitled 'Ten Poets Workshop' (pp. 108–112) give some additional information about the poets we have featured here and suggest several ways of exploring this material.

In the competition for time and attention in the National Curriculum, there is the danger that poetry is squeezed to the margins. When this neglect occurs, pupils are short-changed; they are denied access both to that strand of literary history that has the longest and most distinguished pedigree and to an art form that has a peculiar ability to comment upon the culture and society in which they live. We hope that *New Touchstones First* will encourage teachers and pupils to explore poetry widely, to enjoy the voices they encounter, and to gain a fuller knowledge of how poems work.

Michael and Peter Benton

PART A

Ten Units

Playing with Words

All poetry is playing with words and *images* – the picture those words conjure up in our minds. It might be light-hearted word-play, like a riddle or a game, or it might be serious play. Some writers do it to amuse themselves and us. But even in play they can make us feel, or see or hear, something in new ways. Here are eight different kinds of word-play. Read them – aloud when you can – and work out what each writer is doing.

THREE HAIKU BY SCHOOL STUDENTS

| 1 2 3 4 5 | (5 syllables) |

A kingdom of birds,

| 1 2 3 4 5 6 7 | (7 syllables) |

The voice of wings fluttering

| 1 2 3 4 5 | (5 syllables) |

A tune gathering.

Andrew

A pattern of waves
Across my bedroom curtains
Like a lazy sea.

John

Tall Poplars in Stormy Weather

Green as the stream flows,
Flickering whipcord in the wind,
Lombardy thrashes.

Elisabeth

GUITAR RIDDLE

MY NECK IS LONG

My sinews strong Fire
wood my trunk
is made with- No
arms, no toes
a bridge, no nose.
I may be a guitar- well
who knows? I fret, thogh
I am played with. How can
it be I have no eyes
yet I can C? How
to it that thogh
I an round
can B flat? I

Kevin Dickson (School student)

THE HONEY POT

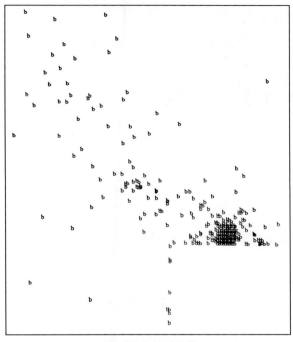

Alan Riddell

THREE LIMERICKS

There was a young lady of Twickenham
Whose shoes were too tight to walk quick in 'em.
   She came back from a walk
   Looking whiter than chalk
And took 'em both off and was sick in 'em.

A tutor who tooted the flute
Tried to tutor two tooters to toot.
Said the two to the tutor,
'Is it harder to toot or
To tutor two tooters to toot?'

A bather whose clothing was strewed
By breezes that left her quite nude
   Saw a man walk along
   And, unless I am wrong,
You expect this last line to be rude.

Anon

HOW TO ADDRESS A GOLDFISH

O goldfish
O goldfish O
goldfish O goldfish
O goldfish O goldfish O
goldfish O goldfish O goldfish
O gold O fish OO gold O fish O
goldfish O goldfish O goldfish
O goldfish O goldfish O
goldfish O goldfish
O goldfish O
goldfish O

Keith Bosley

RIDDLE

My breast is puffed up and my neck is swollen.
I've a fine head and a high waving tail,
ears and eyes also but only one foot;
a long neck, a strong beak, a back and
two sides, and a rod right through my middle.
My home is high above men. When he who moves
the forest molests me, I suffer a great deal of misery.
Scourged by the rainlash, I stand alone;
I'm bruised by heavy batteries of hail,
Hoar frost attacks and snow half-hides me.
I must endure all this, not pour out my misery.

Kevin Crossley-Holland

THE LOCH NESS MONSTER'S SONG

Sssnnnwhuffffll?
Hnwhuffl hhnnwfl hnfl hfl?
Gdroblboblhobngbl gbl gl g g g g glbgl.
Drublhaflablhaflubhafgabhaflhafl fl fl-
gm grawwwww grf grawf awfgm graw gm.
Hovoplodok-doplodovok-plovodokot-doplodokosh?
Splgraw fok fok splgrafhatchgabrlgabrl fok splfok!
Zgra kra gka fok!
Grof grawff gahf?
Gombl mbl bl-
blm plm,
blm plm,
blm plm,
blp.

Edwin Morgan

SONG OF THE POP-BOTTLERS

Pop bottles pop-bottles
   In pop shops;
The pop-bottles Pop bottles
   Poor Pop drops.

When Pop drops pop-bottles,
   Pop-bottles plop!
Pop-bottle-tops topple!
   Pop mops slop!

Stop! Pop'll drop bottle!
   Stop, Pop, stop!
When Pop bottles pop-bottles,
   Pop-bottles pop!

Morris Bishop

In groups

- Try reading 'Pop-Bottlers' as quickly and as clearly as you can. Who is best? Tongue twisters like these are full of *alliteration* (repeated consonants like 'p', 't' and 'l') and *assonance* (repeated vowel sounds – here it is 'o'), which trip us up. Do you know other tongue twisters?
- Each read 'How to Address a Goldfish' aloud. Watch each other. What happens?
- The 'Riddle' is over a thousand years old. What does it describe?
- Practise reading 'The Loch Ness Monster's Song'. Who is best?

On your own/in pairs

- Write your own tongue twister. You just need an alliterative phrase to start you off such as 'Weight-watchers…' or 'Beanie babies…'.
- Make up a riddle to describe an everyday object, e.g. a ruler, a book, a tube of toothpaste.
- Read the 'Guitar' shape poem. Take a *simple* shape (an outline of your hand or footprint, a light bulb, a bottle) and find suitable words to fill it.
- Try writing another verse for 'The Loch Ness Monster's Song' or a song for another creature, using sounds you think are suitable.
- Look at 'The Honey Pot' (p. 3). Use a single letter to make your own picture: 'c', 'j', 'q', 't', 'u' and 'y' are all possibilities.
- Haiku, like those on p. 2, began in Japan but are popular here too. The idea is to capture a single image or feeling in 17 syllables arranged 5–7–5 in just three lines. Try it yourself.
- Limericks like those on p. 3 are funny, five-line poems where the longer lines 1, 2 and 5 rhyme with each other, and so do the shorter lines 3 and 4. Hear them read aloud to get the special rhythm. Can you invent one yourself?

Sounds and Movement

THE CATARACT OF LODORE

The Cataract strong,
Then plunges along,
Striking and raging
As if a war waging
Its caverns and rocks among:
Rising and leaping,
Sinking and creeping,
Swelling and sweeping,
Showering and springing,
Flying and flinging,
Writhing and ringing,
Eddying and whisking,
Spouting and frisking,
Turning and twisting,
Around and around
With endless rebound!
Smiting and fighting,
A sight to delight in;
Confounding, astounding.
Dizzying and deafening the ear with its
    sound,
Dividing and gliding and sliding,
And falling and brawling and sprawling,
And driving and riving and striving,
And sprinkling and twinkling and wrinkling,
And sounding and bounding and rounding,
And bubbling and troubling and doubling,
And grumbling and rumbling and tumbling,

And clattering and battering and shattering;
Retreating and beating and meeting and
    sheeting,
Delaying and straying and playing and
    spraying,
Advancing and prancing and glancing and
    dancing,
Recoiling, turmoiling and toiling and boiling,
And gleaming and streaming and steaming
    and beaming,
And rushing and flushing and brushing and
    gushing,
And flapping and rapping and clapping and
    slapping,
And curling and whirling and purling and
    twirling,
And thumping and plumping and bumping
    and jumping,
And dashing and flashing and splashing and
    clashing,
And so never ending, but always descending,
Sounds and motions for ever and ever are
    blending,
All at once and all o'er, with a mighty
    uproar,
And this way the Water comes down at
    Lodore.

Robert Southey

Robert Southey was very excited when he saw the great waterfall and rapids at Lodore and he tried to catch some of the movement and noise by using sounding, restless words and rhythms.

As a class

- We think that, starting with 'plunges' in line two and 'striking' and 'raging' in line three, the writer uses around one hundred active verbs in this poem to describe the movement of the water. How many do you make it? And how many full stops can you find? What is the effect of these two things on the way we read the poem?
- Rehearse a class reading of the poem, splitting the lines between different people. You could even read it as a 'round', with one voice starting the poem followed by another a second or two later, so that the readings overlap. Tape the result.

Another poet, James Stephens, uses a similar technique in his poem about the deepest, most distant parts of the ocean.

THE MAIN-DEEP

The long-rolling,
Steady-póuring
Deep-trenchéd
Green billów:

   The wide-topped,
Unbróken,
Green-glacid,
Slow-sliding,

   Cold-flushing,
—On—on—on—
Chill-rushing,
   Hush-hushing,

...Hush-hushing...

James Stephens

THE STORM

See lightning is flashing,
The forest is crashing,
The rain will come dashing,
   A flood will be rising anon;

The heavens are scowling,
The thunder is growling,
The loud winds are howling,
   The storm has come suddenly on!

But now the sky clears,
The bright sun appears,
Now nobody fears,
   But soon every cloud will be gone.

Sara Coleridge

In groups

- Practise reading the poems to bring out the sounds and movement of the great waves and the crashing storm. How is the sound of the water in Stephens' poem different from that of Lodore? What kinds of words does 'The Storm' share with Southey's poem?

Ted Hughes' poem 'Gulls' pictures these graceful birds balancing on invisible currents of air. Hear it read aloud and try to say what he does with the words to catch the movement. You could think about alliteration, the verbs he uses, and the number of sentences in the poem.

GULLS

Gulls are glanced from the lift
Of cliffing air
And left
Loitering in the descending drift,
Or tilt gradient and go
Down steep invisible clefts in the grain
Of air, blading against the blow,

Back-flip, wisp
Over the foam-galled green
Building seas, and they scissor
Tossed spray, shave sheen,
Wing-waltzing their shadows
Over the green hollows,

Or rise again in the wind's landward rush
And, hurdling the thundering bush
With the stone wall flung in their faces,
Repeat their graces.

Ted Hughes

CAT

Cat
Purring

four furry paws
walking

delicate-
ly
   between
flower stems
stalking

butter-
flies

Keith Bosley

THE SIDEWALK RACER
Or, On the Skateboard

Skimming
an asphalt sea
I swerve, I curve, I
sway; I speed to whirring
sound an inch above the
ground; I'm the sailor
and the sail, I'm the
driver and the wheel
I'm the one and only
single engine
human auto
mobile.

Lillian Morrison

How do the sound, the movement and the shape of the last two poems help us feel and see the action?

On your own

Write a poem that focuses on the sound and movement of something you know or enjoy. For example, riding a bike, roller-blading, watching motor-racing, playing a particular game. Try to make the sound of words you choose suggest the movement.

Rhythm

By performing songs, dances and poems, you can feel the rhythm. Usually, there is a regular beat and often a repeated pattern in the music, the movements or the words. Sometimes the beat and the pattern are strong, as in a lot of music; at other times, you hardly notice them. However, rhythm of some sort is almost always there.

WHISPER WHISPER

whisper whisper
whisper whisper
goes my sister
down the phone

whisper whisper
go the beech leaves
breathing in the
wind alone

whisper whisper
whisper whisper
slips the river
on the stone

whisper whisper
go my parents
when they whisper
on their own

I don't mind the
whisper whisper
whisper whisper
it's a tune

sometimes though
I wish the whisper
whisperings would
Shut up soon

Kit Wright

In groups

In the poem opposite, Kit Wright catches the rhythm and sound of whispering – on the phone, among leaves, in the river's movement, between parents – and describes it as 'a tune'. In fact, rhythm in poetry might be called 'the tune on the page'.

In order to play the tune on this page, decide how you will split up the poem for reading aloud. Will you have one or two voices repeating the whispers in each verse? Or will you simply divide the verses among the group?

The last two verses are different – how might you read them?

Rehearse your reading and present it to the rest of the class.

One of the liveliest, and often amusing, rhythms is that of the galloping poem. The two best-known examples are William Cowper's 'John Gilpin' and Robert Browning's 'How They Brought the Good News from Ghent to Aix', which begins:

```
x /   x  x  /  x  x  /  x  x  /
```
I sprang to the stirrup, and Joris, and he;
I galloped, Dirck galloped, we galloped all three;
'Good speed!' cried the watch, as the gate-bolts undrew;
'Speed!' echoed the wall to us galloping through;
Behind shut the postern,★ the lights sank to rest,   ★gate
And into the midnight we galloped abreast.

We have marked the heavy (/) and light (x) stresses in line 1 to show you how the galloping rhythm works, but you will hear it best by reading the lines aloud. Try to hear the whole poem; unfortunately it is too long to print here.

In the desperate ride that follows, only the storyteller reaches Aix. No one knows what the good news was; Browning seems more interested in the galloping rhythm! Perhaps this is why the style has often been imitated: the funniest version is entitled 'How I Brought the Good News from Aix to Ghent (or Vice Versa)', which begins:

I sprang to the rollocks and Jorrocks and me,
And I galloped, you galloped, he galloped, we galloped all three...
Not a word to each other; we kept changing place,
Neck to neck, back to front, ear to ear, face to face;
And we yelled once or twice, when we heard a clock chime,
'Would you kindly oblige us, *Is that the right time?*'
As I galloped, you galloped, he galloped, we galloped, ye galloped, they two shall have galloped;
  let us trot.

R.J. Yeatman and W.C. Sellar, *1066 and All That*

Try to write a few galloping lines of your own.

A variation on the galloping poem is R.L. Stevenson's 'Windy Nights'. Listen to it read aloud. The stresses in the first four rhyming lines of each verse are different from those in the final couplet. Why does the rhythm change in this way? The second poem by Stevenson catches the rhythm of a train. Read it aloud and talk about how it creates the sense of the train's movement.

WINDY NIGHTS

Whenever the moon and the stars are set,
  Whenever the wind is high,
All night long in the dark and wet,
  A man goes riding by.
Late in the night when the fires are out,
Why does he gallop and gallop about?

Whenever the trees are crying aloud,
  And ships are tossed at sea,
By, on the highway, low and loud,
  By at the gallop goes he.
By at the gallop he goes, and then
By he comes back at the gallop again.

R.L. Stevenson

FROM A RAILWAY CARRIAGE

Faster than fairies, faster than witches,
Bridges and houses, hedges and ditches;
And charging along like troops in a battle,
All through the meadows the horses and
    cattle:
All of the sights of the hill and the plain
Fly as thick as driving rain;
And ever again, in the wink of an eye,
Painted stations whistle by.

Here is a child who clambers and scrambles,
All by himself and gathering brambles;
Here is a tramp who stands and gazes;
And there is the green for stringing the
    daisies!
Here is a cart run away in the road
Lumping along with man and load;
And here is a mill, and there is a river:
Each a glimpse and gone for ever!

R.L. Stevenson

Comparisons

When we are talking to other people we use comparisons all the time to express our feelings and to describe things we have seen or done. Writers use comparisons too, for similar reasons.

Here is a poem which is simply a list of comparisons, with pairs of contrasting ideas – wet/dry, live/dead and so on.

COMPARISONS

As wet as a fish — as dry as a bone;
As live as a bird — as dead as a stone;
As plump as a partridge — as poor as a rat;
As strong as a horse — as weak as a cat;
As hard as a flint — as soft as a mole;
As white as a lily — as black as a coal;
As plain as a staff — as rough as a bear;
As light as a drum — as free as the air;
As heavy as lead — as light as a feather;
As steady as time — uncertain as weather;
As hot as an oven — as cold as a frog;
As gay as a lark — as sick as a dog;
As savage as tigers — as mild as a dove;
As stiff as a poker — as limp as a glove;
As blind as a bat — as deaf as a post;
As cool as a cucumber — as warm as toast;
As flat as a flounder — as round as a ball;
As blunt as a hammer — as sharp as an awl;
As brittle as glass — as tough as gristle;
As neat as a pin — as clean as a whistle;
As red as a rose — as square as a box;
As bold as a thief — as sly as a fox.

Anon

Some of these phrases are now so common in everyday speech that we hardly think of them as comparisons. Which ones are familiar to you?

Direct comparisons like these which use the words 'as' or 'like' to connect two things are called *similes*. In poetry, similes are not to be taken literally; they are meant to give you a clearer idea of what the poet feels about something. So when Robert Burns writes, 'My love is like a red, red rose', he does not mean that his love is prickly and bright red: he thinks she is beautiful, soft and, perhaps, sweetly perfumed.

A simile says that one thing is like another, whereas a *metaphor* says they are identical. When Douglas Gibson looks across some fields, towards some distant trees where the morning mist is lying thickly, he writes:

On the horizon, heads of trees
Swim with the mist about their knees...

He assumes the tree-tops are swimmers in a sea of mist.

These two types of comparison are ways in which writers look at things in fresh and original ways.

On your own

Read through the following comparisons. They are all extracts from longer poems, apart from 'Winter', which is complete. Take your time, read them slowly, and allow each picture to form in your mind's eye.

WINTER

The winter trees like great sweep's brushes
Poke up from deep earth, black and bare,
Suddenly stir, and shake a crowd
Of sooty rooks into the air.

L.A.G. Strong

CATS

Snowflake – gentle paw
A fist of pins;
Kettles on the purr
Ready to spit;
Black silk then bristled fur.

Phoebe Hesketh

REFLECTIONS

The arched stone bridge
is an eye, with underlid
in the water.

May Swenson

FOUNTAINS

Suddenly all the fountains in the park
Opened smoothly their umbrellas of water,
Yet there was none but me to miss or mark
Their peacock show...

W.R. Rodgers

STREET LIGHTS

Our street lights are all provided
with little shelters, like Mexican hats,
wide-brimmed over their long faces.

Martyn Crucefix

AN ARMY MASSES ITS FORCES FOR ATTACK

The Assyrian came down like a wolf on the
   fold,
And his cohorts were gleaming in purple and
   gold;
And the sheen of their spears was like stars
   on the sea,
When the blue wave rolls nightly on deep
   Galilee.

Lord Byron

Choose an example of a simile and a metaphor and write a sentence about each, saying what appeals to you about the comparison.

As a class

Compare your choices and see which are the most popular similes and metaphors.

   Talk about why the two parts of the comparisons are linked – their shape? Sound? Feel? Movement? Or some mixture of these?

   Finally, here is a short poem written entirely as a metaphor.

FOG

The fog comes
on little cat feet.

It sits looking
over the harbour and city
on silent haunches
and then moves on.

Carl Sandburg

What is cat-like about fog?

On your own

Write your own short poem about another type of weather or time of day and use a comparison. Use Carl Sandburg's poem as a model. You might start:
'The sun rises …'
'The sun sets…'
'The rain pelts…'
'The hail bounces…'
'The snow drifts…'

U N I T   5

Patterns on the Page

Poems come in all sorts of shapes and sizes: fat ones and thin ones, long ones and short ones. There are poems in regular forms like haiku (Unit 1) or ballads (Unit 7), poems whose shape tells you how to read them ('When Hannibal Crossed the Alps', p. 91), and poems which follow a punch-drunk, unpredictable pattern like 'The Fight of the Year' (p. 32). This unit introduces two much-used forms – one simple, the other complicated. They are the couplet and the sonnet.

(i) Couplets

A couplet is a pair of lines, usually of the same length, which rhyme with each other. In the two examples below, one expresses gentleness of feeling, the other makes a witty joke.

MOTHERLESS BABY

Motherless baby and babyless mother
Bring them together to love one another.

Christina Rossetti

THIS ENGLISHWOMAN

This Englishwoman is so refined
She has no bosom and no behind.

Stevie Smith

On your own

● With Stevie Smith's couplet as your model, write your own rhyming couplet. You might start:

'This Englishman is so…' or
'This teacher talks so…'

Couplets can be put together to tell stories. Here are two more examples. The first is based upon the book *Gulliver's Travels*, where Lemuel Gulliver is ship-wrecked and finds himself in the land of Lilliput as a giant among a nation of tiny people only a few inches tall. The second is a modern poem which, with its dark humour, undermines the usual feelings between grandmother, mother and baby. Hear the poems read aloud.

GULLIVER IN LILLIPUT

From his nose
Clouds he blows.
When he speaks,
Thunder breaks.
When he eats,
Famine threats.
When he treads
Mountains' heads
Groan and shake;
Armies quake.
See him stride
Valleys wide,
Over woods,
Over floods.
Troops take heed,
Man and steed:
Left and right.
Speed your flight!
In amaze
Lost I gaze
Toward the skies:
See! and believe your eyes!

Alexander Pope

INFANT SONG

Don't you love my baby, mam,
Lying in his little pram,

Polished all with water clean,
The finest baby ever seen?

Daughter, daughter, if I could
I'd love your baby as I should,

But why the suit of signal-red,
The horns that grow out of his head,

Why does he burn with brimstone heat,
Have cloven hooves instead of feet,

Fishing hooks upon each hand,
The keenest tail that's in the land,

Pointed ears and teeth so stark
And eyes that flicker in the dark?

Don't you love my baby, mam?

Dearest, I do not think I can.
I do not, do not think I can.

Charles Causley

On your own

- Add one or two couplets to 'Gulliver in Lilliput': 'When he smiles…', 'When he cries…'; 'When he hops…'; 'When he sighs…'; 'When he waves…' …

In pairs/as a class

- Rehearse a reading of 'Infant Song', sharing out the lines between the two voices. The baby in the pram is hardly a picture of innocence! How is the baby described and why might the poet create such a picture?

(ii) The sonnet

A sonnet is a poem of 14 lines, usually divided into 8 and 6 lines, and with a regular rhyme scheme. There are often 5 light stresses (x) and 5 heavy stresses (/) to each line – like repeating the word 'again' five times. For example, the first line of a famous war poem, 'The Soldier', is:

x /   x   /   x   /x   /   x   /

If I should die, think only this of me:

In practice, both the rhymes and the rhythms vary a lot from poem to poem according to the subject matter. 'December' (p. 34) and 'The Thrush's Nest' (p. 24) are both regular sonnets. In the following poem, the cat's mistress wants her pet to stay indoors (lines 1–8), and the cat wants to go outside into the darkness (lines 9–14). Because the poem is a conversation, it has the informal rhythm of talk, not the regular pattern.

In pairs

● Read the poem aloud twice, taking turns at the two voices.

ON A NIGHT OF SNOW

Cat, if you go outdoors you must walk in the snow.
You will come back with little white shoes on your feet,
Little white slippers of snow that have heels of sleet.
Stay by the fire, my Cat. Lie still, do not go.
See how the flames are leaping and hissing low,
I will bring you a saucer of milk like a marguerite,
So white and so smooth, so spherical and so sweet—
Stay with me, Cat. Outdoors the wild winds blow.

Outdoors the wild winds blow, Mistress, and dark is the night.
Strange voices cry in the trees, intoning strange lore;
And more than cats move, lit by our eyes' green light,
On silent feet where the meadow grasses hang hoar—
Mistress, there are portents abroad of magic and might,
And things that are yet to be done. Open the door!

Elizabeth Coatsworth

As a class

● What picture do you get of the pet cat in lines 1–8?
● How does the cat see itself and the world outside in lines 9–14?

UNIT 6

Performance

Lots of poems in this book are 'performance poems' – the sort where you can enjoy working out a reading with two or three or even thirty voices. The four poems in this unit in particular need you to perform them. The first, 'This is the Key', is a very old rhyme which was often used in children's games; the second, 'The One Answer' (often known as 'O, No, John'), is a traditional song with a well-known tune.

THIS IS THE KEY

This is the key of the kingdom:
In that kingdom there is a city.
In that city there is a town.
In that town there is a street.
In that street there is a lane.
In that lane there is a yard.
In that yard there is a house.
In that house there is a room.
In that room there is a bed.
On that bed there is a basket.
In that basket there are some flowers.
Flowers in a basket.
Basket on the bed.
Bed in the room.
Room in the house.
House in the yard.
Yard in the lane.
Lane in the street.
Street in the town.
Town in the city.
City in the kingdom.
Of the kingdom this is the key.

Anon

THE ONE ANSWER

On yonder hill there stands a creature,
    Who she is I do not know.
I'll go and ask her hand in marriage,
    And she'll answer yes or no.
"O, no, John; no, John; no, John, no!

"My father was a Spanish captain,
    Went to sea a year ago;
First he kissed me, then he left me,
    Bade me always answer no.
So no, John; no, John; no, John, no!"

Madam, in your face is beauty;
    On your lips red roses grow.
Will you take me for your husband?
    Madam, answer yes or no.
"O, no, John, no, John; no, John, no."

Madam, since you are so cruel,
    And since you do scorn me so,
If I may not be your husband,
    Madam, will you let me go?
'O, no, John; no, John; no, John, no."

Hark! I hear the church bells ringing;
    Will you come and be my wife?
Or, dear madam, have you settled
    To live single all your life?
"O, no, John; no, John; no, John, no!"

Anon

In groups

- Prepare a reading of 'This is the Key' emphasising the rhythms and using voices either in chorus or singly for different lines. Hear each other's versions.

In pairs

- Hear 'The One Answer' read through once and be sure you understand the story, particularly the twist at the end. Now prepare a performance of the poem and try to get the right tones of voice for John and the lady he so admires. Don't be shy!

Allan Ahlberg's poem 'Excuses' is full of life, particularly as the excuses get more and more unlikely:

Excuses

I've writ on the wrong page, Miss,
My pencil went all blunt.
My book was upside-down, Miss,
My book was back to front.

My margin's gone all crooked, Miss,
I've smudged mine with my scarf.
I've rubbed a hole in the paper, Miss,
My ruler's broke in half.

My work's blew out the window, Miss,
My work's fell in the bin.
The leg's dropped off my chair, Miss,
The ceiling's coming in.

I've ate a poison apple, Miss,
I've held a poison pen!
I think I'm being kidnapped, Miss!
So... can we start again?

Allan Ahlberg

In groups

- Rehearse a performance of the poem. You might give each of the lines to four of the people in the group. Try to catch the way the excuses move from normal and everyday things to totally ridiculous ones. Does everybody, or just the teacher, say the last line?

The next poem, about the old lady who makes an unusual find in her garden, is a very old, English story, but this is the later American version.

THE HAIRY TOE

Once there was a woman went out to pick
  beans,
and she found a Hairy Toe.
She took the Hairy Toe home with her,
and that night, when she went to bed,
the wind began to moan and groan.
Away off in the distance
she seemed to hear a voice crying,
'Where's my Hair-r-ry To-o-oe?
Who's got my Hair-r-ry To-o-oe?'

The woman scrooched down,
'way down under the covers,
and about that time
the wind appeared to hit the house,

smoosh,

and the old house creaked and cracked
like something was trying to get in.
The voice had come nearer,
almost at the door now,
and it said,
'Where's my Hair-r-ry To-o-oe?
Who's got my Hair-r-ry To-o-oe?'

The woman scrooched further down
under the covers
and pulled them tight around her head.

The wind growled around the house
like some big animal
and r-r-um-mbled
over the chimbley.
All at once she heard the door cr-r-a-ack
and Something slipped in
and began to creep over the floor.

The floor went
cre-e-eak, cre-e-eak
at every step that thing took towards her
  bed.
The woman could almost feel
it bending over her bed.
There in an awful voice it said:
'Where's my Hair-r-ry To-o-oe?
Who's got my Hair-r-ry To-o-oe?
YOU'VE GOT IT!'

Anon
(Traditional American)

As a class

- Rehearse a reading of the poem with a narrator taking the main part and everybody joining in for the choruses and the last lines. You can add some sound effects too.

Storytelling

Hilaire Belloc wrote lots of story poems warning about children who did dreadful things and suffered terrible consequences. He called them *Cautionary Verses*. Here is the story of Henry King and a modern story of a girl called J—, written in a similar style.

HENRY KING

Who chewed bits of string and was early cut off in dreadful agonies

The Chief Defect of Henry King
Was chewing little bits of String.
At last he swallowed some which tied
Itself in ugly Knots inside.
Physicians of the Utmost Fame
Were called at once; but when they came
They answered as they took their Fees,
'There is no Cure for this Disease.
Henry will very soon be dead.'
His Parents stood about his Bed
Lamenting his Untimely Death,
When Henry, with his Latest Breath,
Cried — 'Oh, my Friends, be warned by me,
That Breakfast, Dinner, Lunch and Tea
Are all the Human Frame requires...'
With that the Wretched Child expires.

Hilaire Belloc

J—

There was a girl — let's call her J—
Who drove her mother quite insane.
Although adorable and sweet
She would not keep her bedroom neat.
She scattered toys and books around,
And covered every inch of ground,
And heaped her clothes upon the floor
So mum could not get in the door,
Or vac the rug, which, as she feared,
Had *entirely* disappeared
Under an avalanche of stuff.
Cried Mum, "I've really had enough
Of wading knee-deep through debris
Of Maths and French books, *tu compris?*
— Pyjamas, tops, and *sixteen* teddies —
I really can't see where her bed is.
Photos, letters, dog-eared jotters;
Not one, but *all* the Harry Potters
Left out with CDs and the player.
Though I love her, I could slay her!
Leonardo — that's young di C.
Not dear artistic old da V. —
His poster's peeling from the wall.
Tights, glitter, and a spangly shawl;
Lipstick, and smarties, crumpled skirt,
Blouses, tiara (!), rugby shirt (!!);
Volvic and Coke; a plastic cup
Half-full — she never washes up —
It's all too much, she does not care."
Said J—, "Please, Mummy don't despair;
Aunt says when you were my age you
Were — just like me — untidy too!"

Peter Benton

Hear the poems read aloud. It's quite easy to write your own in the same style. You need four stresses in each line (and usually, but not always, eight syllables) and pairs of lines that rhyme. Beat out the stresses like this:

x / x /　x　/ x　/
Matilda told such dreadful lies
x /　x / x　/　x　/
It made one gasp and stretch one's eyes

Long ago, many stories were told in poetry, and often sung by minstrels who would play a harp to accompany them as they sang in courts, great houses, taverns, and market places. Such stories are called *ballads* and they often have simple four-line verses and a chorus. The pictures they make in our minds are often very colourful, sharp and clear. You will find other ballads on pp. 55–58.

THE OUTLANDISH KNIGHT

An outlandish knight came out of the North
　To woo a maiden fair,
He promised to take her to the North lands,
　Her father's only heir.

"Come, fetch me some of your father's gold,
　And some of your mother's fee;
And two of the best nags out of the stable,
　Where they stand thirty and three."

She fetched him some of her father's gold
　And some of her mother's fee;
And two of the best nags out of the stable,
　Where they stood thirty and three.

She mounted her on her milk-white steed,
　He on the dapple grey;
They rode till they came unto the sea-side,
　Three hours before it was day.

"Light off, light off thy milk-white steed,
　And deliver it unto me;
Six pretty maids have I drowned here,
　And thou the seventh shall be.

"Pull off, pull off thy silken gown,
　And deliver it unto me;
Methinks it looks too rich and too gay
　To rot in the salt sea.

"Pull off, pull off thy silken stays,
　And deliver them unto me;
Methinks they are too fine and gay
　To rot in the salt sea.

"Pull off, pull off thy Holland smock,
　And deliver it unto me;
Methinks it looks too rich and gay
　To rot in the salt sea."

"If I must pull off my Holland smock,
　Pray turn thy back unto me,
For it is not fitting that such a ruffian
　A woman unclad should see."

He turned his back towards her,
　And viewed the leaves so green;
She caught him round the middle so small,
　And tumbled him into the stream.

He dropped high, and he dropped low,
　Until he came to the tide—
"Catch hold of my hand, my pretty maiden,
　And I will make you my bride."

"Lie there, lie there, you false-hearted man,
　Lie there instead of me;
Six pretty maidens have you drowned here,
　And the seventh has drowned thee."

She mounted on her milk-white steed,
　And led the dapple grey.
She rode till she came to her father's hall,
　Three hours before it was day.

Anon

In groups

● Prepare readings of the poem whilst others mime the story.

Finally, here's a highly unlikely story by Ogden Nash about a cowardly dragon who found he was, for once, braver than he thought. Work out a class reading of the poem.

THE TALE OF CUSTARD THE DRAGON

Belinda lived in a little white house,
With a little black kitten and a little gray
    mouse,
And a little yellow dog and a little red wagon,
And a realio, trulio, little pet dragon.

Now the name of the little black kitten was
    Ink,
And the little gray mouse, she called her
    Blink,
And the little yellow dog was sharp as
    Mustard,
But the dragon was a coward, and she called
    him Custard.

Custard the dragon had big sharp teeth,
And spikes on top of him and scales
    underneath,
Mouth like a fireplace, chimney for a nose,
And realio, trulio daggers on his toes.

Belinda was as brave as a barrel full of bears,
And Ink and Blink chased lions down the
    stairs,
Mustard was as brave as a tiger in a rage,
But Custard cried for a nice safe cage.

Belinda tickled him, she tickled him
    unmerciful,
Ink, Blink and Mustard they rudely called him
    Percival,
They all sat laughing in the little red wagon
At the realio, trulio cowardly dragon.

Belinda giggled till she shook the house,
And Blink said Weeck! which is giggling for a
    mouse,
Ink and Mustard rudely asked his age,
When Custard cried for a nice safe cage.

Suddenly, suddenly they heard a nasty sound,
And Mustard growled, and they all looked
    around.
Meowch! cried Ink, and Ooh! Cried Belinda,
For there was a pirate climbing in the winda.

Pistol in his left hand, pistol in his right,
And he held in his teeth a cutlass bright,
His beard was black, one leg was wood;
It was clear that the pirate meant no good.

Belinda paled, and she cried Help! Help!
But Mustard fled with a terrified yelp,
Ink trickled down to the bottom of the
    household,
And little mouse Blink strategically
    mouseholed.

But up jumped Custard, snorting like an
    engine,
Clashed his tail like irons in a dungeon,
With a clatter and a clank and a jangling
    squirm
He went at the pirate like a robin at a worm.

The pirate gaped at Belinda's dragon,
And gulped some grog from his pocket
    flagon,
He fired two bullets, but they didn't hit,
And Custard gobbled him, every bit.

Belinda embraced him, Mustard licked him,
No one mourned for his pirate victim.
Ink and Blink in glee did gyrate
Around the dragon that ate the pyrate.

Belinda still lives in her little white house,
With her little black kitten and her little gray
    mouse,
And her little yellow dog and her little red
    wagon,
And her realio, trulio little pet dragon.

Belinda is as brave as a barrel full of bears,
And Ink and Blink chase lions down the
    stairs.
Mustard is as brave as a tiger in a rage,
But Custard keeps crying for a nice safe cage.

Ogden Nash

Looking and Seeing

It is often said that some poets can 'see into the life of things': that is, they do not merely look at the surface but see further in, deeper down than most of us and understand more about life. The first two poems are literally about looking closely:

OBSERVATION

Now and then concentrating
On the very small,

focusing my attention
on a very small area

like this crack in sandstone
perpetually wet with seepage,

getting so close
to moss, liverwort and fern

it becomes a forest
with wild beasts in it,

birds in the branches
and crickets piping,

cicadas shrilling.
Someone seeing me

staring so fixedly
at nothing

might be excused
for thinking me vague, abstracted,

lost in introspection.
No! I am awake, absorbed,

just looking in a different direction.

W. Hart-Smith

THE MAGNIFYING GLASS

With this round glass
I can make *Magic* talk –
A myriad shells show
In a scrap of chalk;

Of but an inch of moss
A forest – flowers and trees;
A drop of water
Like a hive of bees.

I lie in wait and watch
How the deft spider jets
The woven web-silk
From his spinnerets;

The tigerish claws he has!
And oh! the silly flies
That stumble into his net –
With all those eyes!

Not even the tiniest thing
But this my glass
Will make more marvellous,
And itself surpass.

Yes, and with lenses like it,
Eyeing the moon,
'Twould seem you'd walk there
In an afternoon!

Walter de la Mare

This little piece is from Dorothy Wordsworth's *Journal* or diary, but it is arranged on the page as a poem:

THE LAKE

The lake was covered all over
With bright silverwaves
That were each
The twinkling of an eye.

Dorothy Wordsworth

As a class

● Hear the poems read aloud and talk about what each poet sees and why looking closely is important.

Next, two poems by writers who were keen observers of nature:

THE THRUSH'S NEST

Within a thick and spreading hawthorn bush,
   That overhung a molehill large and round,
I heard from morn to morn a merry thrush
   Sing hymns to sunrise, and I drank the
     sound
With joy; and, often an intruding guest,
   I watched her secret toils from day to day –
How true she warped the moss to form a
    nest,
   And modelled it within with wood and
    clay;
And by and by, like heath-bells gilt with dew,
   There lay her shining eggs, as bright as
    flowers,
Ink-spotted-over shells of greeny blue;
   And there I witnessed in the sunny hours
A brood of nature's minstrels chirp and fly,
Glad as that sunshine and the laughing sky.

John Clare

HEDGEHOG

His back's all prickles, but his pointed face
Is furry and his soft black-leather snout
Gentle and wrinkled. Sunlong in a ditch
He dozes on dead leaves, till with the dusk
He clambers out, shambling through twilight
   lanes
To scrabble banks for worms. When Autumn
   brings
The first cold winds, he'll find a rabbit hole
And, curled within it, sleep the snow away
Till March comes round to wake him. Then
   he'll crawl
Out to the sunbright rim of the world, and
   stretch
Dazzled and dreaming. But if danger's near
Up go his bristles, and he'll roll himself
Tight as a ball, tough as a blackthorn hedge!

Clive Sansom

As a class

● Hear the two poems read aloud. Pick out details that you particularly like and say why you like them. Can you say which one is a sonnet? (See p. 16 if you need help.)

On your own

- Choose a familiar object: a leaf, a flower, a stone, a piece of bark...
  What does it look like? What does it feel like? What does it remind you of? Write a short poem about it, looking closely at every aspect.

The next three poems all suggest that we should look beyond the surface of things to see their true value. 'The Elixir' was supposed to give eternal life and, like the philosopher's stone, it could turn things to gold.

As a class

- Hear the three poems read aloud. Talk about the kind of looking and seeing these writers are doing. What ideas link the three pieces?

From: THE ELIXIR

Teach me, my God and King,
In all things thee to see,
And what I do in any thing,
To do it as for thee:

A man that looks on glass,
On it may stay his eye;
Or if he pleaseth, through it pass,
And then the heaven espy.

All may of thee partake:
Nothing can be so mean,
Which with this tincture (for thy sake)
Will not grow bright and clean.

A servant with this clause
Makes drudgery divine:
Who sweeps a room as for thy laws,
Makes that and the action fine.

This is the famous stone
That turneth all to gold:
For that which God doth touch and own
Cannot for less be told.★

George Herbert

★valued

TREASURES IN HEAVEN

Lay not up for yourselves treasures upon
  earth,
Where moth and rust doth corrupt,
And where thieves break through and steal:

But lay up for yourselves treasures in heaven,
Where neither moth nor rust doth corrupt,
And where thieves do not break through nor
  steal.
For where your treasure is, there will your
  heart be also.

The Bible, St Matthew, Chapter 6

PRECIOUS STONES

An emerald is as green as grass;
  A ruby red as blood;
A sapphire shines as blue as heaven;
  A flint lies in the mud.

A diamond is a brilliant stone,
  To catch the world's desire;
An opal holds a fiery spark;
  But a flint holds fire.

Christina Rossetti

Making Word-Pictures

You have already seen in Unit 1 how to make word-pictures as tiny, 17-syllable haiku poems. The poems in this unit build up more detailed pictures. Hear the first poem read aloud; then re-read it to yourself, letting the pictures form in your mind's eye.

AMO ERGO SUM*

Because I love
    The sun pours out its rays of living gold
    Pours out its gold and silver on the sea.

Because I love
    The earth upon her astral spindle winds
    Her ecstasy-producing dance.

Because I love
    Clouds travel on the winds through wide skies,
    Skies wide and beautiful, blue and deep.

Because I love
    Wind blows white sails,
    The wind blows over flowers, the sweet wind blows.

Because I love
    The ferns grow green, and green the grass, and green
    The transparent sunlit trees.

Because I love
    Larks rise up from the grass
    And all the leaves are full of singing birds.

Because I love
    The summer air quivers with a thousand wings,
    Myriads of jewelled eyes burn in the light.

Because I love
    The iridescent shells upon the sand
    Take forms as fine and intricate as thought.

Because I love
>   There is an invisible way across the sky,
>   Birds travel by that way, the sun and moon
>   And all the stars travel that path by night.

Because I love
>   There is a river flowing all night long.

Because I love
>   All night the river flows into my sleep,
>   Ten thousand living things are sleeping in my arms,
>   And sleeping wake, and flowing are at rest.

Kathleen Raine

*I love therefore I am

As a class

- Describe the pictures that you imagine from each of the short sections of the poem.
- Why do you think that each sections begins, 'Because I love…'?
- What do you think the mysterious ending means?

On your own

- Add one or two sections of your own to the poem.

Here are two more poems, both on the same subject, which make different word-pictures. Christina Rossetti's poem lists the months of the year; each time she gives a clue about what she sees in her mind's eye.

JANUARY COLD DESOLATE

January cold desolate;
February all dripping wet;
March wind ranges;
April changes;
Birds sing in tune
>   To flowers of May,
Till sunny June
>   Brings longest day;
In scorched July
The storm-clouds fly
Lightning torn;
August bears corn,
September fruit;
In rough October
Earth must disrobe her;
Stars fall and shoot
In keen November;
And night is long
And cold is strong
In bleak December.

Christina Rossetti

On your own

- As you see, the poet gives only brief hints. Take each month in turn and add a line which gives a word-picture of one particular thing that fills out her idea. For example:

  > 'January cold desolate;
  > Puddles quickly freeze and set.'

  > Or, 'Till sunny June
  > Brings longest day;
  > And children after sunset play.'

- Try to keep to the rhyming sounds in the poem.

Now, hear the second poem read aloud.

THE MONTHS OF THE YEAR

January brings the snow;
Makes the toes and fingers glow.

February brings the rain,
Thaws the frozen ponds again.

March brings breezes loud and shrill,
Stirs the dancing daffodil.

April brings the primrose sweet,
Scatters daisies at our feet.

May brings flocks of pretty lambs,
Skipping by their fleecy dams.

June brings tulips, lilies, roses;
Fills the children's hands with posies.

Hot July brings cooling showers,
Strawberries and gilly-flowers.

August brings the sheaves of corn,
Then the Harvest home is borne.

Warm September brings the fruit,
Sportsmen then begin to shoot.

Fresh October brings the pheasant;
Then to gather nuts is pleasant.

Dull November brings the blast,
Then the leaves are falling fast.

Chill December brings the sleet,
Blazing fire and Christmas treat.

Sara Coleridge

As a class

- What is the rhyming pattern in each verse?
- Compare the word-pictures drawn by the two poets for each month. Do the two poems give the same impressions?

On your own

- Make a poster-poem (perhaps a haiku calendar) of the months of the year from your additions to Christina Rossetti's poem, including any parts of Sara Coleridge's poem that you particularly like.
- Illustrate it and display it in your classroom.

Feelings and Thoughts

In one way or another, all poems are about feelings and thoughts. In the rest of this book you will find poems that express a whole range of feelings from happiness ('The Passionate Shepherd to His Love', p. 37)to horror ('John Mouldy', p. 87), and many that contain mixed feelings of different kinds ('Lizzie', p. 39 or 'Holidays at Home', p. 99). There are also a lot of poems with ideas that challenge us to think again about familiar things, or make us look at the world or ourselves in a new way. Look up the following poems, read them to yourself, and think about the ideas they contain: 'Me' (p. 68); 'Thoughts Like an Ocean' (p. 69); 'Hi!' (p. 89); 'The Dewdrop' (p. 91); 'A Bad Princess' (p. 106).

As a class

- Feeling and thinking are not separate; they go together in poems. Hear the following poem read aloud and, as you listen, ask yourself:
  - What is the event that is suggested, but not described, in the poem? What are we meant to think has happened?
  - What are the feelings of the mother and child? How do we know?

TWILIGHT

The twilight is sad and cloudy,
  The wind blows wild and free,
And like the wings of sea-birds
  Flash the white caps of the sea.

But in the fisherman's cottage
  There shines a ruddier light,
And a little face at the window
  Peers out into the night.

Close, close it is pressed to the window,
  As if those childish eyes
Were looking into the darkness,
  To see some form arise.

And a woman's waving shadow
  Is passing to and fro,
Now rising to the ceiling,
  Now bowing and bending low.

What tale do the roaring ocean,
  And the night-wind, bleak and wild,
As they beat at the crazy casement,
  Tell to that little child?

And why do the roaring ocean,
  And the night-wind, wild and bleak,
As they beat at the heart of the mother,
  Drive the colour from her cheek?

Henry Wadsworth Longfellow

- Here are two poems on a similar theme – the unity and value of all creation. Christina Rossetti's poem starts with an idea in line 1 and then illustrates it with a list of creatures. Why do you think they are all tiny insects?
- William Blake's 'The Fly' starts with a 'thoughtless' act and then develops a more difficult argument. Why does he describe himself as 'a happy fly' at the end?

As a class

- Hear the poems read aloud. Talk about the feelings and thoughts they express and try to answer the questions posed above.

HURT NO LIVING THING

Hurt no living thing;
Ladybird, nor butterfly,
Nor moth with dusty wing,
Nor cricket chirping cheerily,
Nor grasshopper so light of leap,
Nor dancing gnat, nor beetle fat,
Nor harmless worms that creep.

Christina Rossetti

THE FLY

Little Fly,
Thy summer's play
My thoughtless hand
Has brushed away.

Am not I
A fly like thee?
Or art not thou
A man like me?

For I dance,
And drink, and sing,
Till some blind hand
Shall brush my wing.

If thought is life
And strength and breath,
And the want
Of thought is death;

Then am I
A happy fly,
If I live
Or if I die.

William Blake

PART B

Ten Themes

Seasons

'THE FIGHT OF THE YEAR'

'And there goes the bell for the third month
and Winter comes out of its corner looking groggy
Spring leads with a left to the head
followed by a sharp right to the body
      daffodils
      primroses
      crocuses
      snowdrops
      lilacs
      violets
      pussywillow
Winter can't take much more punishment
and Spring shows no signs of tiring
      tadpoles
      squirrels
      baalambs
      badgers
      bunny rabbits
      mad march hares
      horses and hounds
Spring is merciless
Winter won't go to the full twelve rounds
      bobtail clouds
      scallywaggy winds
      the sun
      a pavement artist
      in every town
A left to the chin
and Winter's down!

1 tomatoes
2 radish
3 cucumber
4 onions
5 beetroot
6 celery
7 and any
8 amount
9 of lettuce
10 for dinner
Winter's out for the count
Spring is the winner!'

Roger McGough

SPRING

Sound the flute!
Now it's mute,
Birds delight
Day and night:
Nightingale
In the dale,
Lark in sky,
Merrily,
Merrily, merrily, to welcome in the year.

Little boy,
Full of joy;
Little girl,
Sweet and small;
Cock does crow,
So do you;
Merry voice,
Infant noise,
Merrily, merrily, to welcome in the year.

Little lamb,
Here I am;
Come and lick
My white neck;
Let me pull
Your soft wool;
Let me kiss
Your soft face:
Merrily, merrily, we welcome in the year.

William Blake

SUMMER

Winter is cold-hearted,
Spring is yea and nay,
Autumn is a weathercock
Blown every way.
Summer days for me
When every leaf is on its tree.

When Robin's not a beggar,
And Jenny Wren's a bride,
And larks hang singing, singing, singing,
Over the wheat-fields wide,
And anchored lilies ride,
And the pendulum spider
Swings from side to side;

WHAT COULD BE LOVELIER THAN TO HEAR

What could be lovelier than to hear
The summer rain
Cutting across the heat, as scythes
Cut across grain?
Falling upon the steaming roof
With sweet uproar,
Tapping and rapping wildly
At the door?

No, do not lift the latch,
But through the pane
We'll stand and watch the circus pageant
Of the rain,
And see the lightning, like a tiger,
Striped and dread,
And hear the thunder cross the sky
With elephant tread.

Elisabeth Coatsworth

And blue-black beetles transact business,
And gnats fly in a host,
And furry caterpillars hasten
That no time be lost,
And moths grow fat and thrive,
And ladybirds arrive.

Before green apples blush,
Before green nuts embrown,
Why, one day in the country
Is worth a month in town;
Is worth a day and a year
Of the dusty, musty, lag-last fashion
That days drone elsewhere.

Christina Rossetti

LAST WEEK IN OCTOBER

The trees are undressing, and fling in many places
On the gray road, the roof, the window-sill –
Their radiant robes and ribbons and yellow laces;
A leaf each second so is flung at will,
Here, there, another and another, still and still.

A spider's web has caught one while downcoming,
That stays there dangling when the rest pass on;
Like a suspended criminal hangs he, mumming,
In golden garb, while one yet green, high yon,
Trembles, as fearing such a fate for himself anon.

Thomas Hardy

NIGHT-TIME IN MID-FALL

It is a storm-strid night, winds footing swift
    Through the blind profound;
    I know the happenings from their sound;
Leaves totter down still green, and spin and drift;
The tree-trunks rock to their roots, which wrench and lift
The loam where they run onward underground.

The streams are muddy and swollen; eels migrate
    To a new abode;
    Even cross, 'tis said, the turnpike-road;
(Men's feet have felt their crawl, home-coming late):
The westward fronts of towers are saturate,
Church-timbers crack, and witches ride abroad.

Thomas Hardy

DECEMBER

A wrinkled crabbèd man they picture thee,
Old Winter, with a rugged beard as grey
As the long moss upon the apple-tree;
Blue-lipt, an ice drop at thy sharp blue nose,
Close muffled up, and on thy dreary way
Plodding along through sleet and drifting snows.
They should have drawn thee by thy high-heap't hearth,
Old Winter! seated in thy great armed chair;
Watching the children at their Christmas mirth; –
Or circled by them as thy lips declare
Some merry jest, or tale of murder dire,
Or troubled spirit that disturbs the night;
Pausing at times to rouse the smouldering fire,
Or taste the old October brown and bright.

Robert Southey

WINTER DAYS

Biting air
Winds blow
City streets
Under snow

Noses red
Lips sore
Runny eyes
Hands raw

Chimneys smoke
Cars crawl
Piled snow
On garden wall

Slush in gutters
Ice in lanes
Frosty patterns
On window panes

Morning call
Lift up head
Nipped by winter
Stay in bed

Gareth Owen

 Talking and writing

Re-read the two poems about spring (pp. 32–33). 'The Fight of the Year' lists a lot of flowers, animals and vegetables which knock out winter and make spring the winner. The three verses of Blake's 'Spring' are made up of rhyming couplets written in three-syllable rhymes (see Part A, Units 1 & 5).

In pairs

- Take the lists from the first poem and develop them in the style of the second to make your own spring poem.

You might begin:

'Daffodils/
On the hills'

You will need to add words when you have only two syllables, e.g.

'Badgers/ found
Underground,'

and lengthen the lines when you start with four syllables, e.g.

'Pussywillow/
Hanging down low.'

Group poem

- As a class, make lists of all the things you associate with each of the four seasons. Then divide into four groups, one per season. Extend your lists by adding your feelings and thoughts about this particular time of year. Develop a group poem on your season to which everyone contributes a line or two.

Love

NOBODY LOVES ME

Nobody loves me.
Everybody hates me,
Going in the garden
To-eat-worms.

Big fat juicy ones,
Little squiggly niggly ones.
Going in the garden
To-eat-worms.

Anon

VALENTINE'S DAY RHYME

Postman, Postman, at the gate,
Will you take this to my date?
Postman, Postman, for a laugh,
Do the tango up the path.

Anon

AFFECTIONS TRANSFERRED

She frowned and called him Mr.
Because in sport he kr.
　　And so in spite,
　　That very night
This Mr. kr. sr.

Anon

ESAU

I saw Esau kissing Kate,
The fact is we all three saw;
　　For I saw him,
　　And he saw me,
And she saw I saw Esau.

Anon

HOME

Home's not merely four square walls,
　　Though with pictures hung and gilded;
Home is where affection calls, —
　　Fill'd with shrines the heart hath builded!
Home! — go watch the faithful dove,
　　Sailing 'neath the heaven above us;
Home is where there's one to love;
　　Home is where there's one to love us!

Home's not merely roof and room, —
　　It needs something to endear it;
Home is where the heart can bloom, —
　　Where there's some kind lip to cheer it!
What is home with none to meet, —
　　None to welcome, none to greet us?
Home is sweet — and only sweet —
　　When there's one we love to meet us!

Charles Swain

THE PASSIONATE SHEPHERD TO HIS LOVE

Come live with me and be my love,
And we will all the pleasures prove,
That hills and valleys, dales and fields,
And all the craggy mountains yields.

There we will sit upon the rocks,
And see the shepherds feed their flocks,
By shallow rivers to whose falls
Melodious birds sing madrigals.

And I will make thee beds of roses
With a thousand fragrant posies,
A cap of flowers, and a kirtle
Embroidered all with leaves of myrtle;

A gown made of the finest wool
Which from our pretty lambs we pull;
Fair lined slippers for the cold,
With buckles of the purest gold;

A belt of straw and ivy buds,
With coral clasps and amber studs:
And if these pleasures may thee move,
Come live with me and be my love.

The shepherds' swains shall dance and sing
For thy delight each May morning:
If these delights thy mind may move,
Then live with me and be my love.

Christopher Marlowe

THE MILTON ABBAS RHYME

*The chapel at Milton Abbas Abbey in Dorset was
dedicated to St Catherine, who was supposed to have
the power of finding husbands for young women who
wanted to marry if they prayed to her.*

Saint Catherine, Saint Catherine,
O lend me your aid,
And grant that I never
May die an old maid.

A husband, Saint Catherine!
A good one Saint Catherine!
But any one better
Than no one, Saint Catherine!

A husband, Saint Catherine!
Handsome, Saint Catherine!
Rich, Saint Catherine!
Young, Saint Catherine!
SOON, Saint Catherine!

Anon

SERIOUS LUV

Monday Morning

I really luv de girl dat's sitting next to me
I think she thinks like me and she's so cool,
I think dat we could live for ever happily
I want to marry her when I leave school.

She's de only one in school allowed to call
   me Ben
When she does Maths I luv de way she
   chews her pen,
When we are doing Art she's so artistic
In Biology she makes me heart beat so quick.

When we do Geography I go to paradise
She's helped me draw a map of Borneo
   twice!
Today she's going to help me to take me
   books home
So I am going to propose to her when we're
   alone.

The next day

I used to luv de girl dat's sitting next to me
But yesterday it all came to an end,
She said that I should take love more
   seriously
And now I think I really luv her friend.

                    Benjamin Zephaniah

CHILDREN

If children live with criticism
   they learn to condemn

If children live with hostility
   they learn to fight

If children live with ridicule
   they learn to be shy

If children live with shame
   they learn to feel guilty

If children live with tolerance
   they learn to be patient

If children live with encouragement
   they learn confidence

If children live with praise
   they learn to appreciate

If children live with fairness
   they learn justice

If children live with security
   they learn to have faith

If children live with approval
   they learn to like themselves

If children live with acceptance and
   friendship
   they learn to find love in the world

                    Anon

LIZZIE

When I was eleven
there was Lizzie.
I used to think this:

You don't care, Lizzie,
you say
that you're a ginger-nut
and you don't care.

I've noticed
that they try to soften you
   up

they say
you're clumsy

they say
you can't wear shorts
to school

but you say,
'I don't care,
I mean

how can I play football
in a skirt?'

Lizzie,
I'm afraid of saying
I think you're great

because, you see,
the teachers call you
tomboy.

I'm sorry
but I make out, as if
I agree with the teachers

and the other girls
wear bracelets
and I've noticed
they don't shout like you
or whistle,
and, you see,
the other boys
are always talking about

those girls
with the bracelets

So I do too.

So I know
that makes me a coward
but that's why I don't dare
to say you're great,

but I think it to myself
when you're there
but I don't say.

I just try to show
I like you
by laughing
and joking about
and pulling mad faces.

I'm sorry
but I don't suppose
you'll ever know...

Michael Rosen

 Writing

- The two poems 'Serious Luv' (p. 38) and 'Lizzie' (above) capture the mixed feelings that first love can bring. Can you write your own poem about this?
- Valentine's Day is traditionally a time for writing poems to the one we love. Write your own Valentine's Day verse to go in a card.

Class poem

- Four centuries ago, Christopher Marlowe wrote his poem about 'The Passionate Shepherd' (p. 37) and all the delights he could offer his beloved. What might a modern passionate boy or girl have to offer to persuade a girl or boy to be their love? Can you compose a class poem that lists them?

Performance

- Working in groups, practise a reading of 'The Passionate Shepherd'. Try to be as persuasive as you can.

Times have changed since 'The Milton Abbas Rhyme' (p. 37) was written and not every young woman would pray for a husband, but it's still an amusing little piece. A group of four girls' voices, sharing the lines between them, works well.

- In groups, then as a class, put together and record a programme of these poems about different kinds of love; you could add your own poems too.

Family

THE QUARREL

I quarrelled with my brother,
I don't know what about,
One thing led to another
And somehow we fell out.
The start of it was slight,
The end of it was strong,
He said he was right,
I knew he was wrong!
We hated one another.
The afternoon turned black.
Then suddenly my brother
Thumped me on the back,
And said, 'Oh, *come* along!
We can't go on all night—
I was in the wrong.'
So he was in the right.

Eleanor Farjeon

ON MY FIRST SONNE

Farewell, thou child of my right hand, and
   joy;
My sinne was too much hope of thee, lov'd
   boy,
Seven yeeres tho' wert lent to me, and I thee
   pay,
Exacted by thy fate, on the just day.
O, could I loose all father, now. For why
Will man lament the state he should envie?
To have so soone scap'd worlds, and fleshes
   rage,
And, if no other miserie, yet age?
Rest in soft peace, and, ask'd, say here doth
   lye
Ben Jonson his best piece of poetrie.
For whose sake, hence-forth, all his vowes be
   such,
As what he loves may never like too much.

Ben Jonson

BROTHER AND SISTER

'Sister, sister, go to bed!
Go and rest your weary head.'
Thus the prudent brother said.

'Do you want a battered hide,
Or scratches to your face applied?'
Thus his sister calm replied.

'Sister, do not raise my wrath.
I'd make you into mutton broth
As easily as kill a moth!'

The sister raised her beaming eye
And looked on him indignantly
And sternly answered, 'Only try!'

Off to the cook he quickly ran.
'Dear cook, please lend a frying-pan
To me as quickly as you can.'

'And wherefore should I lend it to you?'
'The reason, Cook, is plain to view.
I wish to make an Irish stew.'

'What meat is in that stew to go?'
'My sister'll be the contents!'
                  'Oh!'
'You'll lend the pan to me, Cook?'
                  'No!'
Moral: Never stew your sister.

Lewis Carroll

STEPMOTHER

My stepmother
   is really nice
She ought to wear
   a label.
I don't come in
   with a latch key now —
my tea is on
   the table.
She doesn't nag at me
   or shout.
I often hear her
   singing
I'm glad my dad
   had wedding bells —
and I hope
   they go on ringing.

Stepmothers
   in fairy tales
are hard and cold
   as iron.
There isn't a lie
   they wouldn't tell,
or a trick
   they wouldn't try on.
But MY stepmother's
   warm and true;
she's kind, and cool,
   and clever —
Yes! I've a *wicked*
   stepmother —
and I hope she stays
   for ever!

            Jean Kenward

MR NOBODY

I know a funny little man,
   As quiet as a mouse,
He does the mischief that is done
   In everybody's house.
Though no one ever sees his face,
   Yet one and all agree
That every plate we break, was cracked
   By Mr Nobody.

'Tis he who always tears our books,
   Who leaves the door ajar.
He picks the buttons from our shirts,
   And scatters pins afar.
That squeaking door will always squeak —
   For prithee, don't you see?
We leave the oiling to be done
   By Mr Nobody.

He puts damp wood upon the fire,
   That kettles will not boil:
His are the feet that bring in mud
   And all the carpets soil.
The papers that so oft are lost —
   Who had them last but he?
There's no one tosses them about
   But Mr Nobody.

The fingermarks upon the door
   By none of us were made.
We never leave the blinds unclosed
   To let the curtains fade.
The ink we never spill! The boots
   That lying round you see,
Are not our boots — they all belong
   To Mr Nobody.

            Anon

'FATHER SAYS'

Father says
Never
let
me
see
you
doing
that
again
father says
tell you once
tell you a thousand times
come hell or high water
his finger drills my shoulder
never let me see you doing that
again
My brother knows all his phrases off by heart
so we practise them in bed at night

Michael Rosen

Performance

Fights or arguments between brothers and sisters are quite common. Often they are triggered by trivial things. The first two poems are about such disagreements. Share out the lines between the voices and give live readings of the poems.

- 'Father says' is more difficult to perform. Rehearse, trying out which is the best tone of voice, accent and pace, before letting the rest of the class hear your efforts.

Discussion

Ben Jonson's poem 'On My First Sonne' is an elegy for his son who died aged 7. It dates from a time, four centuries ago, when death in childhood was common and when faith in God was more widespread than it is today.

- Read through the poem and think about the father's feelings. What comfort does he find in the death of his son?

Nonsense

LADIES AND JELLYSPOONS

Ladies and Jellyspoons:
I come before you
To stand behind you
And tell you something
I know nothing about.

Next Thursday,
The day after Friday,
There'll be a ladies' meeting
For men only.

Wear your best clothes
If you haven't any,
And if you can come
Please stay home.

Admission is free.
You can pay at the door.
We'll give you a seat
So you can sit on the floor.

It makes no difference
Where you sit;
The kid in the gallery
Is sure to spit.

Anon

THE GREENGROCER'S LOVE POEM

Do you carrot all for me?
My heart beets for you.
With your turnip nose
And your radish face.
You are a peach.
If we canteloupe,
Lettuce marry:
Weed make a swell pear.

Anon

ALGY

Algy met a bear,
The bear met Algy.
The bear was bulgy,
The bulge was Algy.

Anon

THE FROG

What a wonderful bird the frog are —
When he sit, he stand almost;
When he hop, he fly almost.
He ain't got no sense hardly;
He ain't got no tail hardly either,
When he sit, he sit on what he ain't got —
    almost.

Anon

YE TORTURES

From the document found in the Archives of Bude Monastery during a squirting excavation. It shows a complete list of tortures approved by the Ministry of Works in the year 1438, for failure to pay leg tithe, or sockage.

The prisoner will be:

Bluned on ye Grunions
   and krelled on his Grotts
Ye legges will be twergled
   and pulled thru' ye motts!

His Nukes will be Fongled
   split thrice on yon Thulls
Then laid on ye Quottle
   and hung by ye Bhuls!

Twice thocked on the Phneffic,
   Yea broggled thrice twee.
Ye moggs will be grendled
   and stretched six foot three!

By now, if ye victim
   show not ye sorrow,
Send him home. Tell him,
   'Come back to-morrow.'

       Spike Milligan

WHEN I WAS YOUR AGE

When I was your age, child —
When I was eight,
When I was ten,
When I was two
(How old are you?) —
My father would have gone quite *wild*
Had I behaved the way you
Do.
What, food uneaten on my plate
When I was eight?
What, room in such a filthy state
When I was ten?
What, late
For school when I was two?
My father would have shouted, 'When

THE SNIFFLE

In spite of her sniffle
Isabel's chiffle.
Some girls with a sniffle
Would be weepy and tiffle;
They would look awful,
Like a rained-on waffle,
But Isabel's chiffle
In spite of her sniffle.
Her nose is more red
With a cold in her head,
But then, to be sure,
Her eyes are bluer.
Some girls with a snuffle,
Their tempers are uffle.
But when Isabel's snivelly
She's snivelly civilly,
And when she's snuffly
She's perfectly luffly.

       Ogden Nash

I was your age, child, my father would have
   raved
Had I behaved
The way you
Do.'
When I was
Your age, child, I did not drive us
All perpetually mad
By bashing
Up my little brother and reducing him to
   tears.
There was a war on in those years!
There were no brothers to be had!
Even sisters were on ration!
My goodness, we were pleased

To get *anything* to tease!
We were glad
Of aunts and dogs,
Of chickens, grandmothers and frogs;
Of creatures finned and creatures hooved,
And second cousins twice removed!
When I was your
Age, child, I was more
Considerate of others
(Particularly of fathers and mothers).
I did not sprawl
Reading the *Dandy*
Or the *Beano*
When aunts and uncles came to call.
Indeed no.
I grandly
Entertained them all
With 'Please' and 'Thank you,' 'May I...?'
   'Thank you,' 'Sorry,' 'Please,'
And other remarks like these.
And if a chance came in the conversation
I would gracefully recite a line
Which everyone recognized as a quotation
From one of the higher multiplication
Tables, like 'Seven sevens are forty-nine.'

When I was your age, child, I
Should never have dreamed
Of sitting idly
Watching television half the night.
It would have seemed demented;
Television not then having been
Invented.

When I was your age, child, I did not lie
About the house all day.
(I did not lie about anything at all — no liar
   I!)
I got out!
I ran away!

To sea!
(Though naturally I was back, with hair
      brushed
   and hands washed, in time for tea.)
Oh yes, goodness me,
When I was nine
I had worked already down a diamond mine,
And fought in several minor wars,
And hunted boars
In the lonelier
Parts of Patagonia.
(Though I admit that possibly by then
I was getting on for ten.)
In the goldfields of Australia
I learned the bitterness of failure;
Experience in the temples of Siam
Made me the wise and punctual man I am;
But the lesson that I value most
I learned upon the Coromandel Coast —
Never, come what may, to boast.

When
I was your age, child, and the older generation
Offered now and then
A kindly explanation
Of what the world was like in their young day
I did not yawn in that rude way.
Why, goodness me,
There being no television to see
(As I have, I think, already said)
We were dashed grateful
For any entertainment we could get instead,
However tedious and hateful.

So grow up, child! And be
Your age! (What *is* your age, then?
Eight? Or nine? Or two? Or ten?)
Remember, as you look at me —
When I was your age I was forty-three.

Michael Frayn

Writing

Several of these poems and rhymes work by using words that are close to the ones we use normally but are not quite right: 'Ladies and Jellyspoons' instead of 'ladies and gentlemen'; 'With your turnip nose' instead of 'turned up nose', and so on.

● Can you write your own piece of nonsense like the silly speech on p. 43? You could begin in a similar fashion: 'Ladies and welly-boots', perhaps, and see where it leads you.
● 'Ye Tortures' on p. 44 is complete nonsense but the pictures *suggested* by the words have a kind of idiotic sense that makes people laugh. (Would you like your nukes to be fongled? – Of course not!) Try to write additional verses with tortures that Spike Milligan might have included.

Performance/drama

The pompous adult in Michael Frayn's poem on pp. 44–45 gradually gets more and more bizarre in his claims about what a wonderful child he was compared with today's children. It's a good poem to perform as a group and you can split it up for different voices and act it out with the poor modern child surrounded by accusing grown-ups each saying their bit.

Ghosts and Ghouls

PRAYER

From ghoulies and ghosties and long-leggety beasties
And things that go bump in the night,
  Good Lord, deliver us!

Traditional Cornish

'EACH NIGHT FATHER FILLS ME WITH DREAD'

Each night Father fills me with dread
When he sits on the foot of my bed;
  I'd not mind that he speaks
  In gibbers and squeaks,
But for seventeen years he's been dead.

Edward Gorey

A ROOM BEWITCHED

In a dark, dark wood, there was
  a dark, dark house,
And in that dark, dark house, there was
  a dark, dark room,
And in that dark, dark room, there was
  a dark, dark cupboard,
And in that dark, dark cupboard, there was
  a dark, dark shelf,
And on that dark, dark shelf, there was
  a dark, dark box,
And in that dark, dark box, there was a...

GHOST!

Anon

THREE GHOSTESSES

There were three ghostesses
Sitting on postesses
Eating buttered toastesses
And greasing their fistesses
Right up to their wristesses.
Weren't they beastesses
To make such feastesses!

Anon

POEM

In the stump of the old tree, where the heart has rotted out,/there is a hole the length of a man's arm, and a dank pool at the/bottom of it where the rain gathers, and the old leaves turn into/lacy skeletons. But do not put your hand down to see, because

in the stumps of old trees, where the hearts have rotted out,/there are holes the length of a man's arm, and dank pools at the/bottom where the rain gathers and old leaves turn to lace, and the/beak of a dead bird gapes like a trap. But do not put your/hand down to see, because

in the stumps of old trees with rotten hearts, where the rain/gathers and the laced leaves and the dead bird like a trap, there/are holes the length of a man's arm, and in every crevice of the/rotten wood grow weasels' eyes like molluscs, their lids open/and shut with the tide. But do not put your hand down to see, because

in the stumps of old trees where the rain gathers and the/trapped leaves and the beak, and the laced weasels' eyes, there are/holes the length of a man's arm, and at the bottom a sodden bible/written in the language of rooks. But do not put your hand down/to see, because

in the stumps of old trees where the hearts have rotted out there are holes the length of a man's arm where the weasels are/trapped and the letters of the rook language are laced on the/sodden leaves, and at the bottom there is a man's arm. But do/not put your hand down to see, because

in the stumps of old trees where the hearts have rotted out/there are deep holes and dank pools where the rain gathers, and/if you ever put your hand down to see, you can wipe it in the/sharp grass till it bleeds, but you'll never want to eat with/it again.

Hugh Sykes Davies

THE LONGEST JOURNEY IN THE WORLD

'Last one into bed
has to switch out the light.'
It's just the same every night.
There's a race.
I'm ripping off my trousers and shirt—
he's kicking off his shoes and socks.

'My sleeve's stuck.'
'This button's too big for its button-hole.'
'Have you hidden my pyjamas?'
'Keep your hands off mine.'
If you win
you get where it's safe
before the darkness comes—
but if you lose
if you're last
you know what you've got coming up is
the journey from the light switch
to your bed.
It's the Longest Journey in the World.

'You're last tonight,' my brother says.
And he's right.
There is nowhere so dark
as that room in the moment
after I've switched out the light.

There is nowhere so full of dangerous
  things—
things that love dark places—
things that breathe only when you breathe
and hold their breath when I hold mine.
So I have to say:
'I'm not scared.'
That face, grinning in the pattern on the wall
isn't a face—
'I'm not scared.'
That prickle on the back of my neck
is only the label on my pyjama jacket—
'I'm not scared.'
That moaning-moaning is nothing
but water in a pipe—
'I'm not scared.'

Everything's going to be just fine
as soon as I get into that bed of mine.
Such a terrible shame
it's always the same
it takes so long
it takes so long
it takes so long
to get there.

From the light switch
to my bed.
It's the Longest Journey in the World.

Michael Rosen

GOODBAT NIGHTMAN

God bless all policemen
and fighters of crime,
May thieves go to jail
for a very long time.

They've had a hard day
helping clean up the town,
Now they hang from the mantelpiece
both upside down.

A glass of warm blood
and then straight up the stairs,
Batman and Robin
are saying their prayers.

They've locked all the doors
and they've put out the bat,
Put on their batjamas
(They like doing that)

They've filled their batwater bottles
made their batbeds,
With two springy battresses
for sleepy batheads.

They're closing red eyes
and they're counting black sheep,
Batman and Robin
are falling asleep.

Roger McGough

Performance

At least three of the poems in this section are great fun to perform. You can work either in groups or as a whole class but it may be easier to work in groups, first of all, on each poem in turn.

- 'A Room Bewitched': How many different ways can you find of building up to the climax? Does it have to be a climax or can it get quieter and more deadly? Do you read all together or take lines each? Can it be read as a 'round', with people starting at intervals? What happens if you substitute 'A man trying to mend a fuse' for the word 'Ghost' at the end? (The result is known as an 'anti-climax', or 'bathos' – that is, a feeling of being let down after a big build-up.)
- 'Poem': This is a really sinister poem but it needs practice to get it right. In groups, build up a creepy and threatening reading of the piece.
- 'The Longest Journey in the World': This needs a narrator and two people to play the brothers.

Record the best of these readings and add some other poems in this section, and ones like 'The Hairy Toe' from p. 19 and 'Colonel Fazackerley' on p. 96, and you have a really good radio programme on ghosts and ghouls!

Writing

- What things frightened you most when you were little? Talk about this and then jot down your ideas. Can they be collected together to make a class poem?

Stories

JAMES

Who played computer games but finally got a life

The chief delight of youthful James
Was violent computer games,
Where everything was quite destroyed.
But most of all the lad enjoyed
The buxom charms of Lara Croft,
Despite the fact his sister scoffed
And called him 'weird, a total nerd',
And found his passion quite absurd,
And said he ought to 'get a life'—
Thus causing much familial strife.

(This Lara, if you didn't know,
Creation of the Eidos Co.,
Is no bloodless Space Invader
But heroine of their game Tomb Raider,
Quick-thinking, weapon-toting, strong
—With legs so very, very long...)

But we digress from young James' plight.
He'd stay up playing every night
Until his eyes were raw and red;
For years he hardly went to bed.
He couldn't leave the thing alone
And wore his fingers to the bone
Tapping the keyboard fev'rishly
Trying to get from level three
To four — or was it five to six?
No matter — he'd got to have his fix.

His parents, in complete despair,
Pleaded with him, tore their hair,

Called in a psychiatrist
Who warned the boy he should desist
And go for healthy walks and ride
His bicycle, not lurk inside,
Confined entirely to his room
Whose matt black walls and general gloom
Lit only by his screen display,
Depressed the spirit, were not gay.

Young James grew older, tall and wan,
His energy was almost gone
When (happy chance!) he glanced outside
And saw, a vision slowly glide
Along the sidewalk on her bike,
Laughing and waving, quite unlike
Lara or girls he'd seen before.
A girl called Jill had moved next door.
Immediately, his heart went bump,
Against his ribs he felt it thump.

The rest you know, or you can guess.
No longer now a total mess
In thrall to his computer screen,
James has a real, not virtual, queen.
His old computer gathers dust
And Lara's blasters, legs and bust
Are all forgotten now you see:
And James is just like you and me.
But every day he thanks the fates
That made him happy with Jill Gates!

Peter Benton

THE LION AND ALBERT

There's a famous seaside place called
    Blackpool,
  That's noted for fresh air and fun,
And Mr and Mrs Ramsbottom
    Went there with young Albert, their son.

A grand little lad was young Albert,
    All dressed in his best; quite a swell
With a stick with an 'orse's 'ead 'andle,
    The finest that Woolworth's could sell.

They didn't think much to the Ocean:
    The waves, they was fiddlin' and small,
There was no wrecks and nobody drownded,
    Fact, nothing to laugh at at all.

So, seeking for further amusement,
    They paid and went into the Zoo,
Where they'd Lions and Tigers and Camels,
    And old ale and sandwiches too.

There were one great big Lion called Wallace;
    His nose were all covered with scars
He lay in a somnolent posture,
    With the side of his face on the bars.

Now Albert had heard about Lions,
    How they was ferocious and wild
To see Wallace lying so peaceful,
    Well, it didn't seem right to the child.

So straightway the brave little feller,
    Not showing a morsel of fear,
Took his stick with its 'orse's 'ead 'andle
    And pushed it in Wallace's ear.

You could see that the Lion didn't like it,
    For giving a kind of a roll,
He pulled Albert inside the cage with 'im,
    And swallowed the little lad 'ole.

Then Pa, who had seen the occurrence,
    And didn't know what to do next,
Said 'Mother! Yon Lion's 'et Albert',
    And Mother said 'Well, I am vexed!'

Then Mr and Mrs Ramsbottom
    Quite rightly, when all's said and done,
Complained to the Animal Keeper,
    That the Lion had eaten their son.

The keeper was quite nice about it;
    He said 'What a nasty mishap.
Are you sure that it's *your* boy he's eaten?'
    Pa said 'Am I sure? There's his cap!'

The manager had to be sent for.
    He came and he said 'What's to do?'
Pa said 'Yon Lion's 'et Albert,
    And 'im in his Sunday clothes, too.'

Then Mother said, 'Right's right, young
    feller;
  I think it's a shame and a sin,
For a lion to go and eat Albert,
    And after we've paid to come in.'

The manager wanted no trouble,
    He took out his purse right away,
Saying 'How much to settle the matter?'
    And Pa said 'What do you usually pay?'

But Mother had turned a bit awkward
    When she thought where her Albert had
    gone.
She said 'No! someone's got to be
    summonsed'—
  So that was decided upon.

Then off they went to the P'lice Station,
    In front of the Magistrate chap;
They told 'im what happened to Albert,
    And proved it by showing his cap.

The Magistrate gave his opinion
    That no one was really to blame
And he said that he hoped the Ramsbottoms
    Would have further sons to their name.

At that Mother got proper blazing,
    'And thank you, sir, kindly,' said she.
'What waste all our lives raising children
    To feed ruddy Lions? Not me!'

Marriott Edgar

AFTER BLENHEIM

It was a summer evening,
    Old Kaspar's work was done,
And he before his cottage door
    Was sitting in the sun;
And by him sported on the green
His little grandchild Wilhelmine.

She saw her brother Peterkin
    Roll something large and round
Which he beside the rivulet
    In playing there had found;
He came to ask what he had found
That was so large and smooth and round.

Old Kaspar took it from the boy
    Who stood expectant by;
And then the old man shook his head,
    And with a natural sigh,
''Tis some poor fellow's skull,' said he,
'Who fell in the great victory.

'I find them in the garden,
    For there's many here about;
And often when I go to plough
    The ploughshare turns them out;
For many thousand men,' said he,
'Were slain in that great victory.'

'Now tell us what 'twas all about,'
    Young Peterkin he cries;
And little Wilhelmine looks up
    With wonder-waiting eyes;
'Now tell us all about the war,
And what they fought each other for.'

'It was the English,' Kaspar cried,
    'Who put the French to rout;
But what they fought each other for
    I could not well make out.
But everybody said,' quoth he,
    'That 'twas a famous victory.

'My father lived at Blenheim then,
    Yon little stream hard by;
They burnt his dwelling to the ground,
    And he was forced to fly:
So with his wife and child he fled,
Nor had he where to rest his head.

'They say it was a shocking sight
    After the field was won;
For many thousand bodies here
    Lay rotting in the sun:
But things like that, you know, must be
After a famous victory.

'Great praise the Duke of Marlboro' won
    And our good Prince Eugene;'
'Why, 'twas a very wicked thing!'
    Said little Wilhelmine;
'Nay...nay...my little girl,' quoth he,
'It was a famous victory.

'And everybody praised the Duke
    Who this great fight did win.'
'But what good came of it at last?'
    Quoth little Peterkin.
'Why, that I cannot tell,' said he,
'But 'twas a famous victory.'

                        Robert Southey

Writing

You may have already read a poem like the one about James on p. 51. It is a modern version of one of Hilaire Belloc's *Cautionary Verses* that we met on p. 20.

● Try to write your own. Perhaps, to get you started, you could think about things that irritate others. 'The chief defect of little boys / Is'…What? Hmm…'Noise'? 'Toys'? Maybe: 'always making lots of noise'? 'Breaking all my favourite toys'? – and so on.

Performance

● Listen to 'After Blenheim' read aloud, discuss what the poem is telling us about war, and then prepare a group reading of the poem. There are four voices in the poem: a Narrator, Old Kaspar, Peterkin and little Wilhelmine (who only gets one line.)

'The Lion and Albert' is written as a piece to be read aloud to an audience. It is the sort of comic recitation that some of the old music-hall comedians used to give. It became a 'party piece' and for some time was very well-known.

● Dramatise it with the voices of the Narrator, Mr and Mrs Ramsbottom, the Keeper and the Manager.

Ballads

THE TWO SISTERS OF BINNORIE

There were two sisters sat in a bower;
  Binnorie, O Binnorie;
There came a knight to be their wooer;
  By the bonny mill dams of Binnorie.

He courted the eldest with gloves and rings,
But he loved the youngest above all things,

The eldest was vexed to despair,
And much she envied her sister fair.

The eldest said to the youngest one,
"Will ye see our father's ships come in?"

She's taken her by the lily-white hand,
And led her down to the river strand.

The youngest stood upon a stone;
The eldest came and pushed her in.

"O sister, sister reach your hand,
And you shall be heir of half my land,

"O sister, reach me but your glove
And sweet William shall be your love."

"Sink on, nor hope for hand or glove!
Sweet William shall surely be my love."

Sometimes she sank, sometimes she swam,
Until she came to the mouth of the dam.

Out then came the miller's son
And saw the fair maid swimming in.

"O father, father, draw your dam!
Here's either a mermaid or a swan."

The miller hasted and drew his dam,
And there he found a drowned woman.

You could not see her middle small,
Her girdle was so rich withal.

You could not see her yellow hair
For the gold and pearls that clustered there.

And by there came a harper fine
Who harped to nobles when they dine.

And when he looked that lady on,
He sighed and made a heavy moan.

He's made a harp of her breast bone,
Whose sounds would melt a heart of stone.

He's taken three locks of her yellow hair
And with them strung his harp so rare.

He went into her father's hall
To play his harp before them all.

But as he laid it on a stone,
The harp began to play alone.

And soon the harp sang loud and clear,
"Farewell, my father and mother dear.

"Farewell, farewell, my brother Hugh,
Farewell, my William, sweet and true."

And then as plain as plain could be,
  (Binnorie, O Binnorie)
"There sits my sister who drowned me
  By the bonny mill dams of Binnorie!"

                    Anon

JOHN BARLEYCORN

There were three kings into the east,
　Three kings both great and high;
And they hae sworn a solemn oath
　John Barleycorn should die.

They took a plough and plough'd him down,
　Put clods upon his head;
And they hae sworn a solemn oath
　John Barleycorn was dead.

But the cheerful Spring came kindly on,
　And show'rs began to fall;
John Barleycorn got up again,
　And sore surpris'd them all.

The sultry suns of Summer came,
　And he grew thick and strong;
His head weel arm'd wi' pointed spears,
　That no one should him wrong.

The sober Autumn enter'd mild,
　When he grew wan and pale;
His bending joints and drooping head
　Show'd he began to fail.

His colour sicken'd more and more,
　He faded into age;
And then his enemies began
　To show their deadly rage.

They've ta'en a weapon, long and sharp,
　And cut him by the knee;
Then tied him fast upon a cart,
　Like a rogue for forgerie.

They laid him down upon his back,
　And cudgell'd him full sore;
They hung him up before the storm,
　And turn'd him o'er and o'er.

They fillèd up a darksome pit
　With water to the brim;
They heavèd in John Barleycorn,
　There let him sink or swim.

They laid him out upon the floor,
　To work him further woe;
And still, as signs of life appear'd,
　They toss'd him to and fro.

They wasted o'er a scorching flame
　The marrow of his bones;
But a miller us'd him worst of all—
　He crush'd him 'tween two stones.

And they hae ta'en his very heart's blood,
　And drank it round and round;
And still the more and more they drank,
　Their joy did more abound.

John Barleycorn was a hero bold,
　Of noble enterprise;
For if you do but taste his blood,
　'Twill make your courage rise.

'Twill make a man forget his woe;
　'Twill heighten all his joy;
'Twill make the widow's heart to sing,
　Tho' the tear were in her eye.

Then let us toast John Barleycorn,
　Each man a glass in hand;
And may his great posterity
　Ne'er fail in old Scotland.

Robert Burns

LA BELLE DAME SANS MERCI

'O what can ail thee, knight-at-arms,
    Alone and palely loitering?
The sedge has withered from the lake,
    And no birds sing.

'O what can ail thee, knight-at-arms,
    So haggard and so woe-begone?
The squirrel's granary is full,
    And the harvest's done.

'I see a lily on thy brow
    With anguish moist and fever dew,
And on thy cheeks a fading rose
    Fast withereth too.'

I met a lady in the meads,
    Full beautiful – a faery's child,
Her hair was long, her foot was light,
    And her eyes were wild.

I made a garland for her head,
    And bracelets too, and fragrant zone,
She looked at me as she did love,
    And made sweet moan.

I set her on my pacing steed,
    And nothing else saw all day long,
For sidelong would she bend, and sing
    A faery's song.

She found me roots of relish sweet,
    And honey wild, and manna dew,
And sure in language strange she said –
    'I love thee true!'

She took me to her elfin grot,★
    And there she wept and sighed full sore,
And there I shut her wild, wild eyes
    With kisses four.

And there she lullèd me asleep,
    And there I dreamed – ah! woe betide!
The latest dream I ever dreamed
    On the cold hill's side.

I saw pale kings and princes too,
    Pale warriors, death-pale were they all;
The cried – 'La Belle Dame sans Merci
    Hath thee in thrall!'

I saw their starved lips in the gloam,
    With horrid warning gapèd wide,
And I awoke and found me here,
    On the cold hill's side.

And this is why I sojourn here,
    Alone and palely loitering,
Though the sedge is withered from the lake,
    And no birds sing.

John Keats

★grotto or cave

About ballads

Ballads are narrative poems (they tell a story) and were often sung by wandering minstrels, who would accompany their songs with a harp. The songs were not written down but were known off by heart by the minstrel, who would sing them in taverns, courts and market places. The stories would change over time, particularly as other people learned them and added bits of their own, so one ballad may have many different versions.

Ballads are usually simple in their language, often have very clear images such as 'milk white steed', 'yellow hair' and frequently have a chorus or repeated line. They are usually written down in simple four-line verses in which alternate lines may rhyme (line 1 with 3 and 2 with 4, usually called an a, b, a, b, rhyme scheme). Sometimes they are in rhymed couplets where each pair of lines rhymes (a, a, b, b). They can be very long: the old Robin Hood ballads could be ninety verses or more! It is only through these ballads that we know the stories at all.

There are three ballads in this section: the old Scottish ballad of 'the Two Sisters of Binnorie', which tells a tale of jealousy, treachery, murder and revenge; Robert Burns' story of 'John Barleycorn', which is not about a man at all but about the stages in growing barley and how whisky is made from it; and John Keats's poem 'La Belle Dame Sans Merci', which tells of a wandering knight bewitched by a lovely but cruel enchantress – the beautiful lady without mercy.

Performance

- 'The Two Sisters of Binnorie' is a dramatic story which can be read by a whole class, particularly if everyone joins in the repeated chorus lines which are in italics. (They can be said in every verse if you like.) You will need a Narrator, two Sisters and a Miller's Son to make up the cast.

'La Belle Dame Sans Merci' is a conversation between the person who meets the pale, haggard knight after he has been released by the enchantress, and the knight himself, who tells what happened to him when he was under her spell.

- In pairs, practise a reading of the poem and check, as you read, that you understand the story.
- The fifteen verses of 'John Barleycorn' can be read in groups or around the class. What do the opening two lines of the poem make you think of? Are there any other points in the poem that suggest something similar?

Writing

- Try to compose an opening verse to a ballad of your own. You could model it on 'John Barleycorn'. For example: 'There were two friends at Newlands School…' or 'There was a girl who hated sums…'.

Creatures

THE MOUSE

I hear a mouse,
Bitterly complaining
In a crack of moonlight
Aslant on the floor–

'Little I ask
And that little is not granted.
There are few crumbs
In this world any more.

'The breadbox is tin
And I cannot get in.

'The jam's in a jar
My teeth cannot mar.

'The cheese sits by itself
On the pantry shelf.

'All night I run
Searching and seeking,
All night I run
About on the floor.

'Moonlight is there
And a bare place for dancing,
But no little feast
Is spread any more.'

Elizabeth Coatsworth

MICE

I think mice
Are rather nice.

   Their tails are long,
   Their faces small,
   They haven't any
   Chins at all.
   Their ears are pink,
   Their teeth are white,
   They run about
   The house at night.
   They nibble things
   They shouldn't touch
   And no one seems
   To like them much.

But I think mice
Are nice.

Rose Fyleman

CHOOSING THEIR NAMES

Our old cat has kittens three—
What do you think their names should be?

One is tabby with emerald eyes,
   And a tail that's long and slender,
And into a temper she quickly flies
   If you ever by chance offend her.
      I think we shall call her this—
      I think we shall call her that—
Now, don't you think that Pepperpot
   Is a nice name for a cat?

One is black with a frill of white,
   And her feet are all white fur,
If you stroke her she carries her tail upright

And quickly begins to purr.
   I think we shall call her this—
   I think we shall call her that—
Now, don't you think that Sootikin
   Is a nice name for a cat?

One is a tortoiseshell yellow and black,
   With plenty of white about him;
If you tease him, at once he sets up his back,
   He's a quarrelsome one, ne'er doubt him.
      I think we shall call him this—
      I think we shall call him that—
Now, don't you think that Scratchaway
   Is a nice name for a cat?

Thomas Hood

COWS

Half the time they munched the grass, and all
  the time they lay
Down in the water-meadows, the lazy
  month of May,
    A-chewing,
    A-mooing,
To pass the hours away.

  'Nice weather,' said the brown cow.
    'Ah,' said the white.
  'Grass is very tasty.'
    'Grass is all right.'

Half the time they munched the grass, and all
  the time they lay
Down in the water-meadows, the lazy
  month of May,
    A-chewing,
    A-mooing,
To pass the hours away.

  'Rain coming,' said the brown cow.
    'Ah,' said the white.
  'Flies is very tiresome.'
    'Flies bite.'

Half the time they munched the grass, and all
  the time they lay
Down in the water-meadows, the lazy
  month of May,
    A-chewing,
    A-mooing,
To pass the hours away.

  'Time to go,' said the brown cow.
    'Ah,' said the white.
  'Nice chat.' 'Very pleasant.'
    'Night.' 'Night.'

Half the time they munched the grass, and all
  the time they lay
Down in the water-meadows, the lazy
  month of May,
    A-chewing,
    A-mooing,
To pass the hours away.

              James Reeves

MISTER FOX

A fox went out in a hungry plight,
And he begged of the moon to give him
  light,
For he'd many miles to trot that night,
  Before he could reach his den O!

And first he came to a farmer's yard,
Where the ducks and geese declared it hard
That their nerves should be shaken and their
  rest be marr'd,
  By the visit of Mister Fox O!

He took the grey goose by the sleeve;
Says he, 'Madam Goose, and by your leave,
I'll take you away without reprieve,
  And carry you home to my den O!'

He seized the black duck by the neck,
And swung her over across his back;
The black duck cried out, 'Quack! Quack!
  Quack!'
  With her legs hanging dangling down O!

Then old Mrs Slipper-slopper jump'd out of
  bed,
And out of the window she popp'd her head,
Crying, 'John, John, John, the grey goose is
    gone,
  And the fox is away to his den O!'

Then John he went up to the top of the hill,
And he blew a blast both loud and shrill;
Says the fox, 'That is very pretty music –
    still
  I'd rather be in my den O!'

At last the fox got home to his den;
To his dear little foxes, eight, nine, ten,
Says he, 'You're in luck, here's a good fat
  duck,
  With her legs hanging dangling down O!

He then sat down with his hungry wife;
They did very well without fork or knife;
They'd never ate better in all their life,
  And the little ones pick'd the bones O!

              Anon

UPON THE SNAIL

She goes but softly, but she goeth sure;
She stumbles not as stronger creatures do:
Her journey's shorter, so she may endure
Better than they which do much further go.

She makes no noise, but stilly seizeth on
The flower or herb appointed for her food,
The which she quietly doth feed upon,
While others range and gare, but find no
   good.

And though she doth but very softly go,
However 'tis not fast, nor slow, but sure;
And certainly they that do travel so,
The prize they do aim at, they do procure.

John Bunyan

THE CATERPILLAR

Brown and furry
Caterpillar in a hurry,
Take your walk
To the shady leaf, or stalk,
   Or what not,
Which may be the chosen spot.
   No toad spy you,
Hovering bird of prey pass by you;
Spin and die,
To live again as butterfly.

Christina Rossetti

Talking animals

Two cows talking like two old farmers (p. 60), a fox stealing dinner for his family (p. 60), a mouse complaining because it cannot find any food (p. 59) — there are several ways that you could dramatise these poems.

- Work in groups and prepare a performance of one of the poems to present to the rest of your class.

Discussion and illustration

'Upon the Snail' and 'The Caterpillar' both describe journeys: one goes gently and surely towards her goal, the other is in a hurry.

- According to the poems, why do they travel so differently?
- What is the moral suggested by 'Upon the Snail'?
- Copy out 'The Caterpillar' on a separate sheet and illustrate it to show the stages of its life.

The Pied Piper
of Hamelin

I

Hamelin Town's in Brunswick,
By famous Hanover city;
  The river Weser, deep and wide,
  Washes its wall on the southern side;
  A pleasanter spot you never spied;
But, when begins my ditty,
  Almost five hundred years ago,
  To see the townsfolk suffer so
    From vermin, was a pity.

II

  Rats!
They fought the dogs and killed the cats,
  And bit the babies in the cradles,
And ate the cheeses out of the vats,
  And licked the soup from the cook's
    own ladles,
Split open the kegs of salted sprats,
Made nests inside men's Sunday hats,
And even spoiled the women's chats,
  By drowning their speaking
  With shrieking and squeaking
In fifty different sharps and flats.

III

At last the people in a body
  To the Town Hall came flocking:
"'Tis clear,!" cried they, "Our Mayor's a
  noddy;
  "And as for our Corporation – shocking
"To think we buy gowns lined with ermine
"For dolts that can't or won't determine
"What's best to rid us of our vermin!
"You hope, because you're old and obese,
"To find in the furry civic robe ease?
"Rouse up, sirs! Give your brains a racking
"To find the remedy we're lacking,
"Or, sure as fate, we'll send you packing!"
At this the Mayor and Corporation
Quaked with a mighty consternation.

IV

An hour they sate in council,
    At length the Mayor broke silence:
"For a guilder I'd my ermine gown sell;
    "I wish I were a mile hence!
"It's easy to bid one rack one's brain –
"I'm sure my poor head aches again,
"I've scratched it so, and all in vain.
"Oh for a trap, a trap, a trap!"
Just as he said this, what should hap
At the chamber door but a gentle tap?
"Bless us," cried the Mayor, "what's that?"
(With the Corporation as he sat,
Looking little though wondrous fat;
Nor brighter was his eye, nor moister
Than a too-long-opened oyster,
Save when at noon his paunch grew
    mutinous
For a plate of turtle green and glutinous)
"Only a scraping of shoes on the mat?
"Anything like the sound of a rat
"Makes my heart go pit-a-pat!"

V

"Come in!" – the Mayor cried, looking
    bigger:
And in did come the strangest figure!
His queer long coat from heel to head
Was half of yellow and half of red,
And he himself was tall and thin,
With sharp blue eyes, each like a pin,
And light loose hair, yet swarthy skin,
No tuft on cheek nor beard on chin,
But lips where smiles went out and in;
There was no guessing his kith and kin:
And nobody could enough admire
The tall man and his quaint attire.
Quoth one: "It's as my great-grandsire,
"Starting up at the Trump of Doom's tone,
"Had walked this way from his painted
    tombstone!"

VI

He advanced to the council-table:
And, "Please your honours," said he, "I'm
    able,
"By means of a secret charm, to draw
"All creatures living beneath the sun,
"That creep or swim or fly or run,
"After me so as you never saw!
"And I chiefly use my charm
"On creatures that do people harm,
"The mole and toad and newt and viper:
"And people call me the Pied Piper."
(And here they noticed round his neck
A scarf of red and yellow stripe,
To match with his coat and the self-same
    cheque;
And at the scarf's end hung a pipe;
And his fingers they noticed were ever
    straying
As if impatient to be playing
Upon this pipe, as low it dangled
Over his vesture so old-fangled.)
"Yet," said he, "poor Piper as I am,
"In Tartary I freed the Cham,
"Last June, from his huge swarms of gnats;
"I eased in Asia the Nizam
"Of a monstrous brood of vampyre-bats:
"And as for what your brain bewilders,
"If I can rid your town of rats
"Will you give me a thousand guilders?"
"One? fifty thousand!" – was the exclamation
Of the astonished Mayor and Corporation.

VII

Into the street the Piper stept,
    Smiling first a little smile,
As if he knew what magic slept
    In his quiet pipe the while;
Then, like a musical adept,
To blow the pipe his lips he wrinkled,
And green and blue his sharp eyes twinkled,
Like a candle-flame where salt is sprinkled;
And ere three shrill notes the pipe uttered,
You heard as if an army muttered;
And the muttering grew to a grumbling;
And the grumbling grew to a mighty
    rumbling;
And out of the houses the rats came
    tumbling.
Great rats, small rats, lean rats, brawny rats,
Brown rats, black rats, grey rats, tawny rats,
Grave old plodders, gay young friskers,
    Fathers, mothers, uncles, cousins,
Cocking their tails and pricking whiskers,
    Families by tens and dozens,
Brothers, sisters, husbands, wives –
Followed the Piper for their lives.
From street to street he piped advancing,
And step for step they followed dancing,
Until they came to the river Weser
Wherein all plunged and perished!
– Save one who, stout as Julius Caesar,
Swam across and lived to carry
(As he, the manuscript he cherished)
To Rat-land home his commentary:
Which was, "At the first shrill notes of the
    pipe,
"I heard a sound as of scraping tripe,
"And putting apples, wondrous ripe,
"Into a cider-press's gripe:
"And a moving away of pickle-tub-boards,
"And a leaving ajar of conserve-cupboards,
"And a drawing the corks of train-oil-flasks,
"And a breaking the hoops of butter-casks:
"And it seemed as if a voice
"(Sweeter far than by harp or by psaltery
"Is breathed) called out, "Oh rats, rejoice!

" 'The world is grown to one vast drysaltery!
" 'So munch on, crunch on, take your
    nuncheon,
" 'Breakfast, supper, dinner, luncheon!"
"And just as a bulky sugar-puncheon,
"Already staved, like a great sun shone
"Glorious scarce an inch before me,
"Just as methought it said, "Come, bore me!"
"–I found the Weser rolling o'er me."

VIII

You should have heard the Hamelin people
Ringing the bells till they rocked the steeple.
"Go," cried the Mayor, "and get long poles,
"Poke out the nest and block up the holes!
"Consult with carpenters and builders,
"And leave in our town not even a trace
"Of the rats!" – when suddenly, up the face
Of the Piper perked in the market-place,
With a, "First, if you please, my thousand
    guilders!"

IX

A thousand guilders! The Mayor looked blue;
So did the Corporation too.
For council dinners made rare havoc
With Claret, Moselle, Vin-de-Grave, Hock;
And half the money would replenish
Their cellar's biggest butt with Rhenish.
To pay this sum to a wandering fellow
With a gipsy coat of red and yellow!
"Beside," quoth the Mayor with a knowing
  wink,
"Our business was done at the river's brink;
"We saw with our eyes the vermin sink,
"And what's dead can't come to life, I think.
"So, friend, we're not the folks to shrink
"From the duty of giving you something to
  drink,
"And a matter of money to put in your poke;
"But as for the guilders, what we spoke
"Of them, as you very well know, was a joke.
"Beside, our losses have made us thrifty.
"A thousand guilders! Come, take fifty!"

X

The Piper's face fell, and he cried,
"No trifling! I can't wait, beside!
"I've promised to visit by dinner-time
"Bagdad, and accept the prime
"Of the Head-Cook's pottage, all he's rich in,
"For having left, in the Caliph's kitchen,
"Of a nest of scorpions no survivor:
"With him I proved no bargain-driver,
"With you, don't think I'll bate a stiver!
"And folks who put me in a passion
"May find me pipe after another fashion."

XI

"How?" cried the Major, "d'ye think I brook
"Being worse treated than a Cook?
"Insulted by a lazy ribald
"With idle pipe and vesture piebald?
"You threaten us, fellow? Do your worst,
"Blow your pipe there till you burst!"

XII

Once more he stept into the street,
  And to his lips again

Laid his long pipe of smooth straight cane;
  And ere he blew three notes (such sweet
Soft notes as yet musician's cunning
  Never gave the enraptured air)
There was a rustling, that seemed like a
  bustling
Of merry crowds justling at pitching and
  hustling,
Small feet were pattering, wooden shoes
  clattering,
Little hands clapping and little tongues
  chattering,
And, like fowls in a farm-yard when barley is
  scattering,
Out came the children running.
All the little boys and girls,
With rosy cheeks and flaxen curls,
And sparkling eyes and teeth like pearls,
Tripping and skipping, ran merrily after
The wonderful music with shouting and
  laughter.

XIII

The Mayor was dumb, and the Council stood
As if they were changed into blocks of wood,
Unable to move a step, or cry
To the children merrily skipping by,
– Could only follow with the eye
That joyous crowd at the Piper's back.
But how the Major was on the rack,
And the wretched Council's bosoms beat,
As the Piper turned from the High Street
To where the Weser rolled its waters
Right in the way of their sons and daughters!
However he turned from South to West,
And to Koppelberg Hill his steps addressed,
And after him the children pressed;
Great was the joy in every breast.
"He never can cross that mighty top!
"He's forced to let the piping drop,
"And we shall see our children stop!"
When, lo, as they reached the mountain-side,
A wondrous portal opened wide,
As if a cavern was suddenly hollowed;
And the Piper advanced and the children
  followed,
And when all were in to the very last,
The door in the mountain-side shut fast.

Did I say, all? No! One was lame,
And could not dance the whole of the way;
And in after years, if you would blame
His sadness, he was used to say, –
"It's dull in our town since my playmates
    left!
"I can't forget that I'm bereft
"Of all the pleasant sights they see,
"Which the Piper also promised me.
"For he led us, he said, to a joyous land,
"Joining the town and just at hand,
"Where waters gushed and fruit-trees grew,
"And flowers put forth a fairer hue,
"And everything was strange and new;
"The sparrows were brighter than peacocks
    here,
"And their dogs outran our fallow deer,
"And honey-bees had lost their stings,
"And horses were born with eagles' wings:
"And just as I became assured
"My lame foot would be speedily cured,
"The music stopped and I stood still,
"And found myself outside the hill,
"Left alone against my will,
"To go now limping as before,
"And never hear of that country more!"

XIV

Alas, alas for Hamelin!
    There came into many a burgher's pate
    A text which says that Heaven's gate
    Opes to the rich at as easy rate
As the needle's eye takes a camel in!
The Mayor sent East, West, North, and South,
To offer the Piper, by word of mouth,
    Wherever it was men's lot to find him,
Silver and gold to his heart's content,
If he'd only return the way he went,
    And bring the children behind him.
But when they saw 'twas a lost endeavour,
And Piper and dancers were gone for ever,
They made a decree that lawyers never
    Should think their records dated duly
If, after the day of the month and year,
These words did not as well appear,
"And so long after what happened here

"On the Twenty-second of July,
"Thirteen hundred and seventy-six":
And the better in memory to fix
The place of the children's last retreat,
They called it, the Pied Piper's Street–
Where any one playing on pipe or tabor,
Was sure for the future to lose his labour.
Nor suffered they hostelry or tavern
    To shock with mirth a street so solemn;
But opposite the place of the cavern
    They wrote the story on a column,
And on the great church-window painted
The same, to make the world acquainted
How their children were stolen away,
And there it stands to this very day.
And I must not omit to say
That in Transylvania there's a tribe
Of alien people that ascribe
The outlandish ways and dress
On which their neighbours lay such stress,
To their fathers and mothers having risen
Out of some subterraneous prison
Into which they were trepanned
Long time ago in a mighty band
Out of Hamelin town in Brunswick land,
But how or why, they don't understand.

XV

So, Willy, let me and you be wipers
Of scores out with all men – especially
    pipers!
And, whether they pipe us free from rats or
    from mice,
If we've promised them aught, let us keep
    our promise!

Robert Browning and Kate Greenaway:
The Pied Piper of Hamelin

Robert Browning's famous poem is based upon events that were for a long time thought to be historical. The poet himself mentions 22 July 1376 in part XIV of the poem; others have suggested an earlier date. Whether something like these events occurred, no one really knows, but over the years the story became a well-known legend.

Browning's version is in rhyming verse and was written in 1845 to amuse a child who was ill. It became very popular in Victorian times and, in 1888, Kate Greenaway, who had herself enjoyed the poem as a child, painted these illustrations for a children's edition of the poem.

As a class

* For a first reading, share out the lines among the different characters. You will need:

  – a Narrator (perhaps 2 or 3 people could share this role)
  – the people of Hamelin (4 or 5 voices speaking individual lines, in parts III and XIII)
  – the Mayor and some Council members
  – the Pied Piper
  – the Rat who survives (part VII)
  – the Lame Boy (part XIII)

* Now look carefully at the illustrations and talk about the way Kate Greenaway has portrayed the characters. The men are dressed in tunics to suggest the earlier century in which the story is set; the children all look healthy, fresh-faced and angelic – despite the plague of rats! Is this how *you* saw the characters in your mind's eye?

On your own

* We have been able to reproduce only a few pictures. Choose an episode in the poem and illustrate it yourself. Or, perhaps, you could design a book cover for a new edition of the poem.

* Look again at part II, describing what the rats did. Start with the first two lines and write your own modern version.

In groups

* How would you dramatise the poem? In three groups work on turning the poem into a play script: include only the characters' names, what they say, and simple stage directions. You may well want to make some 'cuts', but be careful to keep all the main events and characters.

* Perform the three versions and discuss their strengths and weaknesses.

Me

There was a naughty Boy
  A naughty Boy was he
He would not stop at home
He could not quiet be—
    He took
    In his Knapsack
    A Book
    Full of vowels
    And a shirt
    With some towels—
    A slight cap
    For night cap—
    A hair brush
    Comb ditto
    New Stockings
    For old ones
    Would split O!
    This Knapsack
    Tight at's back
    He rivetted close
And follow'd his Nose
    To the North
    To the North
And follow'd his nose
    To the North

There was a naughty Boy
  And a naughty Boy was he
He ran away to Scotland
  The people for to see—
    There he found
    That the ground
    Was as hard
    That a yard
    Was as long,
    That a song
    Was as merry,
    That a cherry
    Was as red—
    That lead
    Was as weighty
    That fourscore
    Was as eighty
    That a door
    Was as wooden
    As in England—
    So he stood in
    His shoes
    And he wonder'd
    He stood in his
    Shoes and he wonder'd.

John Keats

ME

As long as I live
I shall always be
My Self – and no other,
Just me.

Like a tree –
Willow, elder,
Aspen, thorn,
Or cypress forlorn.

Like a flower,
For its hour –

Primrose, or pink,
Or a violet –
Sunned by the sun,
And with dewdrops wet.

Always just me.
Till the day come on
When I leave this body,
It's all then done,
And the spirit within it
Is gone.

Walter de la Mare

THOUGHTS LIKE AN OCEAN

The sea comes to me on the shore
On lacy slippered feet
And shyly, slyly slides away
With a murmur of defeat.

         And as I stand there wondering
         Strange thoughts spin round my head
         Of why and where and what and when
         And if not, why, what then?

Where do lobsters come from?
And where anemones?
And are there other worlds out there
With other mysteries?

         Why do *I* walk upon dry land
         While fishes haunt the sea?
         And as I think about their lives
         Do they too think of me?

Why is water, water?
Why does it wet my hand?
Are there really as many stars
As there are grains of sand?

         And where would the ocean go to
         If there were no gravity?
         And where was I before I lived?
         And where's eternity?

Perhaps the beach I'm standing on
Perhaps this stretch of sand
Perhaps the Universe itself
Lies on someone else's hand?

         And isn't it strange how this water and I
         At this moment happened to meet?
         And how this tide sweeps half the world
         Before stopping at my feet?

Gareth Owen

ROMANCE

When I was but thirteen or so
　I went into a golden land,
Chimborazo, Cotopaxi
　Took me by the hand.

My father died, my brother too,
　They passed like fleeting dreams.
I stood where Popocatapetl
　In the sunlight gleams.

I dimly heard the Master's voice
　And boys far-off at play,
Chimborazo, Cotopaxi
　Had stolen me away.

I walked in a great golden dream
　To and fro from school –
Shining Popocatapetl
　The dusty streets did rule.

I walked home with a gold dark boy
　And never a word I'd say,
Chimborazo, Cotopaxi
　Had taken my speech away:

I gazed entranced upon his face
　Fairer than any flower –
O shining Popocatapetl
　It was thy magic hour:

The houses, people, traffic seemed
　Thin fading dreams by day,
Chimborazo, Cotopaxi
　They had stolen my soul away!

Walter James Turner

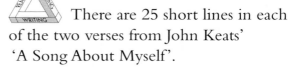

Class reading

There are 25 short lines in each of the two verses from John Keats' 'A Song About Myself'.

- Every member of the class takes one line from each verse to read aloud. You will have to keep your wits about you and practise in order to make a good, continuous reading.

Wondering

'He stood in his/Shoes and he wonder'd' – so ends John Keats's poem. In different ways, too, wondering is the theme of all four poems in this section.

- What is the main idea of 'Me'?
- What impression do you get of the 'golden land' of 'Romance'?

'Thoughts Like an Ocean' is full of the questions that crowd into the mind of the person standing on the sea-shore.

- Do you have any of these thoughts, or any other questions to add?

PART C

Ten
Poets

William Shakespeare
1564–1616

Little is known about Shakespeare's early life except that he was born in Stratford-upon-Avon and probably went to the local grammar school. He married Anne Hathaway in 1582, with whom he had three children during the 1580s, including twins – a boy and a girl. By 1592 he was in London, acting with a theatre company – The Lord Chamberlaine's Men – composing poetry and starting to write the plays which were to make him the world's most famous playwright.

Shakespeare's plays are mostly written in 'blank verse' (unrhymed verse, but with a basic five-beat rhythm – as when you repeat the word 'again' five times), but they also contain passages of prose, chants, and many songs. The lines in 'Drowning' are an example of blank verse. They are spoken by the Duke of Clarence in the play *Richard III* and describe a nightmare that he had just had. 'Full Fathom Five' is one of the songs sung by Ariel in *The Tempest*. Although the subject of both is death by drowning, the first stresses the horror, whereas the second suggests the beauty of this 'sea-change'. There are four more songs in this selection. The two love songs sung by Feste, the clown in *Twelfth Night*, are in different moods: one describes love as something to be accepted and enjoyed when it presents itself; the other is a sad song of a love that is not returned. 'When icicles hang by the wall' is the song about winter which ends *Love's Labour's Lost*; and 'Now the hungry lion roars' also closes a play – it is one of many songs sung by Puck, the mischievous spirit who serves King Oberon, in *A Midsummer Night's Dream*. Finally, we have included the well-known 'Witches Chant' from *Macbeth* for you to rehearse and perform.

'WHEN ICICLES HANG BY THE WALL'

When icicles hang by the wall
  And Dick the shepherd blows his nail,
And Tom bears logs into the hall,
  And milk comes frozen home in pail;
When blood is nipped, and ways be foul,
Then nightly sings the staring owl
      Tuwhoo!
Tuwhit! Tuwhoo! A merry note!
While greasy Joan doth keel the pot.

When all around the wind doth blow,
  And coughing drowns the parson's saw,
And birds sit brooding in the snow,
  And Marion's nose looks red and raw;
When roasted crabs hiss in the bowl –
Then nightly sings the staring owl
      Tuwhoo!
Tuwhit! Tuwhoo! A merry note!
While greasy Joan doth keel the pot.

Love's Labour's Lost, Act 5, sc. ii

THE WITCHES' CHANT

A Cavern: in the middle, a boiling cauldron.
Thunder. Enter the three witches.

1st Witch	Thrice the brinded cat hath mew'd.
2nd Witch	Thrice, and once the hedge-pig whin'd.
3rd Witch	Harpier cries, ''Tis time, 'tis time.'
1st Witch	Round about the cauldron go:
	In the poisoned entrails throw;
	Toad, that under cold stone
	Days and nights has thirty one
	Swelter'd venom sleeping got,
	Boil thou first i' th' charmed pot.
All	Double, double, toil and trouble;
	Fire burn, and cauldron bubble.
2nd Witch	Fillet of a fenny snake,
	In the cauldron boil and bake;
	Eye of newt, and toe of frog,
	Wool of bat, and tongue of dog;
	Adder's fork, and blind-worm's sting,
	Lizard's leg, and howlet's wing;
	For a charm of powerful trouble,
	Like a hell-broth, boil and bubble.
All	Double, double, toil and trouble,
	Fire burn, and cauldron bubble.
3rd Witch	Scale of dragon, tooth of wolf,
	Witches' mummy, maw, and gulf
	Of the ravin'd salt-sea shark;
	Root of hemlock, digg'd i' th' dark;...
	Add thereto a tiger's chaudron,
	For the ingredients of our cauldron.
All	Double, double, toil and trouble,
	Fire burn, and cauldron bubble.

Macbeth, Act 4, sc. i

NOW THE HUNGRY LION ROARS

Now the hungry lion roars,
   And the wolf behowls the moon;
Whilst the heavy ploughman snores,
   All with weary task fordone.
Now the wasted brands do glow,
   Whilst the screech-owl, screeching loud,
Puts the wretch that lies in woe
   In remembrance of a shroud.
Now it is the time of night
   That the graves, all gaping wide,
Every one lets forth his spirite,
   In the church-way paths to glide:
And we fairies, that do run
   By the triple Hecate's team,
From the presence of the sun,
   Following darkness like a dream,
Now are frolic; not a mouse
Shall disturb this hallow'd house:
I am sent with broom before,
To sweep the dust behind the door.

       A Midsummer Night's Dream, Act 5, sc. i

O MISTRESS MINE!

O mistress mine! where are you roaming?
O! stay and hear; your true love's coming,
   That can sing both high and low.
Trip no further, pretty sweeting;
Journeys end in lovers meeting,
   Every wise man's son doth know.

What is love? 'tis not hereafter;
Present mirth hath present laughter;
   What's to come is still unsure:
In delay there lies no plenty;
Then come kiss me, sweet and twenty,
   Youth's a stuff will not endure.

       Twelfth Night, Act 2, sc. iii

COME AWAY, COME AWAY, DEATH

Come away, come away, death,
   And in sad cypress let me be laid;
Fly away, fly away, breath;
   I am slain by a fair cruel maid.
My shroud of white, stuck all with yew,
   O! prepare it.
My part of death, no one so true
   Did share it.
Not a flower, not a flower sweet,
   On my black coffin let there be strown;
Not a friend, not a friend greet
   My poor corse,⋆ where my bones shall be
     thrown.
A thousand thousand sighs to save,
   Lay me, O! where
Sad true lover never find my grave,
   To weep there.

       Twelfth Night, Act 2, sc. iv

⋆corpse

FULL FATHOM FIVE

Full fathom five thy father lies;
   Of his bones are coral made;
Those are pearls that were his eyes:
   Nothing of him that doth fade,
But doth suffer a sea-change
Into something rich and strange.
Sea-nymphs hourly ring his knell:
        Ding-dong.
   Hark! now I hear them –
     Ding-dong, bell!

The Tempest, Act 1, sc.ii

DROWNING

Lord, Lord! methought, what pain it was to drown!
What dreadful noise of waters in mine ears!
What ugly sights of death within mine eyes!
Methought I saw a thousand fearful wrecks;
Ten thousand men that fishes gnaw'd upon;
Wedges of gold, great anchors, heaps of pearl,
Inestimable stones, unvalued jewels,
All scattered in the bottom of the sea:
Some lay in dead men's skulls; and in those holes
Where eyes did once inhabit, there were crept,
As 'twere in scorn of eyes, reflecting gems,
Which woo'd the slimy bottom of the deep,
And mock'd the dead bones that lay scattered by.

Richard III, Act 1, sc. iv

Edward Lear
1812–1888

Many of you have already met Edward Lear and will remember his nonsense verses beginning 'There was an old man of…' or 'There was a young woman of…', and poems such as 'The Jumblies', 'The Owl and the Pussy-Cat', 'The Dong With a Luminous Nose', and 'The Pobble Who Had No Toes'.

He liked to illustrate his poems himself with line drawings in black ink showing preposterous people with enormous noses, ridiculous walks, outlandish hats, or absurd habits. He also liked to draw nonexistent plants such as the *Nasticreechia Krorluppia* and loved to draw his cat, Foss, who lived for seventeen years.

Lear was born in 1812, the last in a family of 21 children. His father had, by this time, lost all his money and was sent to prison for debt. Lear inherited nothing and had to make his own way: he was earning a living as a commercial artist at the age of 15.

Aside from the children's books, he was a serious and respected artist in both oils and water-colours and travelled all over Europe, sketching and painting with enormous energy and trying desperately to make ends meet. At one time he was art master to Queen Victoria.

He was an engaging figure, rather plump ('spherical', he said), with a high dome of a forehead and woolly beard. He wore small spectacles perched on his nose and usually dressed in loose-fitting clothes.

Manypeeplia Upsidownia

Lear was something of a child himself. He loved playing with words and changing their spellings, and making jokes and puns. He delighted in making up new words such as *splendidophoropherostiphongious* and in inventing strange place names: 'I shall go either to Sardinia, or India, or Jumsibobjigglequack this winter…' he wrote in a letter to a friend. Beneath all the humour, though, there sometimes seems to be an underlying sadness – perhaps the penalty for never quite growing up.

But nobody can introduce him as well as he introduces himself in his poem 'Self-Portrait of the Laureate of Nonsense'.

SELF-PORTRAIT OF THE LAUREATE OF NONSENSE

How pleasant to know Mr. Lear!
  Who has written such volumes of stuff!
Some think him ill-tempered and queer,
  But a few think him pleasant enough.

His mind is concrete and fastidious,
  His nose is remarkably big;
His visage is more or less hideous,
  His beard it resembles a wig.

He has ears, and two eyes, and ten fingers,
  Leastways if you reckon two thumbs;
Long ago he was one of the singers,
  But now he is one of the dumbs.

He sits in a beautiful parlour,
  With hundred of books on the wall;
He drinks a great deal of Marsala,
  But never gets tipsy at all.

He has many friends, laymen and clerical;
  Old Foss is the name of his cat;
His body is perfectly spherical,
  He weareth a runcible hat.

When he walks in a waterproof white,
  The children run after him so!
Calling out, 'He's come out in his night-
  Gown, that crazy old Englishman, oh!'

He weeps by the side of the ocean,
  He weeps on the top of the hill;
He purchases pancakes and lotion,
  And chocolate shrimps from the mill.

He reads but he cannot speak Spanish,
  He cannot abide ginger-beer:
Ere the days of his pilgrimage vanish,
  How pleasant to know Mr. Lear!

THERE WAS AN OLD PERSON OF STROUD

There was an old person of Stroud,
Who was horribly jammed in a crowd;
Some she slew with a kick, some she
   scrunched with a stick,
That impulsive old person of Stroud.

Phattfacia Stupenda

THE JUMBLIES

I

They went to sea in a Sieve, they did,
  In a Sieve they went to sea:
In spite of all their friends could say,
On a winter's morn, on a stormy day,
  In a Sieve they went to sea!
And when the Sieve turned round and round,
And everyone cried, 'You'll all be drowned!'
They called aloud, 'Our Sieve ain't big,
But we don't care a button! we don't care a fig!
  In a Sieve we'll go to sea!'
    Far and few, far and few,
      Are the lands where the Jumblies live;
    Their heads are green, and their hands
      are blue,
    And they went to sea in a Sieve.

II

They sailed away in a Sieve, they did,
  In a Sieve they sailed so fast,
With only a beautiful pea-green veil
Tied with a riband by way of a sail,
  To a small tobacco-pipe mast;
And every one said, who saw them go,
'O won't they be soon upset, you know!
For the sky is dark, and the voyage is long,
And happen what may, it's extremely wrong
  In a Sieve to sail so fast!'
    Far and few, far and few,
      Are the lands where the Jumblies live;
    Their heads are green, and their hands
      are blue,
    And they went to sea in a Sieve.

III

The water it soon came in, it did,
  The water it soon came in;
So to keep them dry, they wrapped their feet
In a pinky paper all folded neat,
  And they fastened it down with a pin.
And they passed the night in a crockery-jar,
And each of them said, 'How wise we are!
Though the sky be dark, and the voyage be
  long,
Yet we never can think we were rash or wrong,
  While round in our Sieve we spin!'
    Far and few, far and few,
      Are the lands where the Jumblies live;
    Their heads are green, and their hands
      are blue,
    And they went to sea in a Sieve.

IV

And all night long they sailed away;
  And when the sun went down,
They whistled and warbled a moony song
To the echoing sound of a coppery gong,
  In the shade of the mountain brown.
'O Timballo! How happy we are,
When we live in a sieve and a crockery-jar,
And all night long in the moonlight pale,
We sail away with a pea-green sail,
  In the shade of the mountains brown!'
    Far and few, far and few,
      Are the lands where the Jumblies live;
    Their heads are green, and their hands
      are blue,
    And they went to sea in a Sieve.

V

They sailed to the Western Sea, they did,
  To a land all covered with trees,
And they bought an Owl, and a useful Cart,
And a pound of Rice, and a Cranberry Tart,
  And a hive of silvery Bees.
And they bought a Pig, and some green Jack-
  daws,
And a lovely Monkey with lollipop paws,
And forty bottles of Ring-Bo-Ree,
  And no end of Stilton Cheese.
    Far and few, far and few,
      Are the lands where the Jumblies live;
    Their heads are green, and their hands
      are blue,
    And they went to sea in a Sieve.

VI

And in twenty years they all came back,
  In twenty years or more,
And everyone said, 'How tall they've grown!
For they've been to the Lakes, and the Torrible
  Zone
  And the hills of the Chankly Bore;
And they drank their health, and gave them a
  feast
Of dumplings made of beautiful yeast;
And every one said, 'If we only live,
We too will go to sea in a Sieve, –
  To the hills of the Chankly Bore!'
    Far and few, far and few,
      Are the lands where the Jumblies live;
    Their heads are green, and their hands are
      blue,
    And they went to sea in a Sieve.

THE OWL AND THE PUSSY-CAT

I

The Owl and the Pussy-cat went to sea
  In a beautiful pea-green boat,
They took some honey, and plenty of money,
  Wrapped up in a five-pound note.
The Owl looked up to the stars above,
  And sang to a small guitar,
'O lovely Pussy! O Pussy, my love,
    What a beautiful Pussy you are,
      You are,
      You are!
  What a beautiful Pussy you are!'

II

Pussy said to the Owl, 'You elegant fowl!
  How charmingly sweet you sing!
O let us be married! too long we have
    tarried:
  But what shall we do for a ring?'
They sailed away, for a year and a day,
  To the land where the Bong-tree grows
And there in a wood a Piggy-wig stood
  With a ring at the end of his nose,
    His nose,
    His nose,
  With a ring at the end of his nose.

III

'Dear Pig, are you willing to sell for one
    shilling
  Your ring?' Said the Piggy, 'I will.'
So they took it away, and were married next
    day
  By the Turkey who lives on the hill.
They dined on mince, and slices of quince,
  Which they ate with a runcible spoon;
And hand in hand, on the edge of the sand,
  They danced by the light of the moon,
    The moon,
    The moon,
  They danced by the light of the moon.

Lewis Carroll
(Charles Dodgson), 1832–1898

Lewis Carroll (real name Charles Dodgson) is known the world over for *Alice's Adventures in Wonderland* (published 1865) and *Through the Looking-Glass* (1871). The 'Alice' stories began as a tale that Carroll invented one summer's afternoon to amuse three girls, Alice Liddell and her sisters, whom he had taken on a picnic. Scattered throughout the stories are poems and verses of all kinds such as 'The Mouse's Tale' poem, which is shaped like a tail; the nonsense poem which begins 'You are old, Father William', 'Twinkle, twinkle, little bat' and 'The Lobster Quadrille', which all appear in *Alice's Adventures in Wonderland*. The glorious nonsense verses 'Jabberwocky', 'The Walrus and the Carpenter' and 'The White Knight's Song' are all in *Through the Looking-Glass*. Carroll also wrote many other inventive and often absurd poems, which appeal to adults as well as children. A type of poem he often wrote when he sent gifts to children was the acrostic, where the first letter of each line spells out the letters of the child's name in order. You will find an acrostic like this on p. 82. Carroll was a lecturer in mathematics at Christ Church College, Oxford and loved logic and puzzles. Like so many writers for children, he was able to be himself with young people, and part of him always remained a child. He looked on early childhood as a time of innocence and delight, and as a young man wrote in his poem 'Solitude':

> I'd give all wealth that years have piled,
>   The slow result of life's decay,
> To be once more a little child
>   For one bright summer-day.

Lewis Carroll liked to write amusing imitations (or parodies) of other poets he thought were a bit too serious and stuffy. In 'Father William' he makes fun of a poem by Robert Southey which had the title 'The Old Man's Comforts and How He Gained Them'. Southey's poem begins:

"You are old, Father William," the young man cried,
"The few locks which are left you are gray;
You are hale, Father William, a hearty old man,
Now tell me the reason, I pray."

"In the days of my youth," Father William replied,
"I remembered that youth would fly fast,
And abused not my health, and my vigour at first,
That I never might need them at last."

FATHER WILLIAM

"You are old, Father William," the young
man said,
"And your hair has become very white;
And yet you incessantly stand on your
head –
Do you think, at your age, it is right?"

"In my youth," Father William replied to his
son,
"I feared it might injure the brain;
But now that I'm perfectly sure I have none,
Why, I do it again and again."

"You are old," said the youth, "as I
mentioned before,
And have grown most uncommonly fat;
Yet you turned a back somersault in at the
door –
Pray, what is the reason of that?"

"In my youth," said the sage, as he shook his
gray locks,
"I kept all my very limbs supple
By the use of this ointment – one shilling the
box –
Allow me to sell you a couple."

"You are old," said the youth, "and your jaws
are too weak
For anything tougher than suet;
Yet you finished the goose, with the bones
and the beak –
Pray, how did you manage to do it?"

"In my youth," said his father, "I took to the
law,
And argued each case with my wife;
And the muscular strength, which it gave to
my jaw,
Has lasted the rest of my life."

"You are old," said the youth, "one would
hardly suppose
That your eye was as steady as ever;
Yet you balanced an eel on the end of your
nose –
What made you so awfully clever?"

"I have answered three questions, and that is
enough,"
Said his father, "don't give yourself airs!
Do you think I can listen all day to such
stuff?
Be off, or I'll kick you down stairs!"

As we can see, Southey's Father William was a bit dull and sensible. Carroll's Father William is anything but!

Lewis Carroll even wrote a parody of Father William as an acrostic. He sent this verse to a little girl as an Easter present, along with a copy of his new poem 'The Hunting of the Snark'. What was the girl's name?

> "Are you deaf, Father William!" the young man said,
> "Did you hear what I told you just now?
> Excuse me for shouting! Don't waggle your head
> Like a blundering, sleepy old cow!
> A little maid dwelling in Wallington Town,
> Is my friend, so I beg to remark:
> Do you think she'd be pleased if a book were sent down
> Entitled "The Hunt of the Snark"?'
>
> "Pack it up in brown paper!" the old man cried,
> And seal it with olive-and-dove.★
> I command you to do it!" he added with pride,
> "Nor forget, my good fellow, to send her beside
> Easter Greetings, and give her my love."

> ★his seal, with a picture of a dove with an olive twig in its beak

Another over-serious poet whose work Carroll often parodied was Isaac Watts, who wrote in his 'Divine Songs for Children: Against Idleness and Mischief':

> How doth the little busy bee
>   Improve each shining hour,
> And gather honey all the day
>   From every opening flower!

Carroll's version is rather different!

THE CROCODILE

> How doth the little crocodile
>   Improve his shining tail,
> And pour the waters of the Nile
>   On every golden scale!
>
> How cheerfully he seems to grin,
>   How neatly spreads his claws,
> And welcomes little fishes in,
>   With gently smiling jaws!

And here is another Carroll parody of a very familiar verse:

TWINKLE, TWINKLE

> Twinkle, twinkle, little bat!
> How I wonder what you're at!
> Up above the world you fly,
> Like a tea-tray, in the sky.

THE WHITE KNIGHT'S SONG

I'll tell thee everything I can:
  There's little to relate.
I saw an agèd agèd man,
  A-sitting on a gate.
"Who are you, agèd man?" I said.
  "And how is it you live?"
And his answer trickled through my head,
  Like water through a sieve.

He said "I look for butterflies
  That sleep among the wheat.
I make them into mutton-pies,
  And sell them in the street.
I sell them unto men," he said,
  "Who sail on stormy seas;
And that's the way I get my bread –
  A trifle, if you please."

But I was thinking of a plan
  To dye one's whiskers green,
And always use so large a fan
  That they could not be seen.
So, having no reply to give
  To what the old man said,
I cried "Come, tell me how you live!"
  And thumped him on the head.

His accents mild took up the tale:
  He said "I go my ways,
And when I find a mountain-rill,
  I set it in a blaze;
And thence they make a stuff they call
  Rowland's Macassar-Oil –
Yet twopence-halfpenny is all
  They give me for my toil."

But I was thinking of a way
  To feed oneself on batter,
And so go on from day to day
  Getting a little fatter.
I shook him well from side to side,
  Until his face was blue:
"Come, tell me how you live," I cried,
  "And what it is you do!"

He said "I hunt for haddocks' eyes
  Among the heather bright,
And work them into waistcoat-buttons
  In the silent night.

And these I do not sell for gold
  Or coin of silvery shine,
But for a copper halfpenny,
  And that will purchase nine.

I sometimes dig for buttered rolls,
  Or set limed twigs for crabs:
I sometimes search the grassy knolls
  For wheels of Hansom-cabs.
And that's the way" (he gave a wink)
  "By which I get my wealth –
And very gladly will I drink
  Your Honour's noble health."

I heard him then, for I had just
  Completed my design
To keep the Menai bridge from rust
  By boiling it in wine.
I thanked him much for telling me
  The way he got his wealth,
But chiefly for his wish that he
  Might drink my noble health.

And now, if e'er by chance I put
  My fingers into glue,
Or madly squeeze a right-hand foot
  Into a left-hand shoe,
Or if I drop upon my toe
  A very heavy weight,
I weep for it reminds me so
  Of that old man I used to know –
Whose look was mild, whose speech was
    slow,
Whose hair was whiter than the snow,
Whose face was very like a crow,
With eyes, like cinders, all aglow,
Who seemed distracted with his woe,
Who rocked his body to and fro,
And muttered mumblingly and low,
As if his mouth were full of dough,
Who snorted like a buffalo –
That summer evening long ago,
  A-sitting on a gate.

Robert Louis Stevenson
1850–1894

Robert Louis Stevenson is best known for two of his novels, the children's story *Treasure Island*, and *The Strange Case of Dr Jekyll and Mr Hyde*. Yet, since it was first published in 1885, his collection of poems, *A Child's Garden of Verses*, has rarely been out of print. Stevenson was a great traveller, making canoe tours in Belgium and France, journeying round the Cevennes in South West France on a donkey, travelling to California by ship and train, and spending his last years in Samoa in the Pacific Islands. *Treasure Island* reflects some of the excitement he felt in seeing distant lands and people. If travel was very different in Victorian times, so too was life at home: candles were used to light the stairs up to bed ('Shadow March'), talking and singing in front of an open fire were common evening entertainments ('The Land of Story-Books'), and lead soldiers were some of the most popular children's toys ('The Land of Counterpane' and 'The Dumb Soldier'). Yet, for all the differences, the thoughts and feelings caught in the poems remain fresh and recognisable today. The fear of darkness, the strange worlds of dreams, the magic of story books, and the odd feeling of contentment that can occur when you are ill and have to stay in bed – all are here in Stevenson's poems written over a century ago.

SHADOW MARCH

All round the house is the jet-black night;
   It stares through the window-pane;
It crawls in the corners, hiding from the light,
   And it moves with the moving flame.

Now my little heart goes a-beating like a drum,
   With the breath of the Bogie in my hair;
And all round the candle the crooked shadows come
   And go marching along up the stair.

The shadow of the balusters, the shadow of the lamp,
   The shadow of the child that goes to bed –
All the wicked shadows coming, tramp, tramp, tramp,
   With the black light overhead.

THE LAND OF NOD

From breakfast on all through the day
At home among my friends I stay;
But every night I go abroad
Afar into the land of Nod.

All by myself I have to go,
With none to tell me what to do –
All alone beside the streams
And up the mountain-sides of dreams.

The strangest things are there for me,
Both things to eat and things to see,
And many frightening sights abroad
Till morning in the land of Nod.

Try as I like to find the way,
I never can get back by day,
Nor can remember plain and clear
The curious music that I hear.

THE LAND OF COUNTERPANE

When I was sick and lay a-bed,
I had two pillows at my head,
And all my toys beside me lay
To keep me happy all the day.

And sometimes for an hour or so
I watched my leaden soldiers go,
With different uniforms and drills,
Among the bed-clothes, through the hills;

And sometimes sent my ships in fleets
All up and down among the sheets;
Or brought my trees and houses out,
And planted cities all about.

I was the giant great and still
That sits upon the pillow-hill,
And sees before him, dale and plain,
The pleasant land of counterpane.

ESCAPE AT BEDTIME

The lights from the parlour and kitchen shone out
   Through the blinds and the windows and bars;
And high overhead and all moving about,
   There were thousands of millions of stars.
There ne'er were such thousands of leaves on a tree,
   Nor of people in church or the Park,
As the crowds of the stars that looked down upon me,
   And that glittered and winked in the dark.

The Dog, and the Plough, and the Hunter, and all,
   And the star of the sailor, and Mars,
These shone in the sky, and the pail by the wall
   Would be half full of water and stars.
They saw me at last, and they chased me with cries,
   And they soon had me packed into bed;
But the glory kept shining and bright in my eyes,
   And the stars going round in my head.

THE DUMB SOLDIER

When the grass was closely mown,
Walking on the lawn alone,
In the turf a hole I found
And hid a soldier underground.

Spring and daisies came apace;
Grasses hid my hiding-place;
Grasses run like a green sea
O'er the lawn up to my knee.

Under grass alone he lies,
Looking up with leaden eyes,
Scarlet coat and pointed gun,
To the stars and to the sun.

When the grass is ripe like grain,
When the scythe is stoned again,
When the lawn is shaven clear,
Then my hole shall reappear.

I shall find him, never fear,
I shall find my grenadier;
But for all that's gone and come,
I shall find my soldier dumb.

He has lived, a little thing,
In the grassy woods of spring;
Done, if he could tell me true,
Just as I should like to do.

He has seen the starry hours
And the springing of the flowers;
And the fairy things that pass
In the forests of the grass.

In the silence he has heard
Talking bee and ladybird,
And the butterfly has flown
O'er him as he lay alone.

Not a word will he disclose,
Not a word of all he knows,
I must lay him on the shelf,
And make up the tale myself.

THE LAND OF STORY-BOOKS

At evening when the lamp is lit,
Around the fire my parents sit;
They sit at home and talk and sing,
And do not play at anything.

Now, with my little gun, I crawl
All in the dark along the wall,
And follow round the forest track
Away behind the sofa back.

There, in the night, where none can spy,
All in my hunter's camp I lie,
And play at books that I have read
Till it is time to go to bed.

Walter de la Mare
1873–1956

Ghosts and hauntings, dreams and mysteries, occur frequently in de la Mare's poetry in various moods: 'The Ghost', for example, expresses sadness whereas 'John Mouldy' has the chill of horror. 'The Listeners' is one of the best known of all English poems. Its challenging opening, ghostly atmosphere and unanswered questions (Who is the Traveller? Who was he expecting to meet? Why had he promised to keep his word?) continue to fascinate readers.

No other children's poet writes in such a range of forms, as the remaining poems show. 'Ice', one of many poems about the seasons and the weather, is long and thin like an icicle; 'Echo' hints at some

Walter de la Mare

unhappiness and how everything seems to throw this feeling straight back at you without care or sympathy. 'Hi!' is one of several sharp little poems about blood sports where the light-hearted, almost jolly tone suggested by the rhyming sounds is deliberately at odds with the poet's view of the hunter. Finally, 'All but Blind' is a thoughtful comment in a quite different mood where the physical 'blindness' of three creatures is used as a metaphor (see Part A, Unit 4) for the lack of sympathy and understanding that can exist between people.

ECHO

'Who called?' I said, and the words
  Through the whispering glades,
Hither, thither, baffled the birds –
  'Who called? Who called?'

The leafy boughs on high
  Hissed in the sun;
The dark air carried my cry
  Faintingly on:

Eyes in the green, in the shade,
  In the motionless brake,
Voices that said what I said,
  For mockery's sake:

'Who cares?' I bawled through my tears;
  The wind fell low:
In the silence, 'Who cares? Who cares?'
  Wailed to and fro.

JOHN MOULDY

I spied John Mouldy in his cellar,
Deep down twenty steps of stone;
In the dusk he sat a-smiling,
  Smiling there alone.

He read no book, he snuffed no candle;
The rats ran in, the rats ran out;
And far and near, the drip of water
  Went whisp'ring about.

The dusk was still, with dew a-falling,
I saw the Dog-star bleak and grim,
I saw a slim brown rat of Norway
  Creep over him.

I spied John Mouldy in his cellar,
Deep down twenty steps of stone;
In the dusk he sat a-smiling,
  Smiling there alone.

THE LISTENERS

'Is there anybody there?' said the Traveller,
    Knocking on the moonlit door;
And his horse in the silence champed the grasses
    Of the forest's ferny floor:
And a bird flew up out of the turret,
    Above the Traveller's head:
And he smote upon the door again a second time;
    'Is there anybody there?' he said.
But no one descended to the Traveller;
    No head from the leaf-fringed sill
Leaned over and looked into his grey eyes,
    Where he stood perplexed and still.
But only a host of phantom listeners
    That dwelt in the lone house then
Stood listening in the quiet of the moonlight
    To that voice from the world of men:
Stood thronging the faint moonbeams on the dark stair,
    That goes down to the empty hall,
Hearkening in an air stirred and shaken
    By the lonely Traveller's call.
And he felt in his heart their strangeness,
    Their stillness answering his cry,
While his horse moved, cropping the dark turf,
    'Neath the starred and leafy sky;
For he suddenly smote on the door, even
    Louder, and lifted his head: –
'Tell them I came, and no one answered,
    That I kept my word,' he said.
Never the least stir made the listeners,
    Though every word he spake
Fell echoing through the shadowiness of the still house
    From the one man left awake:
Ay, they heard his foot upon the stirrup,
    And the sound of iron on stone,
And how the silence surged softly backward,
    When the plunging hoofs were gone.

ICE

The North Wind sighed:
And in a trice
What was water
Now is ice.

What sweet rippling
Water was
Now bewitched is
Into glass:

White and brittle
Where is seen
The prisoned milfoil's
Tender green;

Clear and ringing,
With sun aglow,
Where the boys sliding
And skating go.

Now furred's each stick
And stalk and blade
With crystals out of
Dewdrops made.

Worms and ants
Flies, snails and bees
Keep close house-guard,
Lest they freeze;

Oh, with how sad
And solemn an eye
Each fish stares up
Into the sky.

In dread lest his
Wide watery home
At night shall solid
Ice become.

HI!

Hi! handsome hunting man
Fire your little gun.
Bang! Now the animal
Is dead and dumb and done.
Nevermore to peep again, creep again, leap
  again,
Eat or sleep or drink again, Oh, what fun!

ALL BUT BLIND

All but blind
  In his chambered hole
Gropes for worms
  The four-clawed Mole.

All but blind
  In the evening sky
The hooded Bat
  Twirls softly by.

All but blind
  In the burning day
The Barn-Owl blunders
  On her way.

And blind as are
  These three to me,
So, blind to Some-One
  I must be.

THE GHOST

'Who knocks?' 'I, who was beautiful,
  Beyond all dreams to restore,
I, from the roots of the dark thorn am hither,
  And knock on the door.'

'Who speaks?' 'I – once was my speech
  Sweet as the bird's on the air,
When echo lurks by the waters to heed;
  'Tis I speak thee fair.'

'Dark is the hour?' 'Ay, and cold.'
''Lone is my house.' 'Ah, but mine?'
'Sight, touch, lips, eyes yearned in vain.'
  'Long dead these to thine...'

Silence. Still faint on the porch
  Brake the flames of the stars.
In gloom groped a hope-wearied hand
  Over keys, bolts, and bars.

A face peered. All the grey night
  In chaos of vacancy shone;
Nought but vast sorrow was there –
  The sweet cheat gone.

Eleanor Farjeon
1881–1965

Eleanor Farjeon was born and brought up in Hampstead. She never went to school but at home she was surrounded by books and, from an early age, she wrote her own stories and poems. She continued to write mainly for children and her collections of verses include poems as varied as the tiny word-picture 'The Tide in the River' and the well-known story of 'Mrs Malone' (too long to include here), in which this poor, lonely woman shelters the creatures of the wood from the winter snows, shares her bread and drink with them, and gains her reward in heaven.

The selection here includes the rousing poem 'When Hannibal Crossed the Alps', which, with its repetitions and marching beat, needs to be performed aloud. Quite the opposite is 'Keep Still', which makes you want to hold your breath as the words urge you to watch the deer coming down to drink at a pool or stream. 'Here's Spring' and 'The Dewdrop' are both written in couplets (see Part A, Unit 5). One is a word-painting of the most 'fleet-footed' of the seasons; the other tells of the startling idea that goes through the writer's mind as she looks at the reflections in a dewdrop. 'It was Long Ago' captures something that everyone has – an earliest memory. Notice how the three-line verses are themselves arranged in groups of three with repeated rhyming words 'ago', 'know' and 'tree' at the ends of the verses. This childhood memory is so vividly caught in the sense impressions – 'the taste of the berries, the feel of the sun.../And the smell of everything that used to be...' – that, while we listen to the story, we scarcely realise that the word 'remember' appears in the same place in each verse.

THE TIDE IN THE RIVER

The tide in the river,
The tide in the river,
The tide in the river runs deep.
I saw a shiver
Pass over the river
As the tide turned in its sleep.

WHEN HANNIBAL CROSSED THE ALPS

Hannibal crossed the Alps!
Hannibal crossed the Alps!
  With his black men,
  His brown men,
  His countrymen,
  His town-men,
With his Gauls, and his Spaniards, his horses
  and elephants,
Hannibal crossed the Alps!

Hannibal crossed the Alps!
Hannibal crossed the Alps!
  For his bowmen,
  His spear-men,
  His front men,
  His rear men,
His Gauls, and his Spaniards, his horses and
  elephants,
Wanted the Roman scalps!
And *that's* why Hannibal, Hannibal, Hannibal,
Hannibal crossed the Alps!

HERE'S SPRING

Here's Spring,
With green on his wing
And blue in his eye:
With a fly
Caught in his hair:
With a fair
Sky for an hour or so:
With a flower or so
For the garden-bed,
And a spread
Of flowers for the meadows:
With lighter shadows
Of clouds flitting over the land:
With more gold for the sand
On the shore:
With more
Music at morning:
With a shower without warning:
With a step lighter
Than snow, a petal whiter
Than frost,
Here's that most
Sweet-footed,
Fleet-footed
Of the four brothers
The young year mothers
Under her wing:
Here's Spring!

THE DEWDROP

Small shining drop, no lady's ring
Holds so beautiful a thing.
At sun-up in the early air
The sweetness of the world you snare.
Within your little mirror lie
The green grass and the wingèd fly;
The lowest flower, the tallest tree
In your crystal I can see.
Why, in your tiny globe you hold
The sun himself, a midge of gold.
It makes me wonder if the world
In which so many things are curled,
The world which all men real call,
Is not the real world at all,
But just a drop of dew instead
Swinging on a spider's thread.

KEEP STILL

Look, and keep very still,
Still as a tree,
And if you do you will
Presently see
The doe come down to drink
Leading her fawn
Just as they did, I think,
In the first dawn.

Hark, not a sound, my dear,
Be quiet and hark,
And very soon you'll hear
The vixen bark,
And see her cubs at play
As I believe
They played in starlight grey
On the first eve.

Look, and keep very still.
Hark, not a sound!
The pretty creatures will
Soon be around,
At play and drink, as though
They drank and played,
Cub, vixen, fawn and doe,
Ere men were made.

IT WAS LONG AGO

I'll tell you, shall I, something I remember?
Something that still means a great deal to me.
It was long ago.

A dusty road in summer I remember,
A mountain, and an old house, and a tree
That stood, you know,

Behind the house. An old woman I remember
In a red shawl with a grey cat on her knee
Humming under a tree.

She seemed the oldest thing I can remember,
But then perhaps I was not more than three.
It was long ago.

I dragged on the dusty road, and I remember
How the old woman looked over the fence at me
And seemed to know

How it felt to be three, and called out, I remember
'Do you like bilberries and cream for tea?'
I went under the tree

And while she hummed, and the cat purred, I remember
How she filled a saucer with berries and cream for me
So long ago,

Such berries and such cream as I remember
I never had seen before, and never see
Today, you know.

And that is almost all I can remember,
The house, the mountain, the grey cat on her knee,
Her red shawl, and the tree,

And the taste of the berries, the feel of the sun I remember,
And the smell of everything that used to be
So long ago,

Till the heat on the road outside again I remember,
And how the long dusty road seemed to have for me
No end, you know.

That is the farthest thing I can remember.
It won't mean much to you. It does to me.
Then I grew up, you see.

Charles Causley
1917–

Charles Causley was born in Launceston, Cornwall.
He had many different jobs and in 1940 joined the Navy. He served throughout the Second World War and became a teacher in 1946. He has taught and written ever since. His knowledge and fascination with the sea and with the life and legends of his native Cornwall are strong in his poetry. There is often a sense of mystery, magic, and sometimes even terror, lurking behind the poems, which are frequently written in ballad form. The poems 'Green Man in the Garden' and 'Tell Me, Tell Me, Sarah Jane' both suggest this in different ways and also suggest that nature, in the form of the sea or of the Green Man, has a power we cannot control.

On the other hand, Causley can be quite playful, as his modern ballad about Colonel Fazackerley and the ghost shows. His ballad poem 'Mary, Mary Magdalene' is more serious and tells us about an ancient but still living bit of Cornish folklore from the village where he was born. The two poems 'My Mother Saw a Dancing Bear' and 'I Saw a Jolly Hunter' both, in different ways, highlight Causley's love of animals and his strong dislike of anyone who harms them.

GREEN MAN IN THE GARDEN

Green man in the garden
  Staring from the tree,
Why do you look so long and hard
  Through the pane at me?

Your eyes are dark as holly,
  Of sycamore your horns,
Your bones are made of elder-branch,
  Your teeth are made of thorns.

Your hat is made of ivy-leaf,
  Of bark your dancing shoes,
And evergreen and green and green
  Your jacket and shirt and trews.

Leave your house and leave your land
  And throw away the key,
And never look behind, he creaked,
  And come and live with me.

I bolted up the window,
  I bolted up the door,
I drew the blind that I should find
  The green man never more.

But when I softly turned the stair
  As I went up to bed,
I saw the green man standing there.
  Sleep well, my friend, he said.

MARY, MARY MAGDALENE

*On the east wall of the Church of St Mary
Magdalene at Launceston in Cornwall is a granite
figure of the saint. The children of the town say that a
stone lodged on her back will bring good luck.*

Mary, Mary Magdalene
Lying on the wall,
I throw a pebble on your back.
Will it lie or fall?

Send me down for Christmas
Some stockings and some hose,
And send before the winter's end
A brand new suit of clothes.

Mary, Mary Magdalene
Under a stony tree,
I throw a pebble on your back.
What will you send me?

*I'll send you for your christening
A woollen robe to wear,
A shiny cup from which to sup,
And a name to bear.*

Mary, Mary Magdalene
Lying cool as snow,
What will you be sending me
When to school I go?

*I'll send a pencil and a pen
That write both clean and neat,
And I'll send to the schoolmaster
A tongue that's kind and sweet.*

Mary, Mary Magdalene
Lying in the sun,
What will you be sending me
Now I'm twenty-one?

*I'll send you down a locket
As silver as your skin
And I'll send you a lover
To fit a gold key in.*

Mary, Mary Magdalene
Underneath the spray,
What will you be sending me
On my wedding-day?

*I'll send you down some blossom,
Some ribbons and some lace,
And for the bride a veil to hide
The blushes on her face.*

Mary, Mary Magdalene
Whiter than the swan,
Tell me what you'll send me,
Now my good man's dead and gone.

*I'll send to you a single bed
On which you must lie,
And pillows bright where tears may
  light
That fall from your eye.*

Mary, Mary Magdalene
Now nine months are done.
What will you be sending me
For my little son?

*I'll send you for your baby
A lucky stone, and small
To throw to Mary Magdalene
Lying on the wall.*

COLONEL FAZACKERLEY

Colonel Fazackerley Butterworth-Toast
Bought an old castle complete with a ghost,
But someone or other forgot to declare
To Colonel Fazack that the spectre was there.

On the very first evening, while waiting to dine,
The Colonel was taking a fine sherry wine,
When the ghost with a furious flash and a flare,
Shot out of the chimney and shivered, 'Beware!'

Colonel Fazackerley put down his glass
And said, 'My dear fellow, that's really first class!
I just can't conceive how you do it at all,
I imagine you're going to a Fancy Dress Ball?'

At this, the dread ghost gave a withering cry.
Said the Colonel (his monocle firm in his eye),
'Now just how you do it I wish I could think.
Do sit down and tell me, and please have a drink.'

The ghost in his phosphorous cloak gave a roar
And floated about between ceiling and floor.
He walked through a wall and returned through a pane
And backed up the chimney and came down again.

Said the Colonel, 'With laughter I'm feeling quite
    weak!'
(As trickles of merriment ran down his cheek).
'My house-warming party I hope you won't spurn.
You must say you'll come and you'll give us a turn!'

At this the poor spectre – quite out of his wits –
Proceeded to shake himself almost to bits.
He rattled his chains and he clattered his bones
And he filled the whole castle with mumbles and
    moans.

But Colonel Fazackerley, just as before,
Was simply delighted and called out, 'Encore!'
At which the ghost vanished, his efforts in vain,
And never was seen at the castle again.

'Oh dear, what a pity!' said Colonel Fazack.
'I don't know his name, so I can't call him back.'
And then with a smile that was hard to define,
Colonel Fazackerley went in to dine.

I SAW A JOLLY HUNTER

I saw a jolly hunter,
    With a jolly gun
Walking in the country
    In the jolly sun.

In the jolly meadow
    Sat a jolly hare.
Saw the jolly hunter
    Took jolly care.

Hunter jolly eager –
    Sight of jolly prey.
Forgot gun pointing
    Wrong jolly way.

Jolly hunter jolly head
    Over heels gone.
Jolly old safety catch
    Not jolly on.

Bang went the jolly gun.
    Hunter jolly dead.
Jolly hare got clean away.
    Jolly good, I said.

TELL ME, TELL ME, SARAH JANE

Tell me, tell me, Sarah Jane,
   Tell me, dearest daughter,
Why are you holding in your hand
   A thimbleful of water?
Why do you hold it to your eye
   And gaze both late and soon
From early morning light until
   The rising of the moon?

Mother, I hear the mermaids cry,
   I hear the mermen sing,
And I can see the sailing ships
   All made of sticks and string.
And I can see the jumping fish,
   The whales that fall and rise
And swim about the waterspout,
   That swarms up to the skies.

Tell me, tell me, Sarah Jane,
   Tell your darling mother,
Why do you walk beside the tide
   As though you loved none other?
Why do you listen to a shell
   And watch the billows curl,
And throw away your diamond ring
   And wear instead the pearl?

Mother, I hear the water
   Beneath the headland pinned,
And I can see the seagull
   Sliding down the wind.
I taste the salt upon my tongue
   As sweet as sweet can be.

Tell me, my dear, whose voice you hear?

It is the sea, the sea.

MY MOTHER SAW A DANCING BEAR

My mother saw a dancing bear
By the schoolyard, a day in June.
The keeper stood with chain and bar
And whistle-pipe, and played a tune.

And bruin lifted up its head
And lifted up its dusty feet,
And all the children laughed to see
It caper in the summer heat.

They watched as for the Queen it died.
They watched it march. They watched it halt.
They heard the beggar as he cried,
'Now, roly-poly!' 'Somersault!'

And then, my mother said, there came
The keeper with a begging-cup,
The bear with burning coat of fur,
Shaming the laughter to a stop.

They paid a penny for the dance,
But what they saw was not the show;
Only in bruin's aching eyes,
Far distant forests, and the snow.

Elizabeth Jennings
1926–

Elizabeth Jennings was at school in Oxford when she first began to write. The poem 'A Classroom' captures the occasion when, aged 13, she was suddenly fascinated by listening to the sounds and rhythms of a well-known battle poem, 'Lepanto' by G.K. Chesterton. It was the 'spell of words' that enchanted her and, as she tells us, 'That day is still/Locked in my mind'.

In fact, spells appear quite often in her poems. We have included two here – one spell that does not work as a way of getting off to sleep; the other, a more difficult poem about the very air we breathe. Poems about animals and birds, friendships and family relationships are some of her favourite

subjects, as can be seen in 'Hatching', 'Holidays at Home' and 'Old People'. Thoughtful, detailed looking is typical of her writing, whether the focus is upon a newly hatched bird, the hidden feelings of a boy about family holidays, or a child's view of old people.

A CLASSROOM

The day was wide and that whole room was
    wide,
The sun slanting across the desks, the dust
Of chalk rising. I was listening
As if for the first time,
As if I'd never heard our tongue before,
As if a music came alive for me.
And so it did upon the lift of language,
A battle poem, *Lepanto*. In my blood
The high call stirred and brimmed.
I was possessed yet coming for the first
Time into my own
Country of green and sunlight,
Place of harvest and waiting
Where the corn would never all be garnered
    but
Leave in the sun always at least one swathe.

So from a battle I learnt this healing peace,
Language a spell over the hungry dreams,
A password and a key. That day is still
Locked in my mind. When poetry is spoken
That door is opened and the light is shed,
The gold of language tongued and minted
    fresh.
And later I began to use my words,
Stared into verse within that classroom and
Was called at last only by kind inquiry
"How old are you?" "Thirteen"
"You are a thinker". More than thought it
    was
That caught me up excited, charged and
    changed,
Made ready for the next fine spell of words,
Locked into language with a golden key.

HOLIDAYS AT HOME

There was a family who, every year,
Would go abroad, sometimes to Italy,
Sometimes to France. The youngest did not
    dare
To say, "I much prefer to stay right here."

You see, abroad there were no slot machines,
No bright pink rock with one name going
    through it,
No rain, no boarding-houses, no baked beans,
No landladies, and no familiar scenes.

And George, the youngest boy, so longed to
    say,
"I don't *like* Greece, I don't like all these
    views,
I don't like having fierce sun every day,
And, most of all, I just detest the way

The food is cooked – that garlic and that
    soup,
Those strings of pasta, and no cakes at all."
The family wondered why George seemed to
    droop
And looked just like a thin hen in a coop.

They never guessed why when they said,
    "Next year
We can't afford abroad, we'll stay right
    here",
George looked so pleased and soon began to
    dream
Of piers, pink rock, deep sand, and
    Devonshire cream.

AN ATTEMPT TO CHARM SLEEP

A certain blue
A very dark one
Navy-blue
Going to school
Get back to colour
A pale blue
Somebody's eyes
Or were they grey
Who was the person
Did they like me
Go back to colour
An intolerant blue
A very deep
Inviting water
Is it a river
Where is it going
Shall I swim
What is its name
Go back to colour
Go back to waking
The spell doesn't work
As I stare at the night
It seems like blue.

OLD PEOPLE

Why are people impatient when they are
    old?
Is it because they are tired of trying to make
Fast things move slowly?
I have seen their eyes flinch as they watch
    the lorries
Lurching and hurrying past.
I have also seen them twitch and move away
When a grandbaby cries.
They can go to the cinema cheaply,
They can do what they like all day.
Yet they shrink and shiver, looking like old,
    used dolls.
I do not think that I should like to be old.

SPELL OF THE AIR

I am the impulse of all whispers, I
    Am the place for a rush of birds,
I am the whole intention of the sky
    And the place for coining words.

I am your life breathing in and out,
    I set your senses free,
I sort the truth from complicated doubt,
    I am necessity.

HATCHING

His night has come to an end and now he
    must break
The little sky which shielded him. He taps
Once and nothing happens. He tries again
And makes a mark like lightning. He must
    thunder,
Storm and shake and break a universe
Too small and safe. His daring beak does this.

And now he is out in a world of smells and
    spaces.
He shivers. Any air is wind to him.
He huddles under wings but does not know
He is already shaping feathers for
A lunge into the sky. His solo flight
Will bring the sun upon his back. He'll bear
    it,
Carry it, learn the real winds, by instinct
Return for food and, larger than his mother,
Avid for air, harry her with his hunger.

Grace Nichols
1950–

Grace Nichols was born and grew up in the South American country of Guyana. She says that as a child she was a 'regular bookworm' who loved to read by torchlight under the sheets when she was supposed to be asleep, but sometimes she would stay up late listening to jumbie (ghost) stories and almost frighten herself to death!

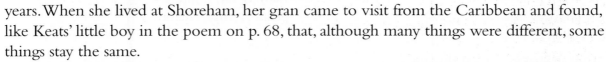

When she left school she worked as a teacher, then as a clerk and finally became a newspaper reporter. It was when she was a reporter that she also started to write short stories and published her first poems.

Grace Nichols moved from Guyana to Britain and has lived near the south coast of England for several years. When she lived at Shoreham, her gran came to visit from the Caribbean and found, like Keats' little boy in the poem on p. 68, that, although many things were different, some things stay the same.

Grace Nichols has published many books for both adults and children and has won the Commonwealth Poetry Prize. Her poems for children are often very active, lively and funny, sometimes using the rhythms of rap. She remembers when she was a child, an old preacher in Guyana urged her: 'Don't be a kyatta-pilla [caterpillar] be a butterfly!'. From reading her poems we can see that she took his advice.

MORNING

Morning comes
   with a milk-float jiggling

Morning comes
   with a milkman whistling

Morning comes
   with empties clinking

Morning comes
   with alarm-clock ringing

Morning comes
   with toaster popping

Morning comes
   with letters dropping

Morning comes
   with kettle singing

Morning comes
   with me just listening.

Morning comes to drag me out of bed
  – Boss-Woman Morning.

WHEN MY FRIEND ANITA RUNS

When my friend Anita runs
she runs straight into the headalong –
legs flashing over grass, daisies, mounds.

When my friend Anita runs
she sticks out her chest like an Olympic
champion – face all serious concentration.

And you'll never catch her looking around,
until she flies into the invisible tape
that says, she's won.

Then she turns to give me
this big grin and hug.

O to be able to run like Anita,
            run like Anita,
Who runs like a cheetah.
If only, just for once, I could beat her.

BABY-K RAP RHYME

My name is Baby-K
An dis is my rhyme
Sit back folks
While I rap my mind;

Ah rocking with my homegirl,
My Mommy
Ah rocking with my homeboy,
My Daddy
My big sister, Les, an
My Granny,
Hey dere people – my posse
I'm the business
The ruler of the nursery

poop po-doop
poop-poop po-doop
poop po-doop
poop-poop po-doop

Well, ah soaking up de rhythm
Ah drinking up my tea
Ah bouncing an ah rocking
On my Mommy knee
So happy man so happy

poop po-doop
poop-poop po-doop
poop po-doop
poop-poop po-doop

Wish my rhyme wasn't hard
Wish my rhyme wasn't rough
But sometimes, people
You got to be tough

Cause dey pumping up de chickens
Dey stumping down de trees
Dey messing up de ozones
Dey messing up de seas
Baby-K say, stop dis –
please, please, please

poop po-doop
poop-poop po-doop
poop po-doop
poop-poop po-doop

Now am splashing in de bath
With my rubber duck
Who don't like dis rhyme
Kiss my baby-foot
Babies everywhere
Join a Babyhood

Cause dey hotting up de globe, man
Dey hitting down de seals
Dey killing off de ellies
for dere ivories
Baby-K say, stop dis –
please, please, please

poop po-doop
poop-poop po-doop
poop po-doop
poop-poop po-doop

Dis is my Baby-K rap
But it's kinda plea
What kinda world
Dey going to leave fuh me?
What kinda world
Dey going to leave fuh me?

Poop po-doop.

I LIKE TO STAY UP

I like to stay up
and listen
when big people talking
jumbie stories

Ooooooooooooooooooh
I does feel so tingly
and excited
inside——eeeeeeeeeeee

But when my mother say
'Girl, time for bed'
then is when
I does feel a dread
then is when
I does jump into me bed
then is when
I does cover up
from me feet to me head

then is when
I does wish
I didn't listen
to no stupid jumbie story
then is when
I does wish
I did read me book instead

GULL

The oil-stricken gull
has struggled ashore,
and although full-grown,
looks like a bewildered
scraggy fledgling.

Her oil-tarred wings
seem heavy as lead
as she totters slightly,
stiff-legged.

Staring out at us
with an unblinking
atomic,
almost comic surprise.

She hasn't taken any sides
but she's lost her natural home
and more. An unanswerable cry
is stuck in her throat
    Why?
     Why?
      Why?

MY GRAN VISITS ENGLAND

My Gran was a Caribbean lady
As Caribbean as could be
She came across to visit us
In Shoreham by the sea.

She'd hardly put her suitcase down
When she began a digging spree
Out in the back garden
To see what she could see

And she found:
That the ground was as groundy
That the frogs were as froggy
That the earthworms were as wormy

That the weeds were as weedy
That the seeds were as seedy
That the bees were as busy
As those back home

And she paused from her digging
And she wondered
And she looked at her spade
And she pondered

Carol Ann Duffy
1955–

Carol Ann Duffy is one of the leading poets of our time. She has published several collections of poems for adults and won many awards for her work. In 1999 she published *Meeting Midnight*, her first collection of poems for young people, which was an immediate success.

The poems that appear in this section were all written especially for this volume of *New Touchstones*. Several of the poems are an unsettling mixture of the ordinary and the strange, where reality blurs with unreality. The images may seem odd, funny, even sinister at first, but also seem to be in some way 'true'. For example, the Bad Princess and the Tree Girl in the poem 'A Bad Princess' are fairy-tale characters from a fairy-tale world at one level, but at another we can recognise them as representing possible aspects of and potential choices for *real* girls. Who we are and who we might be, our identity, is a constant theme of the poems. In 'The Maiden Names' we see the childhood realisation that most women give up their own names when they get married.

The poems stay in the mind long after they are read, teasing us with their meanings and magical images. Above all we realise something of what Carol Ann Duffy means when she writes that 'Language inside me flared, burned'.

THE MAIDEN NAMES

I got a shock
hearing the grown-ups talk
to find that my grandma's name
wasn't her name at all,
only her married name.

I listened hard
till I heard
that the same was true
of Grandmother Two,
who had nearly been left
on the shelf
long ago
when she was cried* something else.

The maiden names
were their real names.
I spoke them aloud –
Mary Wallace, Agatha Hart,
Miss Wallace, Miss Hart –
and saw them as maidens, lassies, girls
in their lost young worlds
with their own names.

Language inside me flared, burned,
then to my mother I turned.

*Scottish dialect for 'called'.

HALO

I was as good as gold, an angel, said ta very
 much, no thanks,
yes *please*, smiled politely
when I said hello, helped out, tried;
so it came to pass I awoke
and there in the bed
next to my head on the pillow
a halo glowed, a hoop-la of gold.
I didn't faint or scream
or wake-up and find it was only a dream,
but went to the mirror
and stared at the icon of me –
acne, bad hair, pyjamas, sticky-out ears, halo.

On the way to school
I swished the halo along with a stick
up the road, down the hill, round the bend
where I frisbeed it to my good friend
 Dominic Gill,
who caught it, said *What's this then, mate?*
A halo, chum, I'm a saint.
No you ain't.

Nevertheless, the halo settled itself
at the back of my head,
shining and bright,
shedding its numinous light all through
 Maths,
double English, RK★, PE, lunch, History,
 silent reading.
The teachers stared,
but left me alone,
and I kept my eyes on the numbers, the
 verbs,
the prophets, the dates, the poem,
till the bell rang, then legged it for home.

But some big kids snatched my halo
as I ran through the park;
tossed it between them, kicked it,
threw it,
far too high for me,
into the outstretched branches of a tree.
Dusk lapped at my feet,
the navy-blue sea of the sky
floated the moon,
as I watched the light of my halo dissolve
to the pinprick glow of a worm,
hearing the loudening shout of a voice
calling, calling my human name.

★Religious Knowledge

A BAD PRINCESS

A bad Princess stomped through the woods
in a pair of boots
                        looking for trouble –
diamond tiara, satin dress, hair an absolute mess,
ready to bubble.

Imagine her shock and surprise
when she bumped straight into
                        her very own double;

a Tree Girl,
with shiny holly-green eyes
and a crown of autumn leaves on her wild head,
the colour of both of their hair.

Don't you dare, screamed Bad,
walk in these Royal woods looking like me!

I shall do as I please, you grumpy old thing,
said Tree.
Give me those emeralds that hang from your ears
or I'll kick you hard
and pinch you meanly.
Then we'll see which one of we two
is cut out
            to be Queenly!

Oh! The bad Princess turned
                        and ran for her life,
ran for her life
into the arms of the dull young Prince
and became his wife.

WALK

Confetti blows
outside the church
as I walk by.

Late summer wind
is dusty, dry.
No children play
in these long streets.

I stare at sweets
locked up behind
thick glass and steel
and want to cry.

The wedding guests
are somewhere else,
like happiness.

THE GOOD FRIEND OF MELANIE MOON

For the first year of my friendship with Melanie Moon
I gave her a cotton worm.
In the second year I gave her a paper spoon.
For the third, a leather piano.
For the fourth, a rose.
In the fifth year of my friendship with Melanie Moon
I gave her a wooden glove.
Year six, an iron hanky.
Year seven, a woollen book.
Year eight, a bronze banana
Year nine, a copper hat.
In the tenth year of my friendship with Melanie Moon
I gave her a tin cat.

In year eleven I gave her slippers of steel.
In year twelve I gave her a silk cheroot.
A lace knife in thirteen.
In fourteen, an ivory wasp.
In the fifteenth year of my friendship with Melanie Moon
I gave her a crystal moth.

Melanie Moon – in our twentieth year I gave her
a china car.
Melanie Moon – in our twenty-fifth year I gave her
a silver tent.
In the thirtieth year, a pearl pear.
In year thirty-five, a coral cake.
In the fortieth year, a ruby boot.
In year forty-five, a sapphire goat.

Melanie, Melanie, Melanie Moon,
in our fiftieth year a golden umbrella.
Melanie, Melanie, Melanie Moon,
in our fifty-fifth year an emerald gun.
In the sixtieth year of our friendship
I gave her a diamond balloon
and then my friendship with Melanie Moon
was done.

Ten Poets Workshop

WILLIAM SHAKESPEARE

Performance

- Working in groups of three, rehearse 'The Witches' Chant' (p. 73). Once you have mastered the words and the rhythm, add some simple movements as you circle round and drop things in the cauldron.

Writing

- Using Shakespeare's lines from *Macbeth* as a model, write a witches' chant of your own. As before, work in groups of three. Use Shakespeare's couplet 'Double, double …' as your chorus, but invent your own horrible ingredients. Try to follow the four-beat rhythm of the lines and the rhyming couplets, if possible. You will need to agree what your menu is for: School Dinners? A potion to keep off homework? A magic brew to stop toothache? When it's finished, perform your chant to the rest of the class.

Illustration

- Several of Shakespeare's songs lend themselves to illustration. 'Now the hungry lion roars' (p. 74), 'When icicles hang by the wall' (p. 72), 'Full Fathom Five' (p. 75) are all vivid word-pictures. Copy out one of them in the middle of a page and illustrate as many details as you can.

EDWARD LEAR

Performance

- Get to know Mr Lear by working in groups of four to produce the best reading you can of his 'Self-Portrait' on p. 77. Take two verses each.
- 'The Jumblies' (p. 78) can be a class performance with single voices introducing the first half of each verse. Another small group of voices can take over when the Jumblies say something, and everybody can join in the chorus.

Writing

- Invent your own Edward Lear style limerick. Notice how he often begins with 'There was an old person of—' and returns in the last line to the 'old person' phrase along with a long word like 'impulsive' or 'mendacious'.

Illustration

- Invent your own strange Nonsense Botany plant, draw it, name it and write a verse about it.

LEWIS CARROLL

Performance

- In threes, practise performing 'Father William' (p. 81), with one taking the part of the inquisitive youth, one taking that of Father William and the third filling in the Narrator's words.
- You can do a similar reading of 'The White Knight's Song' (p. 83), but it is a good idea to all join in together for the last eleven lines.

Writing

- Write your own acrostic poem to spell out your name or the name of a friend.

ROBERT LOUIS STEVENSON

Reading aloud

- In groups of three or four, prepare a live reading of 'Escape at Bedtime' (p. 85) sharing out the lines but all coming together to speak the last two lines.
- 'Shadow March' (p. 84) builds up the tension as the shadows seem more and more threatening and the child's fear mounts. Rehearse a reading where the single voice of the child is 'backed' by other voices, either by repeating the words 'tramp, tramp, tramp' or by whispering the word 'shadows'.

WALTER DE LA MARE

Listening

- 'The Listeners' (p. 88), as its title suggests, is full of sounds. When you have heard the poem read aloud, get into pairs and make a list of all the sounds that are mentioned in the poem. Then, think about the sounds of the words themselves. What do you notice about these three descriptions: '…the forest's ferny floor', '…the leaf-fringed sill/ Leaned over and looked', and '…the silence surged softly'? (See Part A, Unit 2).

Dialogue

- 'The Ghost' (p. 89) is a conversation between two people. Are they men or women? What might be the thoughts and feelings of the person in the lonely house that the ghost visits? Rehearse a reading of the poem for three voices: two for the dialogue in verses one to three, and a third for the final two verses.

ELEANOR FARJEON

Earliest memories

- Hear 'It Was Long Ago' (p. 93) read aloud. The speaker is recalling an incident from when she was three years old. Notice how the repetitions help us to see the 'red shawl', the 'grey cat', the 'house', the 'dusty road' and so on in our mind's eye. Talk about your earliest memories. Choose one event or scene and write your own poem to capture it as clearly as possible.

Choral speaking

- Divide up the lines of 'When Hannibal Crossed the Alps' (p. 91) among different groups in the class so that everyone has at least one line to say. Rehearse the readings and make sure you have the best rhythm and good continuity. Put all the pieces together into a performance.

CHARLES CAUSLEY

Performance

- The poem 'Mary, Mary Magdalene' (p. 95) is a dialogue between St Mary Magdalene and a child as she grows into a girl, a wife, a mother, a widow. Rehearse a reading of the poem, deciding on how you will split the verses. One way would be to have three voices reading the first three verses and then splitting the other verses between different voices. One person reads Mary Magdalene throughout. Some verses are better read by girls' voices; others could easily be boys reading.
- 'Tell Me, Tell Me, Sarah Jane' (p. 97) is a dialogue, a conversation between mother and daughter, but it is strange and magical in tone — even a bit frightening towards the end as we realise how the girl is obsessed by the sea. In pairs, work on a reading trying to catch the strangeness of it. Maybe 'Father' could be substituted for 'Mother' if appropriate.

ELIZABETH JENNINGS

Point of view

● What picture of old people do you get from the poem on p. 99? Talk about the details and why the writer concludes that she does not want to be old. How might an elderly person view young people? List the things that the elderly might notice about the young, and write a poem from their point of view.

Charm

● There is no punctuation in 'An Attempt to Charm Sleep', the long, thin poem on p. 99. Copy it out and put in commas, full stops and questions marks so that you can follow it more easily. Now hear it read aloud. There are three attempts to charm sleep, none of which works. Write your own attempt to charm sleep in the same style, perhaps using a different colour, by counting sheep or pebbles, or by some other trick.

GRACE NICHOLS

Performance

● In groups, practise reading the poem 'Morning' (p. 101) with different voices reading each line and everyone joining in for the last line of all.
● Get the rap rhythms moving in a reading of the poem 'Baby-K Rap Rhyme' on p. 102. Again, split it up between you and all join in where you decide it needs it.

Writing

● In groups, maybe the same groups you had for the performance, create your own poem called 'Evening' to match Grace Nichols' poem 'Morning' (p. 101). Each think of what things you associate with the evening. Remember to find *active* verbs as she does, so that each line ends with something like 'ringing' or 'dropping'. Maybe you will use 'sleeping' or 'yawning' for your evening poem.

CAROL ANN DUFFY

Performance

● Working in threes, practise a performance of 'A Bad Princess' on p. 106. You will need a Narrator, a Bad Princess and a Tree Girl.

● 'The Good Friend of Melanie Moon' (p. 107) is a strange poem but it's fun to perform. Each year Melanie is given the appropriate present (Most of us know that 25 years is a silver anniversary and 50 is a golden one, where you give presents of silver or gold, but not many people know there are other anniversaries like paper and tin and china.) Split the poem up among the class (there are 25 different voices).

Writing

● 'Halo' (p. 105) begins 'I was as good as gold, an angel…' and the writer tells of a day when her halo didn't slip. Write a matching poem about yourself when you were naughty – perhaps beginning 'I was as bad as bad, a devil…' and you grew horns instead of gaining a halo.

The Ten Poets

One of these ten poets may have appealed to you more than the others. Choose one poet and write about what it is that you like about their poems. You could say what lines you particularly enjoy; what images stick in your mind; any things in the poems that you recognise from your life or are important to you. Below, we have also chosen books by the same writer that will take you further into their work.

Shakespeare: *Shakespeare's Songs*, Vista.
Lear: *A Book of Bosh*, ed. Brian Alderson, Puffin.
The Complete Nonsense of Edward Lear, ed. Holbrook Jackson, Faber and Faber.
Carroll: *Alice's Adventures in Wonderland* and *Through the Looking-Glass*, Macmillan.
Stevenson: *A Child's Garden of Verses*, Puffin.
da la Mare: *Collected Rhymes and Verses*, Faber and Faber.
Farjeon: *Invitation to a Mouse*, Pelham Books.
Causely: *Selected Poems for Children*, Macmillan.
Jennings: *A Spell of Words*, Macmillan.
Nichols: *Give Yourself a Hug*, Puffin.
Duffy: *Meeting Midnight*, Faber and Faber.

Acknowledgements

The authors and publishers wish to thank the following for permission to reproduce copyright material:

Copyright text:

Alan Ahlberg: *Excuses* from 'Please Mrs Butler', Kestrel, 1983. Copyright © Allan Ahlberg, 1983.

Hilaire Belloc: *Henry King* from 'Selected Cautionary Verses', Random House UK Ltd. Reprinted by permission of The Peters Fraser and Dunlop Group Limited on behalf of The Estate of Hilaire Belloc, © The Estate of Hilaire Belloc, 1940, 1964.

Peter Benton: *J—* and *James* © Peter Benton 2000. Written for this edition of *New Touchstones*.

Morris Bishop: *Song of the Pop-Bottlers* © 1950, first appeared in 'The New Yorker'.

Keith Bosley: *How to Address a Goldfish* and *The Cat* from 'And I Dance', HarperCollins Publishers Ltd.

Charles Causley: *Infant Song, I Saw a Jolly Hunter, My Mother Saw a Dancing Bear, Tell me, Tell Me, Sarah Jane, Colonel Fazackerley, Mary Mary Magdalene* and *Green Man in the Garden*, by Charles Causley, from 'Collected Poems 1951–2000', Macmillan.

Elisabeth Coatsworth: *On A Night of Snow* and *The Mouse* from 'The Oxford Book of Children's Poems', Oxford University Press; *What Could be Lovelier Than to Hear*, from 'A Year Full of Poems', Oxford University Press, 1991.

Kevin-Crossley Holland: *Riddle* from 'Storm and Other Old English Riddles', Macmillan.

Carol Ann Duffy: *The Maiden Names, Halo, A Bad Princess, Walk* and *The Good Friend of Melanie Moon* © Carol Ann Duffy 2000. Written for this edition of *New Touchstones*.

Marriott Edgar: *The Lion and Albert* from 'The Oxford Book of Narrative Verse', Oxford University Press.

Eleanor Farjeon: *The Quarrel, When Hannibal Crossed the Alps, Here's Spring, The Dewdrop, The Tide in the River, Keep Still* and *It Was Long Ago*, from 'Invitation to a Mouse', Penguin Books UK.

Michael Frayn: *When I Was Your Age* from 'Allsorts 7', Methuen Publishing Ltd.

Edward Gorey: *'Each night Father fills me with dread'* © 1954 Edward Gorey.

Thomas Hardy: *Last Week in October* and *Night-Time in Mid Fall*, from 'Collected Poems', Macmillan.

W. Hart-Smith: *Observation* from 'The Talking Clothes', Angus & Robertson, 1966.

Ted Hughes: *Gulls* from 'The Mermaid's Purse', Faber and Faber.

Elizabeth Jennings: *Old People* from 'The Secret Brother', Macmillan; *A Classroom, Holidays At Home, An Attempt to Charm Sleep, Spell of the Air* and *Hatching*, from 'A Spell of Words', Macmillan.

Walter de la Mare: *The Magnifying Glass*; *Me, Echo, The Listeners, Ice, John Mouldy, The Ghost, Hi*, and *All But Blind* reprinted by permission of The Literary Trustees of Walter de la Mare, and the Society of Authors as their representatives.

Roger McGough: *The Fight Of The Year* from 'Watchwords', Jonathan Cape; *Goodbat Nightman* from 'In The Classroom', Jonathan Cape.

Spike Milligan: *Ye Tortures*, reproduced by kind permission of Spike Milligan Productions Ltd.

Edwin Morgan: *The Loch Ness Monsters Song*, from 'Collected Poems', Carcanet Press Ltd.

Lillian Morrison: *Sidewalk Racer*, from 'The Sidewalk Racer and Other Poems of Sport and Motion' © 1977 by Lothrop, Lee and Shepard Books.

Ogden Nash: *The Tale of Custard the Dragon* from 'Candy is Dandy: the Best of Ogden Nash', Andre Deutsch Ltd; *The Sniffle*, Orion Publishing Company.

Grace Nichols: *Baby-K Rap Rhyme* from 'No Hickory, No Dickory, No Dock', Viking, 1991; *Morning, When My Friend Anita Runs, Gull* and *My Gran Visits England*, from 'Give Yourself A Hug', A&C Black; *I Like To Stay Up*, from 'I Like That Stuff' edited by Morag Styles.

Gareth Owen: *Winter Days*, from 'Salford Road', HarperCollins Publishers Ltd; *Thoughts Like An Ocean*, from 'Song for the City', HarperCollins Publishers Ltd.

Kathleen Raine: *Amo Ergo Sum*, Bloomsbury Publishing Plc.

James Reeves: *Cows* from 'Complete Poems for Children', Heinemann.

Alan Riddell: *Honey Pot* from 'Eclipse', Calder Publications Ltd.

Michael Rosen: *Lizzie* from 'Quick, Let's Get Out of Here', Scholastic Ltd; *'Father says'*, Scholastic Ltd; *The Longest Journey in the World*, from 'You Can't Catch Me', Scholastic Ltd.

Carl Sandberg: *Fog* from 'Chicago Poems', Harcourt Inc., USA.

Clive Sansom: *Hedgehog*, from 'An English Year', Methuen.

Stevie Smith: *This Englishwoman* from 'Our Bog is Dood: Selected Poems for Young Readers', Faber and Faber, 1999.

James Stephens: *The Main-Deep* from 'Collected Poems', Macmillan.

L.A.G. Strong: *Winter* from 'The Body's Imperfection', Methuen Publishing Ltd.

Hugh Sykes: *Poem* from 'Poetry of the Thirties', Penguin Books Ltd.

Walter James Redfern Turner: *Romance* from 'The New Oxford Book of Children's Verse', Oxford University Press.

Kit Wright: *Whisper Whisper* from 'Rabbitting On', HarperCollins Publishers Ltd.

Benjamin Zephaniah: *Serious Luv* from 'Funky Chickens', Viking, 1996. Copyright © Benjamin Zephaniah, 1996; *Stepmother* by Jean Kenward, Bloomsbury Publishing Plc.

Copyright photographs/artwork:

p5 © Kate Harrison, 1998; p7 'Domino' © Emma Ray, 2000; p14 left-hand picture © Corbis; p14 right-hand picture © Stevie Smith, from *Our Bog is Dood*, Faber and Faber; p30 from *1800 Woodcuts by Thomas Bewick and His School*, Dover Publications, Inc, 1962; p42 © Judy Harrison/Format; p46 © Format Partners/Ulrike Preuss; p47 illustration by Edward Gorey; p 54 © Nicholas Bentley, from 'Selected Cautionary Verses' by Hilaire Belloc, by permission of Gerald Duckworth & Co Ltd; p56 from *1800 Woodcuts by Thomas Bewick and His School*, Dover Publications, Inc, 1962; p57 *La Belle Dame Sans Merci* by Sir Frank Dicksee, City of Bristol Museum and Art Gallery; p59 Giovanni Battista Tiepolo, *Two Cats*, The Victoria and Albert Museum; pp62–64, 66 from *The Kate Greenaway Book* by Bryan Holme, Penguin Putnam Inc, New York. © Kate Greenaway; p69 © Life File/Jeremy Hoare; p72 © National Portrait Gallery, London; p73 Fuseli's 'The Witches' © Mary Evans Picture Library; pp76-77, 79 illustrations by Edward Lear; p80 © Mary Evans Picture Library; p84 © Corbis; p86 Drawing by Hans-Georg Rauch in *Hans-Georg Rauch En Masse* © 1974, Rowolt Verlag GmbH, Hamburg; p87 © Mary Evans Picture Library; p90 © Helen Craig, July 1962; p92 © UNEP/Janet Haas/Topham; p94 © Macmillan; p95 Photograph of St. Mary Magdalene, St. Mary's Church, Launceston, Cornwall. © John Neale, Launceston; p97 Hulton Getty/Paul Martin; p98 Carcanet Press; p100 © Bruce Coleman Collection/Jane Burton; p101 © Gillian Cargill/Little Brown publishers; p104 © Sue Alder/Anvil Press.

Every effort has been made to trace copyright holders of material reproduced in this book. Any rights not acknowledged here will be acknowledged in subsequent printings if notice is given to the publisher.

MY FIRST 18 YEARS

18

BORN IN
1965
FROM 1965 TO 1982

My First 18 Years is a brand of TDM Publishing.
The image, brand and logos are protected and owned by TDM Publishing.

www.mijneerste18jaar.nl
info@mijneerste18jaar.nl

My First 18 Years idea and concept: Thars Duijnstee.
Research and text: Lucinda Gosling, Stephen Barnard, Jeffrey Roozeboom, Katherine Alcock.
Composition and image editing: Jeffrey Roozeboom.
Design: Ferry Geutjes, Boudewijn van der Plas, Jeffrey Roozeboom.
Proofreading: Alison Griffiths.

Photos: Sound & Vision, National Archives, Getty images, Mary Evans Picture Library, Shutterstock, BNNVARA, AVROTROS, Veronica, KRO-NCRV, KIPPA, *Mijn eerste 18 jaar* archives.

In writing this series, the authors drew from the following sources: view from 1963-1999, NTS / NOS Annual Review, nueens.nl, vandaagindegeschiedenis.nl, beleven.org, IMDb, Wikipedia, Eye Filmmuseum, Rollingstone.com, image & sound, National Archives, Onthisday.com, Parlement.com. *Complete Book of UK Hit Singles, First Hits 1949-1959* (Boxtree Books), Billboard Books, *Reader's Digest* Music series 1950s-1970s, British Library Newspaper Archive, rogerebert.com

Thanks to: Spotify, Rick Versteeg, Rik Booltink.

The Top 10 list for each year is compiled by Stephen Barnard and is a personal selection of best-selling hits, radio favourites and lesser-known tracks that reflect the popular artists and styles of each year. Some are universally regarded classics, others will be less remembered yet are equally emblematic of the tastes of that year. Each list should provoke many 'Ah yes!' moments, particularly those almost forgotten treasures that are rarely heard even as 'golden oldies' yet tickled the ears in their day.

How to use Spotify playlists:

1. Open Spotify.
2. Click search (the magnifying glass in the image).
3. Click scan (the camera in the picture).
4. Point your camera at the Spotify code in the book.
5. After that, you can play the selected list.

ISBN 978 94 9331 774 1
NUR: 400

SPORT

Arise, Sir Stanley
1st January 1965 Stanley Matthews be-comes the first ever professional football player to receive a knighthood. He will be 50 years old in February, shortly before he plays his last competitive match for Stoke City.

Dawn Fraser banned
1st March 1965 Triple Olympic gold medal-winning Dawn Fraser is suspended by Australia's Amateur Swimming Association for ten years for misconduct during the previous year's Olympic Games in Tokyo. It is punishment for her decision to march in the opening ceremony against their instructions, and for an incident in which she was alleged to have stolen a flag from outside Emperor Hirohito's palace.

An American first
27th March 1965 It's an all-American triumph in the 119th running of the Grand National. Crompton 'Tommy' Smith becomes the first American jockey to win the race, on the US-owned and trained horse Jay Trump, who defeats Freddie in a close finish at 100/6.

DO YOU REMEMBER THIS?

Ministeck

Double triumph for Clark
31st May 1965 Jim Clark is the first non-American driver in 49 years to win the Indianapolis 500. Two months later he wins the German Grand Prix at Nürburgring to take the second of his Formula One World Drivers' Championships, so becoming the only driver in history to win the Indy 500 and the Formula One champion-ship in the same year.

Ali v Liston
25th March 1965 In a rematch to decide the world heavyweight championship, Muhammad Ali (formerly Cassius Clay) beats Sonny Liston once again. Liston falls to the canvas after two minutes of the second round and does not get up.

20 JAN 1965

Lyndon Johnson inaugurated as US President for second term.

23 FEB 1965

Death of Stan Laurel, one half of Laurel and Hardy comedy team.

7 MAR 1965

US Marines arrive in Vietnam as conflict intensifies.

Football firsts

The end of the 1964-65 season sees Manchester United win the league championship for the first time since the 1958 Munich air crash that decimated their playing squad. Liverpool beat Leeds United 2-1 to win the FA Cup for the first time, this in a match that sees Albert Johanneson of Leeds become the first black player to grace a cup final. Debuting in the European Cup Winners' Cup, West Ham beat 1860 Munich 2-0 in the final. An innovation for the 1965-66 season is the allowance of one substitution per side per game, the very first player to take the field as a 'sub' being Keith Peacock (Illustration) of Charlton Athletic. After all these firsts there is a last: the very last Christmas Day fixture is played in England, a derby match between Blackpool and Blackburn Rovers. From now on festive games will be restricted to Boxing Day

DOMESTIC
NEWS

NHS charges end

31st January 1965 The Labour government ends charges for prescriptions available on the National Health Service. The charge had been 2 shillings, but for the next three years prescriptions are free to all, before charges are reintroduced in 1968.

Goldie the Eagle

11th March 1965 The nation is gripped as the infamous 'Goldie the Eagle is finally recaptured by his London Zoo keepers after eleven days on the run'. Goldie's brief bid for freedom dominates the news for a fortnight, after his escape during a routine cage clean. Goldie wasn't done with his life on the run, however, escaping again for five days in December.

Famous foods

1965 sees the launch in the UK of several famous brands, including the very first Pizza Express restaurant, a British brand, which opens in Soho, London, on 27th March. American brand KFC launches in Preston, Lancashire, in May, and in the same month the Asquith brothers launch their new supermarket chain with Associated Dairies, taking the 'As' from Asquith and the 'Da' from dairies to create British brand 'ASDA' (photo).

6 APR 1965

UK government's TSR-2 bomber aircraft project is abandoned.

12 MAY 1965

West Germany and Israel establish diplomatic relations.

1 JUN 1965

The first Certificate of Secondary Education (CSE) examinations take place.

Little Baldon air crash
6th July 1965 Tragedy strikes as a Handley Page Hastings crashes shortly after take-off from RAF Abingdon. The flight is carrying 41 service personel on a parachute training mission and comes down in Little Baldon with no survivors.

E

Ronnie Biggs escapes!
8th July 1965 Ronnie Biggs, one of the thieves convicted of the Great Train Robbery, escapes from Wandsworth prison. Biggs is on the run for 36 years, spending time in Australia and South America, before returning to the UK, and prison, in 2001.

Television morality fears
13th November 1965 Theatre critic Kenneth Tynan becomes the first person to clearly say the F-word on British television. The live debate he is partaking in discusses issues relating to censorship in the theatre, and morality in entertainment becomes a hot topic in 60s Britain.

Sea Gem collapses
27th December 1965 The Sea Gem oil rig collapses in the North Sea killing thirteen people. The rig is in the process of being moved to a new location when two of its ten legs collapse, sending men and equipment into the cold North Sea.

No smoking adverts
1st August 1965 Advertisements for cigarettes are banned from British television, forming the first step in measures designed to curb the nation's smoking habit. Anti-smoking campaigners must wait until the 1990s for further restrictions to be enacted.

Mary's minis!
The world of fashion gets mini skirt fever as designer Mary Quant introduces her shockingly short designs to London's streets. Her shop on the King's Road in Chelsea, 'Bazaar', does a roaring trade and soon the mini skirt becomes synonymous with the 'Swinging' Sixties.

Moors Murderers caught
7 October 1965 Ian Brady is charged with the murder of seventeen-year-old Edward Evans. Over the next month the police arrest Brady's girlfriend, Myra Hindley, and 150 police officers comb Saddleworth Moor, looking for the bodies of further victims. Eventually the remains of Lesley Ann Downey and John Kilbride are discovered, along with tape recordings of the murders, and a horrified nation learns the extent of the pair's crimes.

F

19 JUL 1965

Mont Blanc Tunnel is opened between France and Italy.

5 AUG 1965

A five month war begins between India and Pakistan.

27 SEP 1965

Death of Clara Bow, icon of the silent movie era.

1965

DO YOU REMEMBER THIS?

Hand mixer

Churchill is dead
24th January 1965 Britain's wartime Prime Minister Sir Winston Churchill dies at his London home at the age of 90. He is accorded a huge state funeral at St Paul's Cathedral six days later and is buried in Bladon churchyard in Oxfordshire.

Sir Alec resigns
2nd July 1965 Alec Douglas-Home surprises even his closest colleagues by resigning as Conservative Party leader. Attention turns immediately towards his successor. For the first time Conservative MPs will be able to choose their own leader by secret ballot. The winner is Edward Heath (photo), the first Conservative leader not to have had a public school education.

Death of the Princess Royal
28th March 1965 Mary, Princess Royal, dies at her home, Harewood House in Yorkshire, aged 67. The only daughter of King George V and Queen Mary, sister of King Edward VIII and King George VI and aunt of Queen Elizabeth II, she was known for her strong advocacy of higher education for women.

Race Relations Act
8th December 1965 The Race Relations Act comes into force making it a civil offence to discriminate against people on grounds of colour, race or ethnic or national background.

Government agenda
May - July 1965 With the partial nationalisation of the steel industry narrowly secured, the Labour government's legislative programme includes a promise to introduce a blood alcohol limit to combat drink driving. Further measures include the introduction of a 70 mph speed limit on UK roads and, after the appointment of Roy Jenkins as Home Secretary in December, a raft of social reforms including the planned decriminalisation of homosexuality.

7 OCT 1965

Post Office Tower opens in London.

27 NOV 1965

First major anti-Vietnam war protest in Wahington DC.

22 DEC 1965

Barbara Castle becomes Minister of Transport.

FOREIGN
NEWS

Arafat's new force
1st January 1965 Palestine Liberation Movement leader Yasser Arafat announces the formation of a military wing to pursue a guerilla war against Israel.

Rolling Thunder begins
22nd March 1965 Operation Rolling Thunder begins - aerial bombing of North Vietnam on a daily basis. Over 55,000 missions will be mounted over the next three years and will bring an end to the war no closer. In October, the war escalates with the US bombing of Viet Cong positions in neighbouring (and neutral) Cambodia.

☐☐ Dolby

Dolby system
At his London laboratory, US engineer Ray Dolby develops a system to suppress tape noise that will become a movie and recording industry standard.

Malcolm X shot dead
21st February 1965 Black Power leader Malcolm X is assassinated in New York. Formerly an advocate of black separatism and a member of the Nation of Islam, his formation of the Organisation of Afro-American Unity and his growing advocacy of world brotherhood made him a hate target for black militants.

War in Kashmir
5th August 1965 Pakistan sends thousands of troops disguised as civilians into India and sparks conflict in Kashmir that will lasts five months.

First space walker
18th March 1965 Soviet cosmonaut Alexei Leonov is the first man to walk in space. He floats outside Voskhod 2 for twelve minutes. 'You just can't comprehend it. Only there can you feel the grandeur, the enormous scale of everything around us,' he says later.

Voting Rights Act
6th August 1965 President Johnson signs the Voting Rights Act into law, removing obstacles such as literacy tests that disqualified African-Americans from voting.

Watts aflame
11th August 1965 Mass rioting breaks out in Watts, a poor black neighbourhood of Los Angeles, following a minor traffic incident. The riots last for six days and cause 34 deaths and over a thousand injuries.

1965

ENTERTAINMENT

Short life for London Life

London Life magazine is launched on 9th October by the Thomson organisation, intended as a hip and happening replacement for the *Tatler*. Contributions include fashion advice from Terence Stamp and Jean Shrimpton, Marc Bolan writes the music reviews one issue, photographs are by Terence Donovan and Duffy, and artwork is supplied by a young artist called Ian Dury. By the end of 1966, staff turn up to work one day to be told the title is closing with immediate effect.

Pipe Up

Unusual pipes and long cigarette holders are all the rage with mods in London this year, who keep one 150-year-old Soho tobacconist in business with their demand for strange smoking accoutrements, or 'kinky gear'.

The hills are alive...

Nuns! Nazis! Lederhosen! Singing siblings! It's all here in what many consider the ultimate musical as Julie Andrews takes on the career-defining role of Maria, a novice nun whose restless character leads the Mother Superior at her Austrian convent to send her to become governess to the motherless offspring of gruff disciplinarian Captain von Trapp (Christopher Plummer). Rodgers and Hammerstein's sing-a-long score seals the film's reputation as a future classic.

Big move for Biba

Around sixty models and well-known personalities, including *Ready, Steady Go!* presenter Cathy McGowan and singer Cilla Black, help the cult London fashion store Biba move premises from Abingdon Road to Kensington Church Street in what is a carefully orchestrated publicity stunt.

Magic Roundabout

Adapted from the stop-motion animation French original, the psychedelic world of *The Magic Roundabout* is first introduced to the British public on 18th October. When the programme is moved the following year, from its slot before the 6 O' clock News to an earlier time, the BBC receives a flood of complaints from adults who are unable to get home from work in time to watch it, proving the cross-generational appeal of Florence, Zebedee, Dougal and Brian the Snail.

Ladybird, ladybird

Ladybird is one of the best-selling childrens-wear brands in the 1960s and most children will be dressed in at least one or two Ladybird garments, whether it's dresses and coats for Sunday best, or vests, baby clothes, pyjamas and playsuits from the more affordable Woolworth's range.

Round the Horne

Created by Barry Took and Marty Feldman, radio sketch show *Round the Horne* is first broadcast on 7th March and includes a number of the cast from its predecessor show, *Beyond our Ken*, among them Kenneth Williams and Hugh Paddick. Blazing a trail for shows such as *The Goodies* and *Monty Python's Flying Circus*, *Round the Horne's* cast of nonsensical characters has the urbane straight man Kenneth Horne at its centre, whose smooth patter is liberally laced with innuendo.

Exterminate!

With *Doctor Who* now firmly established as essential viewing, Whovian playthings are in demand from miniature replicas of the Doctor's most dangerous foe to the

AstroRay Dalek Gun made by Bell Toys, essential for keeping at one's side while hiding behind the sofa.

Call My Bluff

Call My Bluff, the much-loved panel game in which participants attempt to explain the meaning of an obscure word in the English dictionary, with only one definition actually true, is broadcast for the first time on 17th October. Debonair wit Frank Muir captains one team, while the magisterial Robert Morley heads the other; the host is Robin Ray, later succeeded by Robert Robinson. For viewers, the show's lasting appeal is not only the amusing banter among contestants but the chance to expand one's vocabulary with a wondrous array of new words from hickboo to ablewhacket.

Up the Junction

The launch of *Wednesday Playhouse* the previous year provides a platform for some of the

decade's most influential dramas, including *Up the Junction* written by Nell Dunn and directed by Ken Loach who shoots it in a drama-documentary style. Following the lives of three female friends from south London, *Up the Junction* tackles some challenging themes, notably backstreet abortion, and after it is broadcast on 3rd November, the BBC receives 400 complaints.

Telling tales

The very first story - Cap of Rushes - is told on Jackanory on 13th December by Lee Montague. *Jackanory's* simplicity is also its power. Storytellers, recruited from the realms of theatre, film and literature, sit

in a chair in front of the camera as they read the autocue and captivate kids with their energetic and characterful readings of stories old and new. Over the years, Kenneth Williams, Michael Hordern, Alan Bennett and Rik Mayall are just some who sit in the Jackanory chair, with Bernard Cribbins (photo) boasting a record-breaking 111 appearances.

A Bright Future

Wannabe science boffins (and anyone quite simply interested in new technology) gets their first taste of *Tomorrow's World* presented by Raymond Baxter on the BBC on 7th July 1955.

Darling Julie

Julie Christie, gorgeous and gifted, is swiftly becoming the 'it' girl of sixties cinema. This year she stars as Lara opposite Omar Sharif, Tom Courtenay and Geraldine Chaplin in *Dr Zhivago*, David Lean's sweeping, Russian revolution romance based on Boris Pasternak's novel. But it's the John Schlesinger film *Darling*, in which she plays a model and actress juggling the attentions of two older men, that bags her an Academy Award. *Darling* has its finger on the pulse of swinging London and Julie Christie is at its beating heart.

Sex a-Peel

Diana Rigg joins the cast of *The Avengers* as Emma Peel, replacing Honor Blackman's Cathy Gale (who leaves to film *Goldfinger*). In partnership with Patrick Macnee's Steed, she's a brilliant secret agent and martial arts expert, rescuing him from a succession of scrapes wearing the best outfits any crime-fighting heroine could wish for.

Thunderbirds are GO!

Tracy Island in the Pacific Ocean is the base for International Rescue, headed by Jeff Tracy whose five sons, Scott, Virgil, John, Gordon and Alan (aided by brilliant scientist Brains) can scramble their high-performance Thunderbird craft at a moment's notice to rescue those in need. Created by Gerry Anderson, also renowned for supermarionation productions *Captain Scarlett*, *Joe 90* and *Stingray*, the Thunderbirds' special British agent, the glamorous Lady Penelope Creighton-Ward, is voiced by Sylvia Anderson, Gerry's wife and co-creator of the show.

Charlie Girl

Singing star Joe Brown co-stars with Anna Neagle in the musical *Charlie Girl*, which opens at the Adelphi Theatre on the 15th December. The show is one of the most successful of the 1960s, running for 2,202 performances until March 1971.

MUSIC

The Byrds take flight

20th January 1965 By setting an acoustic song to a rock accompaniment, California band the Byrds create a whole new style called folk-rock. The song is Dylan's *Mr Tambourine Man*, which former folk singer and twelve-string guitarist Roger McGuinn has embellished with gorgeously dense harmonies. The record tops the US and UK charts and encourages Dylan to embrace rock.

The best of British blues

14th January 1965 In the wake of the Rolling Stones, London's rhythm and blues club scene is awash with talent. Scoring the year's first new No. 1 are Georgie Fame and the Blue Flames, resident band at the Flamingo in Soho, with the Mose Allison song *Yeh Yeh*. Manfred Mann, with Jagger's pal Paul Jones on vocals, are already Top Ten regulars. Cream of the crop are the Yardbirds, whose guitarist Eric Clapton (photo) joined from John Mayall's Bluesbreakers and has an almost messianic following. He leaves the group in March rather than promote what to him is the distastefully commercial *For Your Love*. Another much-talked-about guitar hero, Jeff Beck, joins in his place.

Stones across the water

18th March 1965 After a series of covers, the Rolling Stones finally hit No. 1 with a Jagger-Richards song. They record *The Last Time* with Phil Spector guesting on acoustic guitar but it's just the appetiser for *(I Can't Get No) Satisfaction* on which Jagger rages with frustration and Keith Richards plays a fuzz-toned guitar riff to die for.

A righteous No. 1

4th February 1965 Produced and co-written by Phil Spector, the Righteous Brothers' *You've Lost That Lovin' Feelin'* spotlights the cavernous bass voice of Bill Medley and the high counter singing of Bobby Hatfield, who make the most convincing 'white soul' sound yet heard in pop music.

Jones the voice

13th March 1965 New at No. 1 in the UK is Pontypridd-born Tom Jones with *It's Not Unusual*. Tom's steamroller voice and Presley-like movements stand out in a group-saturated music scene.

Beatles work it out

Another non-stop Beatle year finds Liverpool's best receiving MBEs from the Queen at Buckingham Palace, filming *Help!* in the Bahamas and meeting Elvis at Graceland. The joyless title of the *Beatles for Sale* LP suggests that some world weariness is creeping in, but their music is evolving, influenced by Bob Dylan's iconoclasm and the new musical adventurism of the Byrds and the Beach Boys. Paul even spreads his wings with *Yesterday*, soon to become the most recorded song in history. On the *Rubber Soul* album they start to edge away from boy-girl love songs to reflective pieces like *In My Life* and *Nowhere Man*, while augmenting their instrumentation with piano, organ and even a sitar.

A world of their own

2nd December 1965 Voted best new group by *New Musical Express* readers are an Australian folk group without an electric guitar in sight. The Seekers have had two UK No. 1s so far - *I'll Never Find Another You* and *The Carnival is Over*.

1965

Provincial pop

What Liverpool, Manchester and London can do, so can the rest of Britain. As a full scale Beatles- and Stones-stoked music boom gathers pace, the Moody Blues (photo) and the Spencer Davis Group emerge from the Midlands. From Hertfordshire come the Zombies - bigger stars in the US than in the UK - and Unit Four Plus Two with the chart topping *Concrete and Clay*. Every town and city seems to have its own group scene, making the future of British pop music look very bright indeed.

Doddy beats the Beatles

30th September 1965 The biggest selling single of the year - now at No. 1 for the first of five weeks - is not a Beatles track but the gushing *Tears* by another famous Liverpudlian export, comedian Ken Dodd.

Dylan goes electric

25th July 1965 The Newport Folk Festival witnesses an electrifying moment in every sense. Bob Dylan, enfant terrible of folk music, takes to the stage with a rock band, plugs in and lets rip with *Maggie's Farm* and the rambling but unignorable *Like a Rolling Stone*. Crowd reaction is split between bemused and enraged, someone cuts the power supply but there's no going back.

Protest pop

28th August 1965 A vogue for protest pop begins when Dylan soundalike Barry McGuire of the New Christy Minstrels tops the US chart with *Eve of Destruction*, which rants about everything from segregation to fallout shelters. Almost simultaneously, Sonny and Cher - Phil Spector acolyte Sonny Bono and backing singer Cherilyn Sarkisian - dress like anti-war protesters and declare their mutual besottedness to the world in *I Got You Babe*.

SPORT

Billie Jean's at our door
1st July 1966 Having defeated reigning champion Margaret Smith in the semi-final, Billie Jean King of the US wins the first of her six Wimbledon tennis championships at the age of 22. She beats Brazilian Maria Bueno 6-3 3-6 6-1.

England's greatest day
30th July 1966 On the greatest day in England's football history, the national team defeat West Germany 4-2 at Wembley to win the FIFA World Cup. England are the tournament hosts and overcome Argentina 1-0 in the quarter final and Portugal 2-1 in the semis to reach the final. The star of the final is striker Geoff Hurst who scores a hat trick, his last goal coming at the very end of extra time. As BBC television commentator Kenneth Wolstenholme famously tells the watching millions, 'Some people are on the pitch, they think it's all over ... it is now.' Manager Alf Ramsey will be rewarded with a knighthood in the New Year honours list.

European gold
30th August - 7th September 1966 Great Britain's only two medals in the European Athletics Championships in Budapest are both golds and go to Lynn Davies in the long jump and Jim Hogan in the marathon.

Ali v. the Brits
Reigning world heavyweight boxing champion Muhammad Ali takes on two British opponents during the course of the year. May sees a rematch with Henry Cooper, who three years earlier had put the then Cassius Clay on the canvas before losing to a technical knockout. Ali wins the fight at Arsenal's Highbury stadium by a sixth round technical knockout. while August finds Ali pitched against Geordie fighter Brian London at Earl's Court. The outclassed London lasts for nearly three rounds before succumbing to a knockout punch.

12 JAN 1966

Lyndon B. Johnson says US should stay in South Vietnam until communist aggression ends.

3 FEB 1966

Unmanned Luna 9 is first spacecraft to make rocket-assisted landing on the Moon.

8 MAR 1966

An IRA bomb damages Nelson's Pillar in Dublin.

1966

Action Man launched!
30th January 1966
Palitoy launches 'Action Man' a British licensed version of the American toy 'G.I. Joe'. This posable, dressable soldier doll initially comes in three versions, 'Action Soldier', 'Action Sailor', and 'Action Pilot'.

Britain goes on safari!
11th April 1966 Britain gets its first safari park as the Marquess of Bath opens one on his estate at Longleat. It is the first such experience, outside of Africa, in the world and allows visitors to drive their cars through enclosures containing the 'Longleat lions' and other animals.

Murderers convicted
6th May 1966 The Moors Murderers Ian Brady and Myra Hindley are finally brought to justice for their crimes following a trial that grips and revolts the nation. Both killers receive multiple concurrent life sentences and are never released, Hindley dying in jail in 2002, and Brady in 2017.

Panda on a plane
11 March 1966
London Zoo's panda Chi Chi makes the news as she is flown to Russia to mate with An An at Moscow Zoo. Sadly, the two do not take to each other and the attempts are unsuccessful. Chi Chi proves one of the most popular animals at London Zoo, and her image is immortalised as the logo of the World Wildlife Fund.

Barclaycard launches
29th June 1966
The Barclaycard is launched as Britain's first creditcard. Initially it is a 'charge' card, meaning the balance must be paid in full every month to avoid penalties, but by the end of 1967 it becomes a full credit card. This allows shoppers to purchase items throughout the month and pay their bills on payday, revolutionising shopping.

Pickles saves World Cup!
27th March 1966 Pickles the dog is applauded as a national hero as he sniffs out the stolen FIFA World Cup trophy. The Jules Rimet trophy had been stolen seven days before whilst on display. With the World Cup just four months out, the search is desperate, and Pickles is the hero of the hour as he finds the trophy under a hedge in South London.

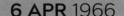

6 APR 1966
Cross-Channel hovercraft service inaugurated between Ramsgate and Calais.

30 MAY 1966
Graham Hill wins the Indianapolis 500.

30 JUN 1966
France leaves NATO.

Independence spreads

More former British colonies and territories gain independence, as British Guiana becomes Guyana, the Bechuanaland Protectorate becomes Botswana, Basutoland becomes Lesotho, and Barbados becomes a Commonwealth realm.

Wage freezes and unemployment

20th July 1966 The government's Prices and Incomes Board gets the legal power to control wages, announcing the beginning of a six-month wage and price freeze. The country's economic troubles continue as unemployment rises by around 200,000 between September and November.

Shepherd's Bush murders

12th August 1966 The country is rocked by the murder of three Metropolitan Police officers. The officers are shot dead in East Acton as they approach a suspicious vehicle. The murderers go on the run. Whilst two are apprehended a few days later, one of them evades a large manhunt that lasts until November, when he is finally apprehended. All three receive life sentences of 30 years.

ROYALTY & POLITICS

Plaid Cymru's first seat

14th July 1966 A by-election in Carmarthen occasioned by the death of sitting MP Megan Lloyd George brings Gwynfor Evans, leader of the Welsh Nationalist party Plaid Cymru, to Parliament. He defeats his Labour opponent and becomes Plaid Cymru's first ever Member of Parliament. The result is a catalyst for the growth of Plaid as a party and suggests that Labour's hold on its heartland of Wales may be under threat.

Pirate radio to be outlawed

27th July 1966 The government introduces the Marine etc Broadcasting Offences Bill to make illegal the unlicensed pirate radio stations operating around the UK coast. It will become law in a year's time. The move is unpopular, given the high broadcasting figures that stations such as Radio Caroline and Radio London attract.

Labour landslide

31st March 1966 With the Labour government's majority reduced to two by recent by-elections, Prime Minister Harold Wilson calls a general election. It is the last to be held with a minimum voting age of 21. Labour returns with a landslide victory over Edward Heath's Conservatives, gaining 48 seats and achieving a majority of 98.

31 JUL 1966

31 drown as pleasure cruiser MV Darlwyne sinks off Cornish coast.

22 AUG 1966

London's Centre Point office block completed and left empty for ten years.

6 SEP 1966

South African premier Hendrik Verwoerd assassinated.

The Queen at Aberfan
29th October 1966 The Queen visits Aberfan in South Wales, eight days after the village school is engulfed by a coal tip landslide causing over 140 deaths, the majority of them children.

France leaves NATO
30th June 1966 Having withdrawn French forces from NATO's Mediterranean fleet and refused to place American nuclear weapons on French soil, President Charles de Gaulle makes good his threat to leave NATO, which is now obliged to move its headquarters from Paris to Belgium.

Democratic fashion
15th September 1966 Having set the tone in haute couture during the 1950s with his trapeze dress with a free waist, Yves Saint Laurent opens a Paris boutique to sell ready-made clothes aimed at democratising fashion, challenging the assumption that London is now the centre of the fashion world thanks to Carnaby Street, Mary Quant and the mini skirt.

FOREIGN
NEWS

Nigerian coup
15th January 1966 The government of Nigeria is overthrown and its Prime Minister murdered in a military coup. In July, a different section of the military seizes power under General Yakubu Gowon. A bloody civil war soon erupts as the eastern province of Biafra fights for independence.

Gandhi elected
19th January 1966 Indira Gandhi, daughter of the late Jawaharlal Nehru, is elected Prime Minister of India in succession to Lal Bahadur Shastri, who died nine days earlier after signing the Tashkent peace agreement with Pakistan.

Let's twist again
Twister, the game where humans are the pieces, and bodily entanglement is an unavoidable result of taking part, is launched this year. Store buyers are initially reluctant, expressing concerns the game is too risqué but the following year, *Twister* (which was originally called Pretzel) sells three million units.

22 OCT 1966
Soviet spy George Blake escapes from prison and is next seen in Moscow.

4 NOV 1966
Devastating floods strike Florence and Venice.

15 DEC 1966
Death of animation pioneer Walt Disney.

Emperor Cannibal?

1st January 1966 Colonel Jean Bodel Bokassa leads a military coup in the Central African Republic and declares himself President. Although he seems to have good intentions for the people of the poverty-stricken country, he soon has opponents eliminated and enriches himself and a small group of associates. A rumour then circulates that Bokassa feasts on the flesh of his political opponents.

Cultural Revolution

16th May 1966 An inflammatory article in the *Chinese People's Daily* calls for the destruction of 'all monsters and demons'. Chinese leader Mao Zedong demands that the country must be cleansed of any form of bourgeoisie and begins the Cultural Revolution, though which Mao, following Lenin's example, aims to secure total power. At least half a million are killed during the revolution, which lasts until Mao's death in 1976.

LSD is outlawed

6th October 1966 The drug LSD - lysergic acid diethylamide - is outlawed in California, though it will continue to be manufactured clandestinely and widely used within the state's hippie communities.

Pogles' Wood

First introduced to viewers as *The Pogles* in the TV programme *Clapperboard* in 1965, *Pogles' Wood* from Smallfilms begins a new series on 7th April under the *Watch with Mother* banner. Created in the barn belonging to Oliver Postgate, Mr and Mrs Pogle, along with their adopted son Pippin and Tog the squirrel, live in a tree hollow. Postgate narrated the series which usually began with the question, 'Now where will we find the Pogles?'

ENTERTAINMENT

DO YOU REMEMBER THIS?

Fondue set

The Frost Report

The Frost Report premieres on BBC1 on 10th March 1966 with writers and performers from the cream of British comedy talent, including John Cleese, Eric Idle, Graham Chapman, Terry Jones and Michael Palin, who find their Python writing style while working on the show.

Till Death Us Do Part

Alf Garnett, a bald, bigoted racist, railing against practically everything in modern Britain, is introduced to an unsuspecting public on 6th June and within two days, the Conservative Party have asked for a copy of the script due to Alf (played to perfection by Warren Mitchell) referring to Edward Heath as, 'a grammar school twit'. Scriptwriter Johnny Speight smartly turned Garnett into a parody of himself, exposing him as a character that embodies the worst aspects of the British.

Alfie

A serial womaniser, Alfie knocks around London, loving and leaving a trail of sexual conquests in his wake, until events cause him to examine his self-centred behaviour with a sense of remorse. Michael Caine, unconventionally but mesmerizingly handsome, breaks the fourth wall and talks to the camera and with that laconic expression and chipper attitude, you can see how he's such a successful seducer.

It's a Knockout

From 7th July 1966, the battle for regional supremacy of the UK is thrashed out on BBC every Saturday evening as amateur athletic teams from around the country don outsized cartoon costumes and tackle obstacle courses, slippery slopes and avoid buckets of slime in a series of baffling races. Still, there is nothing the British population like better than seeing their fellow citizens making fools of themselves, and the slapstick carnage of It's a Knockout is regularly watched by 19 million viewers.

On the Margin

Alan Bennet writes and performs this satirical sketch show with the support of a regular cast including future BBC political commentator John Sergeant, and guest appearances from Michael Hordern and Prunella Scales. Bennett's sardonic comedy is contrasted with more serious poetry readings and, unusually, archive clips of nostalgic music hall performances.

Cathy Come Home

Ken Loach directs another Wednesday Playhouse play, Cathy Come Home, a dramatic exposé highlighting the inhumanity of a social system in which one young woman finds herself trapped. Cathy Come Home follows the devastating descent of one couple into poverty and homelessness, as Cathy finds her marriage destroyed and her children taken from her. The searing impact of the film on the British public means huge support for the charity Shelter which forms shortly afterwards.

Icon of an era

Model Lesley Hornby is 'discovered' when her photograph by Barry Lategan, sporting a chic cropped hairdo by the hairdresser Leonard, is seen by *Daily Express* journalist Deirdre McSharry and published under the headline, 'The Face of 1966'. Aged just 16, Twiggy's androgynous look with her inimitable, gangly frame, freckles, saucer eyes and spider lashes, becomes synonymous with the Swinging Sixties.

Holy smoke Batman!

DC Comics superhero Batman and his sidekick Robin first hit TV screens in America on 12th January. Adam West dons the cape as Bruce Wayne/Batman with Dick Grayson/Robin played by Burt Ward. Together they run around Gotham City fighting crimes committed by an inordinate number of dastardly villains. The series has its tongue firmly in its cheek and Batman's comic-book roots are never forgotten. Lines are delivered with hammy drama and the fight scenes cut with cartoon graphics of punch-up noises. Wham! Ker-pow!

Born Free

Virginia McKenna and Bill Travers play real-life couple George and Joy Adamson, who attempt to introduce an orphaned lion called Elsa back into the wild in Kenya.For McKenna and Travers, the film has a life-changing effect and they go on to become wildlife campaigners, and found the Born Free Foundation. John Barry's song, *Born Free*, sung by Matt Munro with lyrics by Don Black, wins an Academy Award for best original song.

Carry on Screaming

The *Carry On* juggernaut continues with *Carry On Screaming*, the franchise's thirteenth film: a barely-disguised parody of the Hammer Horror genre in a riff on the Frankenstein story.

Live long and prosper

The multi-racial, multi-species crew of the 23rd-century starship, USS *Enterprise*, led by Captain James T. Kirk (William Shatner) are on a mission to 'boldly go where no man has gone before' patrolling the galaxies as a kind of inter-planetary peace-keeping force, but with groovier coordinated uniforms. *Star Trek* ensures that beneath the action and sci-fi kitsch, is a moral and philosophical message in storylines that act as metaphors for current global issues like feminism or the Vietnam War. *Star Trek* gains a cult following and flowers into one of the most successful TV and film franchises of all time.

Prehistoric pin-up

Nobody seems to care much that prehistoric man and dinosaurs are co-existing in *One Million Years B.C.* a fantasy adventure which is released on 25th October, even though dinosaurs died out about 65 million years before early man made an appearance. All eyes instead are on Raquel Welch, who strides around with only a fur bikini cladding her voluptuous frame. The image of Welch as the ultimate in sexy prehistoric womanhood becomes a cultural phenomenon.

MUSIC

Sounds of Simon

1st January 1966 Paul Simon, who is touring UK folk clubs as a singer-songwriter, discovers that a track he made in New York with best pal Art Garfunkel called *The Sound of Silence* is sitting at the top of the US charts. Except it's not quite the same track: someone has added a rock backing to it. Within days he is back in the US and recording again with Art as avatars of the new folk-rock.

What's it all about?

22nd February 1966 Composer Burt Bacharach is a name on everyone's lips. He and lyricist Hal David record mainly with their discovery Dionne Warwick, but Dusty Springfield (*Wishin' and Hopin'*), the Walker Brothers (*Make It Easy on Yourself*) and Tom Jones (*What's New Pussycat?*) have all had hits with their songs. Now Bacharach is in London to oversee Cilla Black's recording of the title song of the film *Alfie*.

Beatles quit performing

These are momentous months for the Beatles. In the middle of an exhausting US tour, John Lennon's opinion that 'we are more popular than Jesus now' provokes an anti-Beatle backlash, convincing the group that they should stop live performing altogether. Their last ever concert is at Candlestick Park in San Francisco in August. The plan now is to focus exclusively on making music in the studio, with a big project in mind that will eventually take shape as *Sgt Pepper*.

James Brown's solo show

11th March 1966 ITV's must-see music show *Ready Steady Go!* departs from its standard format to showcase the inimitable James Brown. The doyen of 60s soul music, Brown receives a Grammy for *Papa's Got A Brand New Bag*, while *It's A Man's Man's Man's World* tops the US R&B chart in May.

In praise of swinging England

16th April 1966 That the UK represents everything that is hip, young and swinging is confirmed by a famous article in *Time* magazine. On cue, Roger Miller's *England Swings* depicts the old country as a place of rosy-cheeked children and friendly bobbies. The tongue-in-cheek song is a gift to the tourist trade and confirms the current American passion for all things British.

Kink commentaries

7th July 1966 The Kinks came out of London's Muswell Hill in 1964 playing a primitive kind of heavy metal on the chart topping *You Really Got Me*. Gradually their sound has mellowed and leader Ray Davies's lyrics have become more observational and satirical, typified by the Carnaby Street send-up *Dedicated Follower of Fashion* and the lament of a bored rock star, *Sunny Afternoon*. Few songs better evoke the long, hot, enervating British summer of 1966.

Frank and Nancy

2nd June 1966 After several years of absence from the singles chart, Frank Sinatra is back with *Strangers in the Night*. He tops both US and UK charts, as does his daughter Nancy with the proto-feminist anthem *These Boots Are Made for Walkin'*, featuring the most famous descending bassline in pop music.

Comings and goings

1st August 1966 Can groups survive the loss of key members? Paul Jones leaves Manfred Mann to go solo and is replaced by Mike D'Abo from Band of Angels, while Jimmy Page joins the Yardbirds in place of Paul Samwell-Smith. Meanwhile the Animals, having already lost Alan Price and Chas Chandler, break up altogether in September, though Eric Burdon keeps the band name with a new line-up.

Spector's masterpiece

25th June 1966 Phil Spector has created another masterpiece. Credited to Ike and Tina Turner but with only Tina heard on the track, *River Deep Mountain High* is the ultimate 'wall of sound' record, made with over twenty musicians in multiple takes over many days.

Beach Boy brilliance

7th November 1966 Some call it the record of the year and even the decade. It may even be the record of the millennium. The UK's new No. 1 is *Good Vibrations* by the Beach Boys, who are now creating the most imaginative soundscapes in pop history. The genius behind this and the head-turning *Pet Sounds* LP is Brian Wilson, who roots the group's sound in sun-kissed harmonies and production techniques learned from Phil Spector.

MY FIRST 18 YEARS TOP10 1966

1. **Summer in the City** *The Lovin' Spoonful*
2. **My Generation** *The Who*
3. **Wouldn't it be Nice** *The Beach Boys*
4. **Reach Out, I'll Be There** *The Four Tops*
5. **Sunny Afternoon** *The Kinks*
6. **Eleanor Rigby** *The Beatles*
7. **Semi-Detached Suburban...** *Manfred Mann*
8. **The Sun Ain't Gonna S...** *The Walker Brothers*
9. **Homeward Bound** *Simon and Garfunkel*
10. **Walk Away Renee** *The Left Banke*

Open 🎧 | Search 🔍 | Scan 📷

Talkin' about their generation

Mod fashions and iconography are all over British pop at the moment, but one band in particular seems to have truly authentic Mod credentials. From the Mod heartland of Shepherds' Bush, the Who have a restless and questioning resident songwriter in Pete Townshend, whose songs like *My Generation*, *Substitute* and *I'm a Boy* distil the Mod experience. Such is the band's aggression on stage that their performances usually end with them destroying their equipment.

Folk-rock evolves

Out of the folk music hub of Greenwich Village burst the Lovin' Spoonful, with good-time songs like *Daydream* and *Do You Believe in Magic* written by John Sebastian and a style evoking old-time jug bands. Sebastian's chum John Phillips forms the Mamas and the Papas who decamp to Los Angeles to add the sweetest of boy-girl harmonies to *Monday Monday* and *California Dreamin'*. Back in the UK, Donovan (photo) evolves from a guitar-playing troubadour with a Bob Dylan cap into a creator of whimsical, fey and faintly psychedelic hits such as *Sunshine Superman* and *Mellow Yellow*.

SPORT

Arise Sir Alf
1st January 1967 Alf Ramsey, manager of the victorious 1966 World Cup-winning England side, is recognised with a knighthood in the New Year honours list. The England captain, Bobby Moore, receives an OBE.

100/1 outsider wins the Grand National
Foinavon, ridden by John Buckingham, is a rank outsider at 100/1 at the start of the 1967 Grand National steeplechase at Aintree on 8th April. But the racing gods are smiling on him and when numerous horses and riders fall at the 23rd fence, Buckingham avoids the melee and takes the lead and romps home to victory.

Grand Slam queen
American Billie Jean King wins the second of her six Wimbledon singles titles against British player Ann Jones, as well as scooping the women's doubles and mixed doubles titles at the tournament.

Arise Sir Francis
Francis Chichester sails his yacht, the *Gipsy Moth IV*, back into Plymouth harbour on the evening of 28th May, 226 days and 28,500 miles after departing. In recognition of his achievement in becoming the first person to sail solo around the world from west to east, he is knighted by the Queen at Greenwich.

Knocked out
9th May 1967 Muhammad Ali is stripped of his World Heavyweight Champion titles and banned from boxing after refusing to be drafted into the US Army at the height of the Vietnam War. Ali argues that as a black Muslim, he is a conscientious objector, but his moral stand comes at great personal cost.

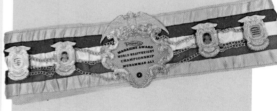

Our 'Enry
Heavyweight boxer Henry Cooper becomes the first person to win three Lonsdale belts outright after his victory over Billy 'Golden Boy' Walker on 7th November. A few weeks later, he wins the first of his two BBC Sports Personality of the Year Awards.

12 JAN 1967
Britain's latest new town is to be built on a 22,000-acre site in Buckinghamshire and called Milton Keynes.

2 FEB 1967
Nicotine-free Bravo cigarettes, made from cured lettuce, go on sale in Tesco supermarket in Brixton.

30 MAR 1967
Photographer Michael Cooper shoots the Peter Blake-designed album artwork for The Beatles' *Sgt. Pepper's Lonely Hearts Club Band*.

1967

Campbell killed

4th January 1967 Donald Campbell, pioneering racing driver, is killed in an attempt to break his own Water Speed World Record in his craft Bluebird. A serial record breaker, Campbell heads to Coniston Water in the Lake District to attempt 300 mph but is killed as Bluebird lifts out of the water and backflips.

European Economic Community

15th January 1967 Britain enters negotiations to discuss joining the European Economic Community. Italy and the Netherlands signal their support for Britain's membership, and a formal application is made from the United Kingdom in May. However, President Charles de Gaulle of France vetoes the move in November.

Outer Space Treaty

27th January 1967 The Outer Space Treaty is signed by the UK, United States, and the Soviet Union in a landmark agreement to prohibit nuclear weapons in space and ensure that no country can claim sovereignty of part of the cosmos. It is also agreed that celestial bodies such as the moon can be used only for peaceful purposes. In light of these agreements, the British launch their Ariel 3 satellite in May, the first satellite to be developed outside either the Soviet Union or the United States.

Torrey Canyon Disaster

18th March 1967 The oil tanker SS Torrey Canyon runs aground off Land's End near the Scilly Isles and begins shedding its cargo of crude oil. 170 miles of British and French coastline are contaminated in one of the world's most serious spills.

Stockport air disaster

4th June 1967 British Midland Flight G-ALHG crashes in Stockport killing 72 passengers and crew in one of Britain's worst air disasters. The crash occurs as the plane is heading into land at Manchester Airport, when two of its engines cut unexpectedly. 12 people survive thanks to the brave efforts of members of the public and police.

New Look Stamps

5th June 1967 British stamps receive a new look as the General Post Office unveils the new 'Machin' series of stamps, replacing the old Wilding series. The new stamps are much simpler than previous designs, and feature Arnold Machin's sculpture of the Queen.

APR 1967

Marion Boyers and John Calder are prosecuted under the Obscene Publications Act for publishing the novel, *Last Exit to Brooklyn*.

MAY 1967

Bird's launch *Angel Delight*, an instant dessert made by magically whipping a sachet of flavoured powder into milk.

27 JUN 1967

The UK's first cash machine opens at a branch of Barclay's Bank on Enfield High Street.

Gay and women's rights

4th July 1967 Following on from the Wolfenden Report's 1957 recommendations, acts of consensual male homosexuality between consenting adults are decriminalised in England and Wales. This first step in gay rights comes just a few months before the Abortion Act is passed in October, legalising abortions up to the 28th week of pregnancy.

Welsh Language Act

27th July 1967 The introduction of the Welsh Language Act takes a step towards protecting Welsh speakers, by enshrining their right to use Welsh in legal proceedings and in official documents in Wales. Alongside the protection of the Welsh language, the Act also importantly repeals an Act from 1746 which defines Wales as part of England.

Britain abroad

10th September 1967 A referendum held on British sovereignty in the Crown colony of Gibraltar returns a huge majority in favour of remaining a British territory. Of the island's 12,000 voters, only 44 vote to become part of Spain. In contrast, in November, British troops finally leave the State of Aden after 128 years, leading to the formation of the republic of Yemen.

Hither Green rail crash

5th November 1967 49 people are killed when the evening express from Hastings to London Charing Cross hits a broken rail and leaves the tracks at the Hither Green Depot.

DO YOU REMEMBER THIS?

Scooter

BBC radio changes

8th November 1967 A month after the BBC renames all its radio networks to accommodate its new pop music station, Radio 1, it launches a new local radio service, starting with BBC Radio Leicester. Both Radio 1 and these local radio stations are designed to replace the newly outlawed 'pirate' radio stations. Eight experimental local stations launch initially, with services to the rest of the country rolled out in the 1970s.

Pound devalued

19th November 1967 The deepening sterling crisis in the UK leads to Prime Minister Harold Wilson taking the drastic action of devaluing the pound by 14%, from $2.80 US dollars to $2.40. The decision is controversial, and Wilson attempts to reassure the nation, stating in a broadcast that the 'pound... in your pocket' will not be affected.

17 JUL 1967

The Keep Britain Tidy campaign launches a dedicated Anti-Litter Week.

2 AUG 1967

A second, southbound bore of the Blackwall Tunnel under the River Thames in east London is opened.

20 SEP 1967

The Queen names the new passenger ship, *Queen Elizabeth 2 (QE2)* at Clydebank.

ROYALTY &
POLITICS

FOREIGN
NEWS

A royal reconciliation?
7th June 1967 Queen Elizabeth, the Queen Mother meets the Duke and Duchess of Windsor for the first time since the 1936 abdication after they had been invited to London for a dedication ceremony for a memorial plaque to Queen Mary at Marlborough House.

Moved to say sorry

On the 11th October, pop group the Move are obliged to issue a formal apology in the High Court to Prime Minister Harold Wilson after they had featured a caricature of the P.M. in the nude on a promotional postcard for their single, *Flowers in the Rain*. The band are ordered to pay all royalties from the single to a charity of the Prime Minister's choice.

Flower power's first shoots
14th January 1967

Something is brewing in San Francisco, where a 'Human Be-In' takes place in Golden Gate Park. It's a gathering of hippies who live in the city's bohemian district of Haight-Ashbury and reject what they see as the bourgeois, well-behaved lifestyle of their parents' generation. The hippie movement has its roots in the nomadic west coast community led by Ken Kesey, author of *One Flew Over the Cuckoo's Nest*. Many hippies believe in free love, communal living and the mind-expanding drug LSD. They're against capitalism, materialism, and war. Their music as played by groups like the Grateful Dead and Jefferson Airplane is free form, unruly, loud and mind expanding. Everything is set for a legendary 'summer of love', as radio vibrates to the sounds of the Frisco bands and the cult of flower power goes international.

The student prince
9th October 1967 Prince Charles begins his first term as an undergraduate student at Trinity College where he reads Archaeology and Anthropology in his first year, followed by two years of History. Arriving in true sixties style as a passenger in a red Mini, the bashful eighteen-year-old is met by a crowd of vocal well-wishers and the inevitable flashbulbs of the press.

8 OCT 1967
Death of Clement Attlee, Britain's Prime Minister from 1945 to 1951.

27 NOV 1967
John Noakes gamely models a chest wig on Blue Peter while Valerie Singleton tells young viewers they are all the rage in the US.

4 DEC 1967
The Royal Smithfield Show opens at Earl's Court with no animals and mechanical exhib its only, due to an outbreak o foot-and-mouth disease.

Astronaut deaths

27th January 1967 A tragic setback in the space race: three astronauts are killed in a fire in their Apollo spacecraft during a test launch. Designated Apollo 1, this was to be the first attempt at a manned crew mission. Crewed flights are suspended for twenty months.

Oppenheimer dies

18th February 1967 Robert Oppenheimer dies of throat cancer aged 62. The director of the Manhattan Project that created the atom bomb, his concerns over nuclear proliferation and his earlier left-wing political affiliations led to the removal of his security clearance in 1954.

Svetlana defects

9th March 1967 In one of the Cold War's most surprising twists, Svetlana Aliluyeva, daughter of Joseph Stalin, defects to the west at the US Embassy in New Delhi.

Coup in Greece

21st April 1967 A military coup in Greece ousts Prime Minister Andreas Papandre-ou. The new regime headed by Colonels George Papadopoulos and Stylianos Pattakos imposes martial law, suspends democracy and even outlaws beards and mini skirts. The infamous Colonels rule until 1974.

Six-Day War

5th - 10th June 1967 To prevent encirclement by the Arab states, Israel launches what becomes known as the Six-Day War against Egypt, Syria, Iraq and Jordan. Virtually all of the Arab air defences are destroyed on the first day and Israeli forces sweep into Sinai and the West Bank. The war ends when Israel and Syria agree to a UN-mediated truce.

Che is dead

8th October 1967 Revolutionary leader Che Guevera, whose relations with Fidel Castro's Cuban regime have cooled, is captured and executed by government forces in Bolivia.

First heart transplant

3rd December 1967 In Cape Town, a team of surgeons led by Christiaan Barnard performs the first heart transplant. A 57-year-old Polish immigrant named Louis Washkansky receives the heart of a young woman who died in an accident. He will die eighteen days later from pneumo-nia due to a weakened immune system.

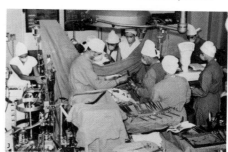

Ceaușescu in power

9th December 1967 Nicolae Ceaușescu becomes Chairman of the Romanian State, with dictatorial powers. Initially his regime seems liberal and mild compared to the rest of the Soviet Bloc, but by the late 1970s Ceaușescu is the strictest of Stalinist dictators running the most repressive regime in Eastern Europe.

Holt disappears

17th December 1967 Australian Prime Minister Harold Holt disappears while swimming near Portsea, Victoria. His body is never found.

ENTERTAINMENT

Eurovision winner

8th April 1967 After nearly a decade of trying, the UK finally wins the Eurovision Song Contest with *Puppet on a String* by Sandie Shaw. Sandie (real name Sandra Goodrich) has been a chart regular for three years and secretly feels that this song is beneath her, yet it is her most lucrative record ever.

Top *Trumpton*

The stop-animation children's series *Trumpton* first airs on 3rd January 1967, with gentle stories from Trumpton-shire, a place originally introduced to young viewers in *Camberwick Green* the previous year. Pivotal to each episode, narrated by Brian Cant, is an emergency call-out by Trumpton's trusty fire brigade led by Captain Flack, whose team dutifully responded to their memorable roll call of 'Pugh, Pugh, Barney McGrew, Cuthbert, Dibble, Grub.'

Derring done

Since its launch in 1879, the *Boy's Own Paper* has fed successive generations of young men with a diet of stirring tales of derring-do, public school stories and advice on wholesome, practical pursuits.

But in 1967, its publisher decides a paltry circulation of 24,000 (compared to 190,000 in its 1890s heyday) cannot justify its continuation in a vastly changed market.

The Jungle Book

Disney's full-length animation based loosely on the 1894 stories of Rudyard Kipling opens in the UK on 17th November 1967. With its lush artwork and uplifting jazz tunes including the toe-tapping *Bare Necessities*, *The Jungle Book* is a critical and commercial success.

Monkee business

It is Beatlemania all over again when manufactured pop foursome The Monkees touch down at Heathrow on 28th June to perform in Britain for the first time. They are greeted by what one news report describes as 'a highly trained team of hysterical mini-skirters' as Manchester-born frontman Davy Jones is rugby tackled by one particularly determined lovestruck fan. The following day, Davy, Peter, Mike and Mickey are woken to a dawn chorus of hundreds of screaming girls outside the Royal Garden Hotel in Kensington.

The test card girl

When BBC engineer George Hersee asks his daughter Carole to pose for photographs with a blackboard and her clown doll, Bubbles, little does she know it will make her one of the most recognisable faces in British television history. Her picture subsequently becomes the test card image for the BBC and it is Carole (and the rather sinister Bubbles) who viewers see on-screen until 1998.

Calamity the Cow

Children's Film Foundation release *Calamity the Cow*, which stars a terribly well-spoken teenage Phil Collins three years before he joins prog-rock band Genesis.

Battleship is launched

Budding naval strategists can test out their skills with the launch of the board game *Battleship*. The aim of the game for two players is to hunt, sink or destroy your opponent's (imaginary) fleet of ships, using nothing more than a plastic board with pegs.

BBC2 embraces colour

Television viewers begin to see the world in glorious technicolour on 1st July 1967 when BBC2 is the first channel in Europe to show programmes in colour, starting with its coverage of the Wimbledon Lawn Tennis Championships. But with just 5,000 colour television sets in circulation among the population it will be a few more years before colour TV becomes the norm.

Just a Minute

22nd December 1967 Three months after the launch of Radio 4, a new panel show, *Just a Minute*, takes to the airwaves, hosted by Nicholas Parsons. The show's insanely simple format - that contestants should speak on any given topic, 'without hesitation, repetition or deviation' proves to be a winning formula. Parsons remains the host until shortly before his death in 2020 at the age of 96.

Fiddler on the Roof

Fiddler on the Roof opens at Her Majesty's Theatre on 16th February 1967 starring Israeli actor Topol in the role of Tevye; he would later be nominated for an Academy Award for playing the same role in the 1971 film adaptation. The £80,000 production is the hit of the year, eventually running for 2030 performances.

Fashion on film

Two major films of 1967, *Far from the Madding Crowd* starring Julie Christie, Alan Bates and Terence Stamp, and *Bonnie and Clyde* with Faye Dunaway and Warren Beatty, have a major influence on fashion, as trim silhouettes and mini skirts give some ground to hippysh Victoriana and Depression-era style dresses.

Blow Up!

For his first English-speaking film, Michaelangelo Antonioni plunges headfirst into a strange and sometimes seedy world of swinging London with a tale about a fashion photographer, played by David Hemmings, who thinks he witnesses a murder. The film's fashionable themes and sexual content quickly make it into a cult classic, with its racy reputation enhanced by a scene with Jane Birkin, in which female pubic hair is glimpsed for the first time in mainstream cinema.

Sixties comedy favourite

Not in Front of the Children becomes one of the year's most popular sitcoms. Wendy Craig stars as Jennifer Corner in her first sitcom, playing the role of a harassed, middle-class wife and mother, a 'type' in she which comes to excel. *Not in Front of the Children* runs for 39 episodes over 4 series until 1970 and wins Craig a BAFTA for Best Actress in 1969.

Dee Time

Radio disc jockey Cyril Nicholas Henty-Dodd, better known as Simon Dee, attracts 18 million viewers with his early evening chat show *Dee Time* on BBC1. In a scene that is to become something of a sixties cliché, at the end of each programme, Dee is filmed driving off in a white E-type Jaguar beside blonde model Lorna Macdonald.

It happens in Monterey

16th - 18th June 1966 Monterey in California is the site of the first true rock festival, which showcases not just star names like the Who and the Byrds but also acts from the mushrooming San Francisco scene who haven't even signed with a record label yet. Janis Joplin (photo) and her band get a big-money deal, while Jefferson Airplane, the Grateful Dead, Moby Grape and a jaw-dropping Jimi Hendrix seize the chance to launch themselves on a bigger stage. Ending with Scott McKenzie singing his 'summer of love' hippie anthem *San Francisco*, Monterey is the start of a new rock era in which the music is louder, druggier and more provocative than ever.

The Beatles

Britain's Summer of Love

Between the 26th and 28th August, the Festival of the Flower Children takes place at Woburn Abbey in Bedfordshire, seat of the Duke of Bedford, where acts include the Small Faces, the Bee Gees and Eric Burdon from The Animals. Britain's Summer of Love is centred largely in London, where clubs like the UFO (where Pink Floyd play) or The Middle Earth Club attract hippies and musicians who embrace drug culture, psychedelic sounds and 'flower power'. While the Beatles and the Rolling Stones become steeped in the scene, for most young people, the Summer of Love is a news story in which they are observers rather than participants.

Beatles in Pepperland

Two very different but complementary songs about their Liverpool childhoods, *Penny Lane* and *Strawberry Fields Forever*, launch the Beatles as an exclusively studio-based band. Two months of recording produce *Sgt. Pepper's Lonely Hearts Club Band*, an all-bells-and-whistles, LSD-tinged album of songs inspired by news stories (*A Day in the Life, She's Leaving Home*), comic characters (*Lovely Rita, When I'm 64*) and even a child's drawing (*Lucy in the Sky with Diamonds*). The LP sets new standards in production and packaging and inspires all manner of bands to create their own *Pepper* equivalent. After this peak, the late-summer suicide of Brian Epstein leaves the band rudderless, while their self-made television movie *Magical Mystery Tour* is poorly received.

MUSIC

It's a mystery

One of the biggest records of the year is surely among the most mysterious in chart history. Based on a Bach organ fugue with lyrics referencing Chaucer and Greek mythology, *A Whiter Shade of Pale* is the first hit for Procol Harum (photo), who were once an Essex beat group called the Paramounts.

Hendrix unveiled

11th January 1967
At a press reception in Soho, ex-Animal Chas Chandler reveals his new discovery, blues guitarist Jimi Hendrix. Jimi is an instant sensation and charts with

Hey Joe and *Purple Haze* before touring the UK as the Jimi Hendrix Experience. *Are You Experienced* is one of the albums of the year, while Jimi's festival-stealing appearance at Monterey shows his native US what they have been ignoring. A second album, *Axis Bold as Love*, keeps up the momentum in December.

1967

Stones are busted
12th February 1967 Mick Jagger and Keith Richards are arrested on drugs charges at Redlands, Keith's home. At the subsequent court hearing, Richards is sentenced to a year in prison while Jagger gets three months. On appeal, Richards' conviction is quashed and Jagger's sentence is reduced to a conditional discharge. In a separate case, Brian Jones is sentenced to three months, reduced on appeal to three months' probation. Even *The Times* voices disquiet over the apparent police witch hunt against the Stones.

Brothers in harmony
24th February 1967 The Bee Gees arrive from Australia sounding very like their Beatle idols. Managed by Brian Epstein associate Robert Stigwood, harmonising brothers Barry, Robin and Maurice Gibb debut with *New York Mining Disaster 1941* and close out the summer with the chart-topping *Massachusetts*.

Engelbert emerges
4th March 1967 Keeping the Beatles' *Penny Lane* off No. 1 and staying there for six weeks is *Release Me* by Gerry Dorsey – or, as he has renamed himself, Engelbert Humperdinck. His country-tinged ballads are aimed squarely at an older female audience. He has more weeks on the chart in 1967 than any other artist.

MY FIRST 18 YEARS
TOP10   1967

1. **Paper Sun** *Traffic*
2. **See Emily Play** *Pink Floyd*
3. **Respect** *Aretha Franklin*
4. **Heroes and Villains** *The Beach Boys*
5. **Matthew and Son** *Cat Stevens*
6. **Excerpt from a Teenage Opera** *Keith West*
7. **Waterloo Sunset** *The Kinks*
8. **Don't Sleep in the Subway** *Petula Clark*
9. **Itchycoo Park** *Small Faces*
10. **Flowers in the Rain** *The Move*

Open 🟢 | Search 🔍 | Scan 📷

Otis killed in air crash
10th December 1967 Five months after winning legions of hippie fans at Monterey, Otis Redding is killed with four members of his backing group the Bar-kays in an air crash in Wisconsin. His last record, made just three days before his death, is *Sittin' on the Dock of the Bay*, a departure from his usual style and a sign of his wish to develop a broader audience.

EMI think pink
July 1967 One of EMI's first 'progressive' signings, Pink Floyd enjoy a meteoric rise. Originally a blues band, they surface in London's underground clubs with an expansive, electronics-driven approach and eccentric Syd Barrett songs. They record debut LP *The Piper at the Gates of Dawn* at Abbey Road with ex-Beatles engineer Norman Smith, though by year end there is increasing concern about Syd's mental state and LSD intake.

SPORT

Manchester United best in Europe

On 29th May, Manchester United face Benfica of Portugal in the European Cup final at Wembley Stadium. Three goals in extra time, from George Best, Brian Kidd and Bobby Charlton, secure a 4-1 victory and make Manchester United the first English team to win the title. On 24th December, Best is awarded the Ballon D'Or as European player of the year.

What a flop

American high jumper Dick Fosbury revolutionises the high jump event at the Olympic Games by adopting a 'back first' technique which will become known as the Fosbury Flop.

Tragedy at Hockenheim

32-year-old Scottish farmer and racing driver Jim Clark, Formula One World Champion in 1963 and 1965, and winner of 25 Grand Prix races, is killed at Hockenheim race circuit when his Lotus-Cosworth somersaults off the track and into woods at 170 mph.

Hemery hurdles to gold

David Hemery wins the Olympic gold medal in 400m hurdles in Mexico City on 15th October. Commentator David Coleman (photo), in a frenzy of excitement as Hemery nears the finish line, neglects to notice his GB teammate John Sherwood gets bronze, and utters words he will long regret: 'Hemery takes the gold, in second place Hennige and who cares who's third? It doesn't matter.'

Winning on equal terms

Billie Jean King wins her third Wimbledon ladies' singles title, her first of the Open era, and receives a cheque for £750 compared to the £2,000 received by the men's champion, Rod Laver. The disparity triggers King's crusade to achieve parity of earnings for women in the game.

Black Power salute at Mexico Olympics

On 16th October, during the medal ceremony for the men's 200 metres at the Mexico Olympic Games, American athletes Tommie Smith and John Carlos, who have won gold and bronze medals respectively, each raise a black-gloved fist during the playing of the *Star Spangled Banner*.

---

15 JAN 1968

'Irretrievable breakdown of marriage' becomes legal grounds for divorce in the UK.

13 FEB 1968

Escaping discrimination in newly independent Kenya, up to 1,500 Kenyan Asians are arriving in Britain each week.

21 MAR 1968

Road deaths in the UK have fallen by 23% after introduction of breathalyser tests in January 1966.

DOMESTIC
NEWS

Ford launch the Escort
January 1968 Ford announce their replacement for the Ford Anglia, the 'Escort', which, like the Anglia, will be manufactured at the Halewood plant. The two-door base model features rear-wheel drive, but headlights are an additional extra, included in the De Luxe model.

The new Ford Escort Colour and Price Guide

Dagenham ladies strike!
7th June 1968 Sewing machinists go out on strike to protest their classification as 'unskilled' workers. Labelled as such, they earn only 85% of what male 'skilled' employees at the plant earn. The strike is successful, leading to their pay being increased to 92% of the men's earnings, and sets in motion events that will lead to the 1970 Equal Pay Act.

DO YOU REMEMBER THIS?

Vacuum cleaner

Mining ends in Black Country
2nd March 1968 300 years of coal mining in the Black Country come to an end as the Baggeridge Colliery near Sedgley closes. Whilst a handful of open-cast mines survive, the way of life that had fuelled the Industrial Revolution, and earned the area its nickname, is on the decline in what was once its heartland.

Dust falls
1st & 2nd July 1968 England and Wales are struck by severe 'dust' storms that combine mineral dust from the Sahara with cold and wet weather. Some areas are thrown into near total darkness by the clouds, and the UK suffers one of its worst and most widespread hailstorms on record. Three people are struck by lightning and one person drowns in flood water.

Five and ten pence
23 April 1968 The country wakes with new coins in its pockets, as it moves toward the decimalisation of the currency. New five and ten pence pieces are introduced, replacing the shilling and the florin, in an attempt to get the public used to the new currency before the process is completed in 1971.

18 APR 1968
New London Bridge, opened 1831, is sold to US millionaire Robert McCulloch for £1 million.

16 MAY 1968
15-year-old Alex Smith becomes Britain's first lung transplant patient but dies 12 days later.

24 JUN 1968
Comedian Tony Hancock dies in Sydney after taking an overdose, aged 44.

Last steam service
11th August 1968 The very last of British Rail's steam locomotives makes its final journey from Liverpool to Carlisle, signalling an end to the age of steam. From now on the only operating steam trains in the UK are on heritage railways or special services.

The Great Flood of 1968
15th September 1968 Severe storms lead to the worst floods in the Home Counties in over 100 years as large parts of the south east are affected. In Edenbridge Railway Station, the service from London's Charing Cross become stranded by flood water, with passengers stuck on board for 12 hours.

Second-class post
16th September 1968 The General Post Office launches a change in services, splitting post into first and second class for the first time. New second-class stamps cost 4d, while first class is 5d.

Derry march
5th October 1968 400 people gather to march through Derry in protest at discrimination in housing. They are supported by the fledgling Northern Ireland Civil Rights Association and the march is attended by several prominent MPs. Trouble breaks out when the Royal Ulster Constabulary use batons to drive the crowd across the river and engage violently with young people. Many are injured, and the extensive media presence leads to images of police brutality being shared widely across the country.

Race Relations Act
26th November 1968 Building upon the Race Relations Act of 1965, the new Act makes it illegal to discriminate against people on racial grounds in issues relating to employment, housing, or public services.

Hong Kong flu
December 1968 Cases of the Hong Kong flu, present in Britain since August, begin to rise in the country. The pandemic will last into 1970, claiming millions of lives globally and around 80,000 within the UK.

9 JUL 1968
The Queen opens the Brutalist Hayward Gallery on London's South Bank.

8 AUG 1968
Princess Margaret makes the inaugural journey on board the Mountbatten-class hovercraft from Dover to Boulogne.

1 SEP 1968
The first section of the London Underground's Victoria line opens between Walthamstow and Highbury & Islington.

ROYALTY &
POLITICS

Rivers of Blood
20th April 1968 Shadow Secretary for Defence Enoch Powell makes his infamous 'Rivers of Blood' speech when addressing a meeting of the Conservative Political Centre in Birmingham. The speech is in opposition to the proposed Race Relations Act and immigration from the Commonwealth and proves enormously controversial both for its theme and its rhetoric.

Anti-Vietnam demo
In a year characterised by protests around the world, on 17th March, demonstrators protesting against the United States, involvement in the Vietnam War, and Britain's support of US action, converge on Grosvenor Square where many clash with riot police outside the American embassy.

Death of Princess Marina
Princess Marina, Duchess of Kent, dies at Kensington Palace on 27th August aged 61, a month after being diagnosed with an inoperable brain tumour.

FOREIGN
NEWS

Thatcher on track
Margaret Thatcher gives her first House of Commons speech as shadow transport minister this year, arguing for investment in British Rail. More than two decades later, in a premiership that had implemented the privatisation of most state-owned services, when Thatcher resigns as Prime Minister, British Rail is the only one that remains. It too is finally privatised under John Major's government.

Prague Spring
4th January 1968 In Czechoslovakia, newly appointed Communist Party secretary Alexander Dubček pushes for 'socialism with a human face'. His political and social reforms are too much for the country's Soviet masters whose tanks invade on the night of 20th August. Dubček is replaced by hardliner Gustav Husak and 'the Prague Spring' comes to an abrupt end as.

18 OCT 1968

US athlete Bob Beamon sets an astonishing world record of 8.90m in the long jump at the Mexico Olympics.

28 NOV 1968

Death of prolific children's author Enid Blyton.

30 DEC 1968

Judy Garland begins a residency at the Talk of the Town in London in what will be her final performances.

Horror photo

1st February 1968 The most horrifying photograph of the Vietnam War is published, catching the moment a Viet Cong prisoner is executed by a South Vietnamese police chief.

Gagarin killed

27th March 1968 Yuri Gagarin, the first man in space, is killed on a training flight near Kirzhach in Russia. His ashes are interred in the walls of the Kremlin.

Baader-Meinhof

2nd April 1968 A new anarchist group announces itself with bomb attacks on department stores in Frankfurt. Andreas Baader and Ulrike Meinhof give their name to the gang, which is soon regarded as the biggest terrorist threat to mainland Europe. Also known as the Red Army Faction, these anti-imperialist urban guerrillas will get progressively more daring - and lethal - with assassinations and kidnappings before the leaders' capture in 1977.

King and Kennedy

4th April 1968 Martin Luther King Jr is murdered in Memphis, Tennessee. The killing of the most articulate and charismatic of civil rights leaders ignites days of rioting across the US. In Indianapolis, New York Senator Robert Kennedy calms his audience with a call for peace between the races.

Presidential candidate Kennedy is cultivating young and disaffected voters with a promise to end the Vietnam War and plans for deep rooted social change. Two months later, following victory in the Californian Democratic primary, he is shot by Palestinian immigrant Sirhan Sirhan. He dies in hospital the next day. Millions line the route as a funeral train brings his body west for burial in Arlington Cemetery, Washington DC, where his brother was laid to rest five years before.

DO YOU REMEMBER THIS?

Slide projector

May '68 revolt

3rd May 1968 Inspired by a global wave of anti-war and anti-capitalist dissent, student protests erupt and bring France close to revolution. On 13th May, a million march through the streets of Paris. By the last week of May, two-thirds of French workers are on strike in sympathy, paralysing the world's fifth largest economy. On 30th May, with the government on the brink of collapse, President de Gaulle dissolves the National Assembly, promises reforms and calls an election. His gamble works: some normality returns and de Gaulle's party increases its majority. But while he holds the country together (just), his own days as leader are numbered.

Pope rejects birth control

25th July 1968 In an encyclical that dismays many, Pope Paul VI signals no change to the Catholic Church's position on artificial birth control. Catholics are advised to exercise abstinence and restraint. Sex is for procreation not recreation.

Nixon is President

5th November 1968 Republican candidate Richard Milhous Nixon, who after losing the presidential election to John Kennedy in 1960

told reporters that they 'won't have Nixon to kick around anymore', finally wins the race for the White House. His election marks a decisive turn to the right in US politics.

Greetings from the Moon

25th December 1968 Apollo 8 is the first manned spacecraft to orbit the Moon. On Christmas Day a quarter of the world's population, at this point the largest television audience ever, watch the three astronauts deliver a seasonal message. Apollo 8's

mission is to search for landing sites for future missions to the Moon. President Kennedy's promise that the US will put the first man on the Moon before the end of the decade is close to being realised.

ENTERTAINMENT

One for sorrow, two for joy

Magpie airs for the first time on 30th July as ITV's answer to the BBC's *Blue Peter*. *Magpie* is a bit more hip than its wholesome rival. It covers music and fashion, has a rock-tinged theme song based on the traditional rhyme about magpies and presenters like Mick Robertson (who joins in 1972 and looks a bit like Brian May) and Jenny Hanley find their faces pinned up on teenage bedroom walls.

Garden greats

TV gets out in the garden this year. The first episode of *Gardener's World*, presented by Ken Burras from the Oxford Botanical Gardens, is broadcast on 5th January. The following year, Percy Thrower (photo) takes over as presenter with filming taking place in his own garden, The Magnolias in Shrewsbury. *The Herbs*, which debuts on BBC1 on 12th February, has Parsley the Lion, Dill the Dog, Tarragon the Dragon et al living in the walled kitchen garden of a country house. The magical password to gain entry to this horticultural wonderland? Herbidacious.

Home front humour

The members of Walmington-on-Sea's Local Defence Volunteers make their first appearance on 31st July. *Dad's Army*, penned by David Croft and Jimmy Perry, is a comic tribute to those who served in the Home Guard during the Second World War. Arthur Lowe plays pompous bank manager and self-appointed leader of the group, Captain Mainwaring, who heads a superb cast that deliver Croft and Perry's lines with immaculate timing and create some of British comedy's finest moments. The interaction between Mainwaring and Ian Lavender's hapless innocent, Private Pike ('You stupid boy') is particularly memorable.

Going ape

Hollywood make-up artist John Chambers is given a budget of $50,000 to transform Roddy McDowell, Maurice Evans and cast into unnervingly convincing simian overlords for the film, *Planet of the Apes*, adapted from Pierre Boulle's novel *La Planète des singes*. Charlton Heston, who spends most of the film in a loin cloth, is in the minority as a human, one of three astronauts who crash land on a planet where they discover, to their alarm, man is subjugated by monkey. Chambers is awarded an honorary Oscar for his work on the film.

Twinkle

The first issue of *Twinkle*, 'a picture paper for little girls', comes out on 27th January, with a free bracelet and St. Christopher charm on the cover to tempt buyers.

Hair at last

The 1968 Theatres Act is given royal assent on 26th July and finally ends censorship in the theatre. One of the first shows to benefit from the lifting of restrictions is the rock musical *Hair*, which contains nudity and pro-fanities. Hair opens at the Shaftesbury Theatre on 27th September with a cast that includes Paul Nicholas, Elaine Paige, Marsha Hunt, Tim Curry and Richard O'Brien. *Hair* runs for 1,997 performances, closing when the roof of the Shaftesbury Theatre collapses.

Chocs away

Cadbury's Milk Tray show their first TV advertisement in which actor and model Gary Myers is the thoughtful action man who thinks nothing of beating avalanch-es or plunging into waves in his bid to secretly deliver a box of chocolates, 'all because the lady loves Milk Tray'.

Chitty Chitty Bang Bang

After a heart attack in 1961, Ian Fleming's wife confiscates his typewriter in an attempt to force him to rest. So he simply writes a children's novel, *Chitty Chitty Bang Bang - The Magical Car* in longhand. In 1967, Albert R. Broccoli decides the story has potential as a film and recruits Dick Van Dyke to play inventor Caractacus Potts, while Sally Anne Howes stars as Truly Scrumptious. But perhaps more terrifying than any Bond villain is ballet dancer Robert Helpmann as the evil Childcatcher. *Chitty Chitty Bang Bang* goes on to become a children's classic.

It's The Basil Brush Show - Boom boom!
After appearances of the garrulous Basil Brush on magician David Nixon's shows, *The Basil Brush Show* begins on BBC on 14th June. Basil is a talkative fox with an upper-class accent, a terrible habit of interrupting, and a tendency to laugh hysterically at his own jokes. In his traditional tweeds and cravat, he's a typical English gent (if you don't count the fact he's actually a fox AND a puppet) and charms the guests who willingly appear on his show. Ivan Owen, who provides Basil's voice, models it on the actor Terry-Thomas.

Wacky Races
Hanna-Barbera's latest cartoon features the wackiest motor racing competition in the world as an unusual set of competitors line up on the grid every episode, with some using more underhand means to win than others. *Wacky Races* introduces us to miniature gangsters the Anthill Mob, pink-loving southern belle Penelope Pitstop and moustache-twirling arch-villain Dick Dastardly and his snickering asthmatic sidekick Muttley.

Festival first
A year before Woodstock happens, 10,000 people descend on Ford Farm, Godshill for the first Isle of Wight festival. Among the acts on the bill are Jefferson Airplane, the Move, Smile and Fairport Convention. The following year, Bob Dylan plays the festival after a long absence and in 1970, the festival has swelled to such a size, the island is overrun with 100,000 festival-goers.

(Morecambe and) Wise move
Eric and Ernie's move to the BBC, after seven successful years in ATV's *Two of a Kind*, is driven by the comedy duo's desire to have their show in colour at a time when BBC2 is still the only channel transmitting in colour. The first episode of the *Morecambe and Wise Show* airs on 2nd September, and soon becomes the jewel in the BBC's light entertainment crown, with up to 28 million people settling down to watch their annual Christmas Day shows.

Hop to it
The Spacehopper hits UK shops in the spring of this year. Originally called 'Pon-Pon', this large inflatable with ball with ribbed horns to use as handles is manufactured by Corgi-Mettoy in the UK and soon streets, driveways, parks and cul-de-sacs are overrun with kids hopping about on them. The fact the Spacehopper has a fearsome face etched on its front and is possibly the most exhausting and inefficient way to get from A to B does little to dent its popularity.

Cilla
Cilla is broadcast on BBC1 on 30th January and marks the beginning of Cilla Black's transition from singing star to TV personality, in a deal brokered by Brian Epstein shortly before his premature death; *Cilla* will run for eight series until 1976.

Oliver!
Lionel Bart's 1960 stage musical comes to cinema screens in this big, loud and colourful adaptation of Dickens' *Oliver Twist*. Ron Moody, anxious to distance his character Fagin from the anti-semitic stereotype of the novel, plays the role with a light mischievous touch, while Jack Wild's Artful Dodger is full of chirpy confidence, Oliver Reed as Bill Sikes glowers with brooding menace and Mark Lester is guileless innocence in the title role. Add to that a bulging songbook of sensational tunes, and it's no surprise that *Oliver!* wins six Academy Awards.

MUSIC

Petula breaks a taboo
2nd April 1968 America's favourite British music star of the moment is former child star Petula Clark. Thanks to hits like *Downtown* and *Don't Sleep in the Subway* and the movies *Goodbye Mr Chips* and *Finian's Rainbow*, she now has a top-rated prime-time TV show. During a duet on the show with Harry Belafonte, she takes his arm and breaks an unwritten ban on interracial touching on US TV. The show sparks uproar but Petula is unrepentant.

Changes for the Beatles
15th May 1968 As the Beatles put the extravagances of *Sgt. Pepper* behind them to navigate life without Brian Epstein, they set up Apple Corps, to release Beatle records and promote new talent. George persuades the others to join him in India for a transcendental meditation course run by Mahirishi Mahesh Yogi. Although they no longer write collaboratively, a positive of the trip is the number of songs which John and Paul create. Many appear on a double album with a plain white cover simply titled *The Beatles*.

Small Faces, big sound
24th May 1968 A fine Mod band always slightly in the shadow of the Who and the Kinks, the Small Faces make Ogden's *Nut Gone Flake*, with a circular sleeve in the style of a tobacco tin. It includes *Lazy Sunday*, a comic take on their East London roots and a sequel to 1967's *Itchycoo Park*.

The king is back
3rd December 1968 Heralding Elvis Presley's re-emergence after years of so-so movies and records is the one-off television special *Elvis*. Singing live on stage for the first time since 1960, he looks lean and lithe and in great voice.

Cream goes sour
26th November 1968 After a productive but fretful year, Cream play their last gig to a packed Royal Albert Hall. Eric Clapton and Ginger Baker form another supergroup in Blind Faith (photo) with Stevie Winwood from Traffic.

Cliff does Eurovision

6th April 1968 The UK hosts the Eurovision Song Contest, with hopes pinned on Cliff Richard and the bouncy *Congratulations*. Cliff comes second by one point to Spain's entry, *La La La* by Massiel.

Mary's opportunity

4th May 1968 Eighteen year old-Welsh folk singer Mary Hopkin appears on the ITV talent show *Opportunity Knocks* and is noticed by Paul McCartney, who's looking for artists to sign to Apple Records. He chooses a song for her based on a Russian folk tune, *Those Were the Days*, which is at No. 1 within weeks.

Here's to you, *Mrs Robinson*

1st June 1968 Contracted to supply songs to the movie *The Graduate*, Paul Simon writes one verse of *Mrs Robinson* for use on the soundtrack. Fully fleshed out and released as a Simon and Garfunkel single, the song is a satirical put-down of status-conscious middle America just as a wave of student protests hits its peak.

Led Zeppelin formed

7th July 1968 The Led Zeppelin story starts here with the break-up of the Yardbirds and Jimmy Page's formation of a new hard rock band - initially called the New Yardbirds - with Chris Dreja, John Paul Jones and Robert Plant. Debuting live in October and signing a massive deal with Atlantic Records, they record their hugely influential self-titled first album for release in January.

Fleetwood Mac

6th July 1968 Adding a third guitarist to an already much talked-about line-up is the most outstanding new British blues band in years, Fleetwood Mac. Danny Kirwan joins ex-John Mayall's Bluesbreakers Peter Green and Jeremy Spencer, drummer Mick Fleetwood and bassist John McVie completing the band.

Dusty in Memphis

24th November 1968 US TV's *Ed Sullivan Show* plays host to Dusty Springfield, fresh from recording in Memphis under top soul producer Jerry Wexler. It's a marriage made in heaven that yields the album *Dusty in Memphis* and possibly the greatest single ever by any white soul singer, *Son Of A Preacher Man*.

SPORT

Sir Matt Steps back
Sir Matt Busby, who has managed Manchester United since 1945, announces his retirement on 14th January. During his time in charge of the club he has collected thirteen trophies including five league championships and the European Cup but finds he is not quite ready for his pipe and slippers. As well as becoming a director of Manchester United he has one final stint in charge, as interim manager in the first half of 1971 after Wilf McGuinness is sacked in December 1970.

Grand Slam greats
Rod Laver defeats fellow Australian Tony Roche in the US Open Men's Singles final on 9th September and in doing so, becomes one of only a handful of players to win all four Grand Slam titles in a single year. In tennis news closer to home, Birmingham-born Ann Jones becomes the Wimbledon Ladies' Singles champion after beating Billie Jean King in the final and goes on to also win the mixed doubles title with Australian Fred Stolle. As a result of her achievements, she is voted Sports Personality of the Year for 1969.

Gentleman Jack
In a Ryder Cup competition riven with animosity between the two sides, in the final round at the Royal Birkdale Golf Club in Southport, Jack Nicklaus concedes a three-foot putt to Britain's Tony Jacklin, meaning the tournament ends in a tie (although America retain the Cup). Nicklaus's gesture is viewed as the pinnacle of decent sportsmanship.

Stewart wins at Silverstone
Jackie Stewart is victorious at the British Grand Prix at Silverstone on 19th July, putting more than a lap between him and the other drivers. He dominates the 1969 Formula One season and becomes World Champion.

King Eddie
Belgian cycling supremo Eddy Merckx utterly dominates this year's Tour de France, and gives a historic, superhuman performance in the mountainous seventeenth stage from Louchon to Mourenx, stretching his lead by another eight minutes.

24 JAN 1969

Ford unveil their sporty new saloon, the Capri at the Brussels Motor Show.

19 FEB 1969

The High Court awards compensation to children born with deformities caused by thalidomide drug.

13 MAR 1969

Scientists at Cambridge University announce that human eggs have been fertilised in a test tube.

Pot Black

Snooker is a fairly niche sport in Britain until David Attenborough, in his role as BBC2 controller, sees the potential in showing a game with coloured balls as a way to promote the channel's colour broadcasts. The first *Pot Black* tournament is recorded at the BBC's Birmingham studios and broadcast on 23rd July. Unlike traditional snooker tournaments, *Pot Black* is fast-paced with each match played in just one frame. Ray Reardon emerges the winner out of the eight competitors.

DOMESTIC NEWS

Northern Ireland

1969 sees an increase in violence in Northern Ireland, as marches and protests are broken up by police and, from April, British troops. August witnesses a three-day riot known as the Battle of the Bogside, with trouble continuing for several days. The Irish Taoiseach calls for a United Nations peacekeeping force on 13th August, and more British troops are deployed. In October, the British government accepts the recommendation to abolish the Ulster Special Constabulary.

First B&Q store opens

March 1969 Richard Block and David Quayle launch their first 'B&Q' DIY superstore in Southampton. The one-stop shop for all things home improvement proves enormously popular and shapes the do-it-yourself home improvement craze of the 70s.

Reggie Kray

Ronnie Kray

Kray twins guilty

4th March 1969 Notorious gangsters and celebrity nightclub owners, the Kray twins, are found guilty of murdering George Cornell and Jack 'the Hat' McVitie and are sentenced to life imprisonment with a minimum term of 30 years. Ronnie and Reggie become almost legendary characters, celebrated and despised by their community in equal measure.

Victoria line opens

7th March 1969 London's new underground line, named for Queen Victoria, becomes the first new tube line in over 60 years. The section from Walthamstow to Victoria is formally opened by the Queen, with the extension to Brixton not completed for a further two years.

22 APR 1969

Sailor Robin Knox-Johnson becomes the first person to make a solo, non-stop circumnavigation of the world.

7 MAY 1969

The Cunard liner *Queen Elizabeth 2* (*QE2*) sails into New York harbour for the first time.

14 JUN 1969

The Queen's black horse, Burmese, makes his first appearance at Trooping the Colour a will continue to take part in th ceremony until 1986.

Harrier jump jet
1st April 1969 The RAF announce their acquisition of the new Hawker Siddeley Harrier 'jump jet'. The jet is ground-breaking in its ability to take off and land vertically and becomes a popular image of British Aerospace innovation.

Concorde prototype
9th April 1969 The prototype for Concorde, the very first supersonic passenger jet, makes its maiden British flight just a few weeks after the French test theirs in March. The project is a joint endeavour between the British and the French governments and will enter service in 1976, revolutionising cross-Atlantic travel.

Welsh bombings
30th June 1969 The Movement for the Defence of Wales, Mudiad Amddiffyn Cymru, continues the bombing activity that has seen tax offices, water pipes and conference centres damaged. The day before the investiture of Prince Charles as Prince of Wales, two members are killed when the bomb they are attempting to plant explodes prematurely. Two bombs are also planted on the day of the investiture, one of which seriously injures a ten-year-old boy.

Raleigh Chopper
April 1969 The Raleigh 'Chopper' bike is launched in the UK. Available in five colours, the bike proves to be a cultural icon for decades, featuring in television and films such as the *Back to the Future* movies. It is the most desired bike of the 70s, and remains so until overtaken by the BMX in the 1980s.

More currency changes
1st August 1969 The halfpenny, in circulation since 1717, ceases to be legal tender as the country takes another tentative step towards decimalisation. In October, the new 50 pence piece is introduced. This seven-sided coin is to replace the ten-shilling note and leaves much of the public sceptical.

DO YOU REMEMBER THIS?

Standing ashtray

3 JUL 1969
Swansea is granted city status to mark the investiture of Prince Charles.

8 AUG 1969
Iain Macmillan photographs the Beatles on the zebra crossing near the Abbey Road studios for their new album cover.

28 SEP 1969
'Book 'em, Danno'. American crime series *Hawaii 5-0* is broadcast for the first time on ITV Yorkshire.

45

London Street Commune evicted
21st September 1969 Police move in and evict the squatters of the London Street Commune, who have been occupying 144 Piccadilly for several days. Earning the street the nickname 'Hippy-dilly', the protesters are calling for improvements to housing, after homelessness charity Shelter announces 3 million people are living in poor conditions across the country.

ROYALTY &
POLITICS

Ballot Box Babies
On 17th April, the Representation of the People Act lowers the voting age in the UK from 21 to 18.

Devlin becomes youngest MP
Twenty-one-year-old Bernadette Devlin wins the Mid Ulster by-election and becomes the young M.P. to take a seat in the House of Commons, taking the Oath of Allegiance on 22nd April, and shortly afterwards making her maiden speech.

Royal family on film
The royal family's experimentation with publicity finds its full expression when they star in a fly-on-the-wall documentary, *Royal Family*, stirring up voyeuristic interest among the Queen's subjects. When it is transmitted on BBC1 on 21st June, viewing figures estimate that 68 per cent of the British population tune to see previously private moments like the Queen buying Prince Edward an ice cream in the shop near Balmoral, or the royals preparing for a family barbecue.

Investiture of the Prince of Wales
Investiture of the Prince of Wales takes place at Caernarfon Castle on 1st July, in a ceremony that has its roots in the medieval age but is beamed into the country's living rooms through modern technology.

15 OCT 1969

Media tycoon Rupert Murdoch purchases the *Sun* newspaper.

25 NOV 1969

In protest at the British government's involvement in Biafra and support of the Vietnam War, John Lennon returns his MBE.

18 DEC 1969

The House of Lords vote to abolish the death penalty in England, Scotland, and Wales.

Jan Palach

16th January 1969 Czech student Jan Palach sets himself on fire in Wenceslas Square in Prague in protest against the reversed reforms of the Prague Spring. He dies three days later from his injuries.

Bed-in for peace

25th March 1969 Five days after John Lennon marries avant-garde artist Yoko Ono, the couple honeymoon in Amsterdam and take over the presidential suite of the Hilton hotel. Welcoming the world press, John and Yoko spend the entire time in bed and talking peace.

Exits and entrances

28th March 1968 As the US says a final goodbye to former President Dwight D. Eisenhower (photo), the year sees far-reaching changes in leadership elsewhere. Also in March, Golda Meir becomes the first female Prime Minister of Israel. In April, Charles de Gaulle steps down as President of France when a referendum goes against him and is succeeded by Georges Pompidou. In September, North Vietnam's President Ho Chi Minh dies and Colonel Muammar Gaddafi seizes power in a coup in Libya.

Man on the Moon

21st July 1969 The time has come. In the media, at work and at school, the talk is about nothing else. The Columbia command module carrying astronauts Neil Armstrong, Buzz Aldrin and Michael Collins launches on 16th July and takes four days to reach the Moon. The Eagle lunar capsule undocks and the descent to the surface begins. Two and a half hours later, Armstrong confirms: 'The Eagle has landed.' Over six hours pass before Armstrong and Aldrin release air from the Eagle's cabin and the hatch opens. At 3:56pm UK time, Neil Armstrong is the first man on the Moon and utters the famous words: 'That's one small step for a man, one giant leap for mankind.' After two hours and fifteen minutes on the Moon, the astronauts take off and link up again with Columbia. They splash down south of Hawaii on 24th August. The achievement is historic. Will the world ever be quite the same again?

The Manson family

9th August 1969 Horrific scenes greet police at film director Roman Polanski's home in Los Angeles, where they find his pregnant actress wife Sharon Tate and four others stabbed to death. A day later, Leno and Rosemary LaBianca are found dead at their home in the city, apparently by the same perpetrators. Two months later, failed musician Charles Manson is arrested on other charges and implicated in the murders by members of his sinister cult. The killings shake the music and movie worlds to their core as it emerges that other celebrities were on Manson's death list.

Chappaquiddick

19th August 1969 Mary Jo Kopechne, an aide to Senator Edward Kennedy, drowns when the car he is driving leaves a bridge at Chappaquiddick Island, Massachusetts. He fails to report the accident for nine hours, for which he receives a two-month suspended jail sentence. Although the incident does not end his political career, it scuppers his chances of ever becoming President.

Internet in embryo

29th October 1969 Four computers are linked to form the US Department of Defense's Advanced Research Projects Agency Network. As the first computer network of its kind, ARPANET is the pre-cursor of the internet.

Taylor-Burton diamond

23rd October 1969
The jewellery house Cartier buys a special diamond at auction for just over $1 million. Richard Burton misses out by underbidding but, determined to acquire it for his diamond-loving wife Elizabeth Taylor, nego-tiates with Cartier to buy it for $1.1 million the following day.

Jumbo journey

2nd December 1969 The Boeing 747 makes its first passenger flight from Seattle to New York. As the largest aircraft in the world and the first with a wide fuselage, allowing more than double an airliner's usual load, it changes aviation history.

ENTERTAINMENT

Shelling peas

The UK's first colour TV commercial - for Birds Eye peas - airs at 10:05am on ITV in the Midlands in a break

during *Thunderbirds*. Unilever, who own the Birds Eye brand, had bought the slot for just £23.

Mary, Mungo & Midge

John Ryan, creator of Captain Pugwash, is asked to create a new up-to-date animation for modern children. The result is *Mary, Mungo and Midge*, which is first broadcast on 30th December. Mary lives in on the eighth floor of a tower block with her sensible old dog, Mungo, and inquisitive mouse, Midge. The joys of modern, urban living are very much at the forefront of *Mary, Mungo and Midge*.

Lulu the elephant

Lulu the baby elephant delights viewers when she goes rogue, wreaking havoc in the *Blue Peter* studio in its 3rd July episode. She defecates on the floor and as she lumbers about the studio, barely controlled by her keeper (whose training stick had been confiscated by producer Biddy Baxter), Lulu steps on John Noakes's foot causing him to hop in agony into the pile of elephant poo. As chaos plays out around her, Valerie Singleton remains the epitome of professionalism, continuing to talk calmly about their forthcoming summer expedition to Ceylon.

Waggoners Walk

The tenants in the various flats of no. 1 Waggoners Walk, Hampstead are the subject of a new Radio 2 soap opera, first broadcast on 28th April. *Waggoners Walk* replaces the long-running radio serial *The Dales*, and aims to exchange stories of cosy, rural life with a more dynamic and fast-paced world, where taboo subjects like abortion, illegitimacy, homosexuality and even murder are tackled.

Art for the masses

Art historian Kenneth Clarke presents *Civilisation,* a major 13-part documentary series about Western art, culture and progress first shown on 23rd February. Initially suggested by David Attenborough (who was BBC2 controller at the time), the series, in which great paintings are discussed, greatly benefits from being broadcast in colour.

BBC1 in colour

BBC1 is the first channel in Europe to offer full broadcast in colour from 15th November, kicking off this auspicious landmark with a Petula Clark concert from the Royal Albert Hall. Colour TV licenses become available for a higher price than those for black and white TV.

Kes

Ken Loach's second feature film, *Kes*, demonstrates the power of film to tell an unflinching truth and is intended to expose the injustices of the country's divided educational system where secondary modern schools are viewed as second-rate. When Billy adopts and trains a kestrel, it shows that every one of us has the potential to shine. The film flops in America where the thick south Yorkshire accents are unfathomable, but in the UK, word of mouth ensures this quiet, powerful, heartbreaking film will become one of the most highly regarded in British cinema.

Hats off

Children's programme *Hattytown Tales* is, quite literally, about a town where all the characters are hats, from a police officer's helmet to a Mexican sombrero. Even the buildings are hat shaped. This Filmfair production for Thames Television is one of the decade's more bizarre children's TV concepts, but it runs for four years, clocking up 52 episodes in total.

The micemen cometh

The Clangers, which makes its debut on BBC1 on 16th November, is another delight conjured up by Oliver Postgate and Peter Firmin's Smallfilms. This is the year of the Moon landings so perhaps it is no surprise that their latest creation is about a group of knitted pink, mouse-like aliens who live on (and inside) a lunar type planet. *The Clangers* characters are based on a Moonmouse who appeared in one episode of *Noggin the Nog*, they're nourished by blue string pudding and Green Soup, which is kindly provided by the Soup Dragon, and communicate through a musical, whistling language. Wonderfully strange yet charming, *The Clangers* becomes a cherished cult classic.

Something completely different

Monty Python's Flying Circus crashes on to BBC1 on 5th October at 10:55pm, the kind of time where something odd and experimental could easily be buried and forgotten about. Not so with the absurd, anarchic comedy dished up by John Cleese, Graham Chapman, Terry Jones, Eric Idle, Michael Palin and Terry Gilliam (who creates animations in which pop art, Dadaism, the Victorian engraving process and slapstick all gloriously collide). The Pythons are seen as subversive and silly, anti-establishment and avant garde, the natural inheritors of Spike Milligan.

The Liver Birds

The Liver Birds, written by Carla Lane and Myra Davis, begins on BBC1 on 14th April with a theme tune by the Scaffold. Sandra and Beryl negotiate the ups and downs of their love lives, their jobs and their parents, including a magnificent Mollie Sugden as Sandra's overbearing mother, who steals every scene she's in.

Diddy, Doddy, go

Tickling stick at the ready. Ken Dodd's Diddymen have been part of the Liverpool entertainer's stage act for a while but now he and the Diddymen puppets get their own TV show, which is first shown on BBC1 on 5th January. Doddy's imagination and penchant for the absurd is encapsulated by the the Diddymen who have names like Dicky Mint, Mick the Marmaliser and the Hon. Nigel Ponsonby Smallpiece. They go to work in the Jam Butty Mines or the Broken Biscuit Repair Factory, all in the fictional Knotty Ash.

The Very Hungry Caterpillar

Will the very hungry caterpillar ever be satisfied? Kids will have to read to the end of this banquet of a book to find out. Written and illustrated by American Eric Carle, *The Very Hungry Caterpillar* is published on 3rd June and goes on to sell fifty million copies worldwide.

The delicate matter of Miss Jean Brodie

The Prime of Miss Jean Brodie, for which Maggie Smith in the title role wins an Oscar, is chosen for the Royal Film Performance on 24th February. The film has been passed by film censors with an X-certificate but organisers of the royal performance decide to cut a ten-second scene in which a drawing of a naked man appears. The *Daily Mirror* suggests the organisers should stick to organising ice cream and ticket sales, 'And leave the Queen Mother to enjoy the film. Sexy bits and all.'

Carry On topless

By the end of the decade, the laboured innuendo of Carry On films is perhaps beginning to pall. Nevertheless, *Carry on Camping*, which is released in cinemas on 29th May, includes one of the franchise's most memorable moments when bubbly blonde Babs, played by Barbara Windsor, has a surprising bikini malfunction during a campsite keep fit session.

MUSIC

Rod joins the Faces
1st January 1969 Steve Marriott leaves the Small Faces to form the much more heavy rock-leaning Humble Pie with Peter Frampton. His old band team up with little known but well-regarded blues singer Rod Stewart as the Faces.

King Crimson reign
9th April 1969 Performing live in London are King Crimson who, without fanfare or promotion, have become kingpins of progressive rock with In *The Court of the Crimson King*. The LP is a jazz-rock-classical hybrid with a much imitated sleeve by artist Barry Godber.

Beatles get back
29th January 1969 The Beatles finally return to performing live - on the roof of the Apple offices in London's Savile Row. *Get Back*, introduced during the session, maintains the roots-driven feel of 1968's 'white album'. Though management issues are pulling the band apart - John, George and Ringo have brought in Allen Klein, when Paul wanted father-in-law Lee Eastman - they can still create an album as elegantly contained as *Abbey Road*, on which *Here Comes the Sun* and *Something* reveal George in particularly impressive form.

Jethro Tull
9th May 1969 Prog rock trio Jethro Tull are rapturously received at the Royal Albert Hall. The band blend jazz, blues and folk. Complaints pour in when Tull appear on *Top of the Pops* in response to wild-man Ian Anderson's lecherous demeanour and one-legged dancing.

Tommy released
23rd May 1969 Ever since *Sgt. Pepper*, bands have been using the LP medium to develop concepts and tell stories.

Pete Townshend of the Who creates *Tommy* - the story of a deaf, dumb and blind boy with brilliant pinball skills who becomes a religious leader. The album's success revitalises the band, while witnessing the Who perform *Tommy* live becomes one of rock music's all-time great experiences.

Sound of the Underground
12th March 1969 The Velvet Underground's self-titled third album is released to general indifference. Since forming in 1965 as part of Andy Warhol's circle, the New York band with their lowlife lyrics and bare guitar sound have offered a chilly counterpoint to expansive, laid-back west coast rock. This is their first release without John Cale who has fallen out with Lou Reed over the band's direction. Over time they will prove one of the most influential bands in rock history.

Troubled times for the Stones

3rd July 1969 A month after leaving the Rolling Stones, Brian Jones is found dead in his swimming pool. The inquest verdict is death by misadventure. Two days later the Stones play a free concert in London's Hyde Park (photo) where Mick Jagger reads a poem by Shelley as a tribute. Brian's replacement is Mick Taylor from John Mayall's band, who stays with the Stones for five years. Although the Stones have released their most blues-based album to date, *Beggar's Banquet*, their troubled year ends with a free festival at the Altamont speedway track in San Francisco which is meant to outdo Woodstock. The decision to trust security to a local chapter of Hell's Angels backfires when they murder a spectator in full view of the band.

Three days of peace and love

15th August 1969 'Three days of peace and music' begin at Max Yasgur's farm in upstate New York. Attended by nearly half a million, the Woodstock festival is a symbolic moment for the counter culture, made indelible by performances from rock's finest - Sly and the Family Stone, Grateful Dead, Santana, Jimi Hendrix, the Who and many more. Two weeks later 150,000 converge on the Isle of Wight for the UK's biggest festival to date, where Bob Dylan - who shunned Woodstock, even though it was close to his home - plays live with the Band.

MY FIRST 18 YEARS

TOP10 1969

1. **For Once in My Life** *Stevie Wonder*
2. **Blackberry Way** *The Move*
3. **You Got Soul** *Johnny Nash*
4. **Games People Play** *Joe South*
5. **Something** *The Beatles*
6. **Tracks of My Tears** *Smokey Robinson*
7. **Bad Moon Rising** *Creedence Clearwater Rev.*
8. **Born to be Wild** *Steppenwolf*
9. **Ruby, Don't Take Your Love** *Kenny Rogers*
10. **Honky Tonk Women** *The Rolling Stones*

Open 🟢 | Search 🔍 | Scan 📷

Spaced out Bowie

20th September 1969 David Bowie has his first hit with *Space Oddity*, which BBC TV uses in its Moon mission coverage. Three years will pass before he charts again but *Space Oddity* has all the Bowie attributes the world will come to know - the Tony Newley-like voice, space age subject matter and his adoption of an alter ego.

SPORT

World Cup, Mexico '70
England travel to the World Cup in Mexico as defending champions, and kids around the country get busy collecting bubblegum and Panini cards and Esso medallions featuring their England heroes. England's first ever World Cup song, '*Back Home*' proves prophetic and they are indeed back home sooner than anticipated after being knocked out in the quarter-finals by West Germany. In the group play-offs, they are also beaten by a magnificent Brazilian side who go on to win the tournament.

Commonwealth Games
The British Commonwealth Games are held from the 16th to 25th July in Edinburgh. England come second in the medal table, behind Australia, with a good haul of medals in track and field.

£200K move for Martin
Martin Peters becomes the first £200,000 footballer when he makes a move from West Ham to Tottenham Hotspur. The investment proves worthwhile for the North Londoners on 21st March, when he scores on his first appearance for his new team against Coventry City.

A vintage year for Jacklin
1970 is a year to remember for Tony Jacklin who receives an OBE in the New Year honours list, then goes on to win the US Open at Hazaltine, Minnesota. Away from the golf course, he even records an album of American songbook standards, *Tony Jacklin Swings Into*.

Dominance on Court
Australian Margaret Court wins all four Grand Slam tennis tournaments.

England vs. Rest of the World
The South Africa cricket team are scheduled to play England this summer but mounting pressure over apartheid leads to a cancellation of their tour. With no international fixtures for England's 1970 cricket season, a Rest of the World team is formed, captained by Gary Sobers (photo). The World XI win the test match series 4-1 but Ray Illingworth's England side put in an impressive performance against a team featuring the cream of the world's cricketers.

18 JAN 1970
The grave of Karl Marx in Highgate Cemetery is vandalised and daubed with swastikas.

11 FEB 1970
Plans are announced to decentralise the NHS by creating ninety separate regional health authorities.

6 MAR 1970
A rabies outbreak in Newmarket, Suffolk leads to a ban on imported animals to the UK.

DOMESTIC
NEWS

Northern Ireland
In June there are riots in Derry over the arrest of MP Bernadette Devlin, imprisoned for incitement to riot during the Battle of the Bogside in 1969, and in July three civilians and a journalist are killed by the British Army in clashes with the Irish Republican Army in Belfast. On 23rd July, Irish Nationalists throw two cans of CS or 'tear' gas into the House of Commons chamber, leading to an evacuation and one MP being hospitalised.

Virgin gets going
February 1970 Richard Branson launches his first Virgin Group business. The Virgin brand begins with a mail-order business offering popular records at a discount. The business' first store will open in 1971, before other products and businesses are added under the Virgin name.

DO YOU REMEMBER THIS?

Reel-to-reel tape recorder

Thalidomide scandal
23rd March 1970 The courts award nearly £370,000 to eighteen victims of the thalidomide scandal. Thalidomide, which was marketed as an anti-nausea drug to treat morning sickness in pregnant women, caused birth defects in some 10-20,000 children worldwide.

Goodbye Minor - hello Range Rover!

You should find the Rover you want from the six you see here.

18th April 1970 British Leyland announce beloved classic the Morris Minor, in production since 1948, is to be discontinued. As fans say goodbye to the Minor, a new success is on the books for Leyland with the launch of the Range Rover in June. The new vehicle proves popular as a sleeker, more urban version of the classic Land Rover.

Bridge disasters
23rd May 1970 Two bridges are heavily damaged within two weeks, as a fire in the Britannia Bridge over the Menai Strait is followed by the collapse of the Cleddau Bridge in Pembrokeshire. The fire in the Britannia Bridge is caused by schoolboys playing in the structure, whilst the collapse at Cleddau occurs during construction and results in the deaths of four workers.

4 APR 1970
Gay Trip wins the Grand National at Aintree.

19 MAY 1970
Government agrees to bail out Rolls Royce to the tune of £20 million as it struggles with cost of developing new aero-engines.

27 JUN 1970
The Bath Festival of Blues and Progressive Festival takes place and includes a headline set by Led Zeppelin.

Babes in the wood

17th June 1970 The nation is horrified as the bodies of two children, Susan Blatchford and Gary Hanlon, are found in woodland at Sewardstone, Essex, 78 days after the friends disappeared on a walk. What happened to the children remains a mystery for over twenty years, until their murderer, Ronald Jebson, finally confesses in 1998.

Docks strike

15th July 1970 Dock workers across the United Kingdom go on strike, calling for an increase in wages of £11 a week. A state of emergency is declared as the strikes get underway, with the army standing ready to protect food imports. The strike is finally settled on the 30th, with an agreed increase in pay of 7%.

Mangrove marches

9th August 1970 Members of the black community in Notting Hill march to the local police station in protest at the frequent raids conducted on the Mangrove, a Caribbean restaurant that served as an important meeting place for black activists. Violence breaks out, and nine protesters are arrested and charged with incitement to riot. All are acquitted of incitement in a trial that sheds light on allegations of racism and brutality within the police force.

Dawson's Field hijacks

6th September 1970 As hijackings become part of the methodology of what are terrorists to some and freedom fighters to others, the Popular Front for the Liberation of Palestine (PFLP) hijack four passenger aircraft and force two of them to land at Dawson's Field, an airstrip in Jordan, where they are joined by a third a few days later. During intense negotiations, most of the hostages are released while the hijackers blow up the empty planes. While the Jordanian military move against Palestinian groups in the kingdom, the remaining hostages, all British, are released in exchange for captured hijackers.

Goodbye to narrowboat freight

15th October 1970 An era draws to a close, as the last narrowboats to carry commercial freight on UK canals deliver their final load of coal from Atherstone to West London. This delivery brings to an end a way of life and transport in existence since the eighteenth century.

8 JUL 1970	24 AUG 1970	12 SEP 1970
Painter Dame Laura Knight dies at the age of 92.	A section of Windscale power station is sealed off due to a suspected radiation leak.	Residents complain of noise following first landing of Concorde at Heathrow.

Iceland stores open

18th November 1970 Malcolm Walker opens his very first Iceland store in Oswestry, Shropshire. Iceland specialises in frozen food, initially loose items, later launching its own-label packaged food in 1977. It quickly becomes a staple of the British high street, providing cheap dinners to price-conscious shoppers.

In the Navy

Prince Charles graduates from the University of Cambridge with a 2:2 in History and joins the Royal Navy.

FOREIGN
NEWS

ROYALTY &
POLITICS

For a better tomorrow vote Conservative

Surprise at the polls

A General Election takes place on 18th June, the first where people aged 18 or over can vote following the lowering of the age of majority from 21 to 18 in the Representation of the People Act the previous year. After six years of a Labour government and against expectations, Edward Heath's Conservatives win a surprise victory.

Margaret Thatcher, milk snatcher

Free school milk in secondary schools is abolished by Ted Heath's Conservative government. The proposal is passed on to Secretary of State for Education Margaret Thatcher who argues the savings can be used to improve school buildings. Rather than abolishing all school milk, she reaches a compromise. Milk is no longer provided in secondary schools, but nursery and primary school children continue to receive a ½ pint of milk each day, dished out by whichever pupil is given the weighty responsibility of being 'milk monitor'.

East and West meet

19th March 1970 For the first time since the division of Germany after the Second World War, West and East German leaders meet in person. West German Chancellor Willy Brandt is received warmly by East German Deputy Prime Minister Willi Stoph, heralding a normalisation of relations between the two countries. On a visit to Poland in December, Brandt is applauded when he unexpectedly kneels at the memorial to the uprising in the Warsaw ghetto in 1944.

MAGGIE THATCHER MILK SNATCHER

Coup in Japan

25th November 1970 An attempted coup in Japan by right-wing militia leader Yukio Mishima fails. After making a public address, he commits *seppuku* - ritual suicide.

19 OCT 1970

BP announce they have found oil in British waters of the North Sea 110 mile east of Aberdeen.

27 NOV 1970

The Gay Liberation Front stage their first demonstration in London.

15 DEC 1970

MPs vote for an Industrial Relations Court in a bid to curb strikes.

'Houston, we have a problem'

11th April 1970 Apollo 13 launches to take men to the Moon for the third time. Two days after launch, the oxygen tank explodes. Captain Jim Lovell reports the issue with the words 'Okay, Houston, we've had a problem here'. The Moon landing is aborted and all efforts are focused on improvising a way to get the three astronauts safely back to Earth. This involves sending the craft into Moon orbit, shutting down the command module's systems to conserve its resources for re-entry and transferring the crew to the lunar module, which acts as a life-boat. They splash down on 17th April at 18:07pm UK time. The men are safe, their rescue as breathtaking and ingenious as the original Moon landing itself.

Earth Day

22nd April 1970 The first Earth Day is celebrated to show support for protecting the globe's threatened environments. More than 20 million take part in peaceful protests across the US, beginning what becomes an annual global event that is still marked a half century later.

📺 ENTERTAINMENT

Divorced, beheaded, died

The BBC stakes its position as an expert creator of quality period dramas with *The Six Wives of Henry VIII,* which begins on 1st January with Annette Crosbie playing the first of the spouses, Catherine of Aragon. Keith Mitchell turns in an Emmy Award-winning performance as the complex Tudor king and has to age throughout the series, transforming from cultured, athletic young prince to bloated, bitter middle-aged monarch. Lavish costumes and Tudor music all enhance the authentic period atmosphere.

Nasser and de Gaulle

Two of the post-war world's most controversial politicians are no more. In September the death of General Gamal Abdel Nasser of Egypt changes the dynamic in the Middle East, as the outwardly more western-minded Anwar Sadat (photo) takes over as President. In November, the last of the Second World War leaders, former French President Charles de Gaulle, dies suddenly at the age of 80.

Who changes colour

Doctor Who regenerates for the second time on 3rd January and emerges in the form of Jon Pertwee. This new version of the Doctor has the air of a flamboyant Victorian dandy, with his velvet frock coats, frilly jabots and dramatic capes, much of which is harvested from Pertwee's own wardrobe. The transformation also coincides with the sci-fi drama being shown in colour for the first time.

The Railway Children

The Railway Children, which is released on 21st December, tells the story of the three Waterbury children. When their beloved father is wrongly imprisoned, their mother (Dinah Sheridan) is obliged to leave behind a comfortable middle-class existence in suburban London and move to a modest cottage in Yorkshire. The film and its success has easily eclipsed E. Nesbit's original 1905 novel and includes a final scene guaranteed to ensure there isn't a dry eye in the cinema.

Words and Pictures

Words and Pictures, the BBC Schools programme dedicated to helping children learn to read phonetically through animations and stories, is first broadcast on 17th October.

Britain's fittest pit their wits

What will become Britain's longest-running sports quiz begins on BBC1 on 5th January. *A Question of Sport* is hosted by David Vine with boxer Henry Cooper and Welsh rugby international Cliff Morgan as team captains. The very first guests to share their sporting knowledge are footballers George Best and Tom Finney, cricketer Ray Illingworth and track and field athlete Lillian Board.

Side-splitting

The Banana Splits Adventure Hour has been on American TV for two years before it is first shown in the UK on 20th February. Coming from the Hanna-Barbera stable, *The Banana Splits* features comedy sketches and cartoons, all topped off with an ear-worm of a theme tune. It's fast-paced and action-packed so it's no surprise that one of its directors, Richard Donner, goes on to make several Hollywood blockbusters including *The Goonies* and the *Lethal Weapon* series.

Scooby Dooby Doo

September sees the introduction of two new cartoon characters in the UK. On the 17th, *Scooby-Doo, Where Are You!* is shown on BBC1. Scooby is a dim but lovable Great Dane who accompanies a gang of teens who drive around in the Mystery Machine solving spooky crimes. Two days after Scooby's debut, slinky, rose-tinted sophisti-cat *The Pink Panther* prowls nonchalantly onto screens, accompanied by Henry Mancini's famous creeping saxophone theme tune.

Cat-napped

The Aristocats, the last Disney Studios film to be approved by Walt Disney himself before his death in 1966, is released in cinemas on 27th December.

Sing and bear it

Although he doesn't look a day over 10, Rupert Bear is already 50 years old when he stars in *The Adventures of Rupert Bear* on ITV this year. Now, Rupert, who lives with his mother and father in Nutwood, is brought to life as a string puppet along with his friends Bill Badger, Podge the Pig, Pong Ping the Pekingese and a host of other characters. Just thirteen episodes of *The Adventures of Rupert Bear* are initially made (the first airs on 28th October) but the series is such a success, it eventually runs for six years and 156 episodes.

The Street reaches 1,000th episode

Coronation Street celebrates its 1,000th episode on 19th August but on 30th June, actor Arthur Leslie, who plays Rovers Return landlord Jack Walker, dies suddenly of a heart attack, obliging the Street's writers to come up with a storyline to explain his absence (it is decided Jack would suffer the same fate off-screen). Key characters departing for whatever reason is a recurring issue in a long-running soap but as the novelist John Braine concludes in a piece he writes in a special 1,000th episode issue of the *TV Times*, 'the most important character in the Street is the Street itself. No matter who comes and goes, the Street remains.'

Scouting for jobs

With the advent of decimalisation, the Scout Association decide to change the name of their annual Bob-A-Job Week to the less snappy-sounding Scout Job Week.

PLEASE GIVE A SCOUT A JOB IN

BOB JOB WEEK

Goodie, Goodie yum-yum

Cambridge Footlights alumni Tim Brooke-Taylor, Graeme Garden and Bill Oddie aka *The Goodies* are let loose on TV screens on 8th November. Cycling around on their 'trandem' their cartoonish humour has huge, cross-generational appeal. Viewers can't get enough of sketches like Kitten Kong (using chroma-key, green screen technology), Bill practising the ancient martial art of 'Ecky Thump' and their catalogue of silly songs including stone-cold classic, 'The Funky Gibbon'.

Page 3 provocation
Editor of the *Sun* newspaper, Larry Lamb, starts publishing a daily photograph of a topless glamour model on page 3, a controversial move that helps to double the newspaper's circulation to 2.5 million within a year. Page 3 understandably provokes protests against the sexualisation of women in what is marketed as a 'family newspaper' but it will be 45 years before the *Sun* removes Page 3 girls from its printed paper in 2015 after increasing pressure from campaigners. By 2017, topless models also disappear from its web site.

Scent of the seventies
The fragrance Aqua Manda's musky blend of mandarin, coriander, jasmine and aromatic herbs pervades every party, club and disco in the land. With its distinctive orange floral packaging and reasonable price point, Aqua Manda is the undisputed smell of the seventies.

Creedence opt out
26th March 1970 Woodstock, the film of the 1970 music festival, goes on global release. Missing from the movie is a group who performed there but vetoed their inclusion in the film - Creedence Clearwater Revival. Originally from San Francisco and one of the top groups on the planet right now, Creedence's music is barnstorming rock'n'roll that conjures up a southern landscape of swamps, riverboats and highways in piledrivers like *Proud Mary* and *Up Around the Bend*.

Butch Cassidy and the Sundance Kid
Paul Newman and Robert Redford make a pair of devastatingly handsome Wild West outlaws in *Butch Cassidy and the Sundance Kid*, which arrives in UK cinemas on 6th February. The inclusion of the Burt Bacharach song *Raindrops Keep Falling on my Head* is controversial yet the track, which is used to accompany the famous bicycle scene in the film, goes on to become a huge hit reaching No. 1 in the US Billboard chart.

The Beatles split
10th April 1970 Paul McCartney has left the Beatles. The band's dissolution is finalised in the courts at the end of the year. The *Let it Be* album is a mixed epitaph, disliked by Paul for the production sheen added by John's buddy Phil Spector. Paul is first to release a solo album with *McCartney*, while Ringo makes an LP of swing era songs as a present for his mum. John records as the Plastic Ono Band but it is a rejuvenated George who wins the most plaudits with the Spector-produced *All Things Must Pass*.

MUSIC

Jackson Five
25th April 1970 At No. 1 in the US with *ABC* are the Jackson Five, the soul-singing siblings discovered by Diana Ross. Originally from Gary, Indiana, the group are as dazzling to watch as they are to listen or dance to - much of which is down to twelve-year-old Michael's precociously emotive voice and stage presence.

Simon says

28th February 1970 As news breaks that Simon and Garfunkel have parted company, their sonic masterpiece *Bridge over Troubled Water* begins its hold on the single and LP charts in the US and UK. Its soul-searching introspection has touched a real chord with America's post-Woodstock generation.

'Four dead in Ohio'

4th May 1970 Crosby, Stills, Nash and Young are America's supergroup of the moment. Formed by members of the Byrds (David Crosby), Buffalo Springfield (Steve Stills, Neil Young) and the Hollies (Graham Nash), their music is homespun but spiky - especially the impassioned *Ohio*, one of the most political songs ever to reach the US Top 40. It is Young's response to the shooting by National Guardsmen of four protesting students at Kent State University.

Everything's all Wight

26th - 31st August 1970 The second Isle of Wight Festival attracts 500,000 people. The most glowing reviews go to Emerson, Lake and Palmer, the supergroup playing live for only the second time. The most lingering memory is of Jimi Hendrix making what will be his very last live performance.

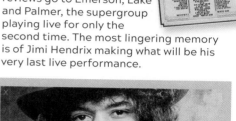

Just a word

3rd June 1970 Making a 6,000-mile round trip today to re-record just one word of his song *Lola* is Ray Davies of the Kinks. BBC Radio won't play the track unless its reference to Coca-Cola is changed. So Ray flies to London, enters a recording studio and sings 'cherry cola' instead, then hotfoots it back to the US. It's surprising that the BBC is prepared to play it at all, given that Lola is a transvestite.

Hendrix is dead

18th September 1970 Jimi Hendrix dies in London aged 27 after taking an overdose of barbiturates and choking on his own vomit. The coroner returns an open verdict. As demonstrated indelibly by his *Are You Experienced* and *Electric Ladyland* albums, Hendrix was simply the most imaginative, most technically adept and most instinctively creative guitarist of his generation.

Janis is dead

4th October 1970 Still reeling from the death of Jimi Hendrix, the rock world is shaken by the death of Janis Joplin at the same age of 27. The greatest white female blues voice of her time, her death is attributed to a heroin overdose. She had only been solo for a year, having stuck with the San Francisco band Big Brother and the Holding Company longer than she needed to.

1970

Singer-songwriters on the rise

Singer-songwriters are the flavour of the year, many of them recording for the hippest California record label, Warner Reprise. Some have been around for a while - James Taylor recorded for Apple in London, Joni Mitchell made her first LP in 1968, and Van Morrison has his roots in the UK beat boom - but the introspective nature of their songs suits the new decade's sombre mood. Taylor's *Sweet Baby James* outsells them all but August sees a young UK singer-pianist make his live US debut at the Troubadour in Los Angeles. His name is Elton John.

Eric becomes Derek

15th June 1970 Having joined Delaney and Bonnie Bramlett's touring band to expunge the excesses of his Cream and Blind Faith days, Eric Clapton forms Derek and the Dominoes with the Bramletts' rhythm section. The revitalised Clapton plays in a subtler, more concise and low-key style typified by *Layla*, a love song to George Harrison's wife Patti, who he will marry after their divorce.

MY FIRST 18 YEARS
TOP10 1970

1. **Layla** *Derek and the Dominoes*
2. **Big Yellow Taxi** *Joni Mitchell*
3. **Fire and Rain** *James Taylor*
4. **Mama Told Me Not to Come** *Three Dog Night*
5. **Spirit in the Sky** *Norman Greenbaum*
6. **Tears of a Clown** *Smokey Robinson*
7. **Woodstock** *Matthews Southern Comfort*
8. **I Hear You Knockin'** *Dave Edmunds*
9. **Let it Be** *The Beatles*
10. **Abraham, Martin and John** *Marvin Gaye*

Open 🟢 | Search 🔍 | Scan 📷

Happy families

23rd September 1970 From Screen Gems, makers of *The Monkees*, comes a television music show that makes a huge star of showbiz kid David Cassidy. *The Partridge Family* is about a pop group of young siblings and their mother, played by Hollywood songstress Shirley Jones, heartthrob David's real life stepmother.

Guitar heroes

If Jimi Hendrix defined the term 'guitar hero', other axe-playing stars are ready to take on the mantle such as Rory Gallagher of Taste, Alvin Lee of Ten Years After and Led Zeppelin's Jimmy Page. For Peter Green, the adulation is too much and he leaves Fleetwood Mac before the band makes a career-changing move to the US.

SPORT

Tragedy at Ibrox

66 people are killed and 200 more are injured during the 'Old Firm' match between Glasgow Rangers and Celtic at the Ibrox Stadium in Glasgow on 2nd January, due to a crush as fans exit the game. The stadium had suffered tragedy once already when a wooden stand collapsed during an international match in 1902, killing 25. The 1971 disaster is the worst in British football history to that point and leads to a rebuilding of Rangers ground.

Arsenal win the double

Five days after becoming League champions of the 1970-1 football season Arsenal face Liverpool at Wembley on 8th May in front of a crowd of 100,000 for the FA Cup Final. They win 2-1 with goals in extra time from Eddie Kelly (helped by George Graham) and Charlie George. The win makes Arsenal only the fourth team to secure the double.

V for victory?

Show jumping rebel Harvey Smith, son of a Yorkshire builder, loses a major title and £2000 in prize money after allegedly flicking the 'V' sign at the judges at the British Show Jumping Derby with horse Mattie Brown on 15th August. Smith protests he was making a 'V for victory' gesture. Notorious for clashing with judges and officials, Smith is a great favourite with the public and after two days his disqualification is reversed.

DOMESTIC NEWS

Northern Ireland

Troubles in Northern Ireland continue with violent riots throughout the year. In August, hundreds of people are arrested by British forces and are interred in Long Kesh prison, where they are held without trial. Known as 'Operation Demetrius', this policy leads to the Ballymurphy Massacre, where eleven people are killed by British forces. The autumn sees a fourteen-year-old girl, Annette McGavigan, killed when caught in crossfire, and two women shot dead at a checkpoint in Belfast. The worst incident of the Troubles so far occurs on 4th December, when a bomb destroys McGurk's bar in Belfast killing fifteen.

The lion roars

The British Lions rugby tour of New Zealand between 12th May and 14th August sees them play in four Test series against the mighty All Blacks. The British side, captained by John Dawes and comprised of the best players from the England, Ireland, Wales and Scotland teams, win two, lose one and draw in a final, nail-biting match to secure a historic Test series win.

15 JAN 1971

George Harrison releases his first solo single *My Sweet Lord*.

6 FEB 1971

Apollo 14 astronaut Alan Shepard hits a golf ball on the moon during a two-day moonwalk.

8 MAR 1971

Brian Faulkner becomes Prime Minister of Northern Ireland.

Divorce Reform

1st January 1971
The year begins with changes to divorce laws in the UK, allowing couples to divorce if they have been living separately for two

years. For the first time divorce can be granted on the grounds that the relationship has irretrievably broken down, with no need for one partner to be proven at fault.

Postal workers strike

20th January 1971 Postal workers go out on strike for the first time in their history, demanding a better pay deal. The strike lasts seven weeks and sees a variety of alternatives spring up in the space left by the Post Office.

Angry Brigade bombs

12th January 1971 The home of the Secretary of State for Employment, Robert Carr, is bombed along with his offices at the Department of Education. Responsibility is claimed by a left-wing group calling themselves the 'Angry Brigade'. Before the year is out, they will have struck the Biba store in Kensington, London, and the Post Office Tower.

Seabed treaty

11th February 1971 Countries including the UK, USA and Soviet Union sign the Seabed Arms Control Treaty which agrees to outlaw the use of nuclear weapons on the ocean floors. The treaty covers the seabed within 12 miles of the coast and seeks to prevent the escalation of nuclear tensions.

Decimalisation day

15th February 1971 The UK and the Republic of Ireland complete the switch to a decimal currency. Pounds are now worth 100 pence, replacing the 'old money' system of 20 shillings to the pound and 12 pence to the shilling. Initially people can still pay in old money, but they receive their change in the new currency. As of September, the old penny and threepence are no longer legal tender.

15 APR 1971

City of London announces plans for the building of the Barbican Centre.

11 MAY 1971

Closure of 62-year-old paper, *The Daily Sketch*.

19 JUN 1971

Viewing figures show talent show Opportunity Knocks is the country's most popular TV programme.

Industrial Relations Act protests

1st March 1971 The proposed Industrial Relations Act prompts huge protests in London where between 120,000 and 250,000 people join 'kill the bill' strikes across the capital. The Act will ensure that only registered trade unions have negotiating power, something workers fear will lead to restrictions upon industrial action. Despite this, the bill is passed and receives royal assent in September.

Spaghetti Junction opens

10th November 1971 The infamous Gravelly Hill Interchange or 'Spaghetti Junction' opens for the first time. Initially featuring 10 routes, including the A38, A5127, and M6, it later expands to 12 in 1972.

ROYALTY &
POLITICS

UK to join EEC

The House of Commons approves the UK's entry into Europe by a majority of 112 votes on 28th October. In his speech to the Commons, Anthony Barber, Chancellor of the Exchequer says, 'We shall join the Six as a proud and powerful country, able and ready to make its full contribution.'

Royal winner

After winning the individual medal at the world 3-day eventing championship at Burghley, aged 21, Princess Anne is voted BBC Sports Personality of the Year.

Paisley forms DUP

Protestant minister, hardline Unionist and MP for North Antrim Ian Paisley founds the Democratic Unionist Party (DUP).

Queen gets a big pay rise

Parliament debates an increase to the Civil List from £475,000 to £980,000. The Commons Select Committee, which makes the recommendation, justifies the increase of more than 100% stating, 'there is little further scope for economies in the Royal Household'.

6 JUL 1971	27-28 AUG 1971	3 SEP 1971
Crash helmets are to become compulsory for motorcyclists.	Clashes break out between police and Hell's Angels at Weeley Festival in Essex.	Qatar gains independence from the United Kingdom.

Starbucks starts
30th March 1971 The first branch of coffee shop giant Starbucks opens in Seattle, Washington, as a store selling varities of coffee beans.

First space station
19th April 1971 Salyut 1, the world's first space station, is launched by the Soviet Union. The first crew of cosmonauts is unable to dock while the second crew are also forced to abort after 23 days aboard in June. When their craft, Soyuz 11, returns to Earth, all three cosmonauts are found dead from an air supply leak. The decision to abandon the station is taken in October.

Idi the cruel
25th January 1971 General Idi Amin Dada seizes power in Uganda when President Milton Obote makes a trip abroad. The former boxing champion is welcomed at first but soon establishes a destructive dictatorship which earns him the nickname 'Slaughterer of Africa'. During his reign, Amin has 300,000 opponents eliminated.

Pentagon Papers
30th June 1971 The US Supreme Court rules that the *New York Times* can publish the Pentagon Papers, overruling objections from the Nixon administration. The Papers are classified studies made for the Department of Defense which reveal the double-dealing and secret machinations that brought the US to war in Vietnam. The revelations strengthen opposition to the war still further in a year in which Australia and New Zealand withdraw their troops from Vietnam, the US resumes bombing of North Vietnam and the conflict spreads to Laos.

The first email
In the US, 23 computers located at various universities are now connected to the ARPANET, the forerunner of the internet. Computer programmer Ray Tomlinson sends the first message over the network from one computer to another. He comes up with the @ sign to distinguish the domain and the recipient. The medium we know as email is born.

Bangladesh goes alone
31st May 1971 Four months after the devastating Cyclone Bhola, the former East Pakistan - now Bangladesh - declares its independence from Pakistan, which brutally crushes the rebellion and creates two million refugees. After Pakistan declares war on India in December, India invades Bangladesh with Bengali rebel support. Pakistan surrenders on 15th December.

1 OCT 1971
The CAT scan is first used in patient diagnosis in Wimbledon.

28 NOV 1971
51-year-old farmer, Ray Covine, uncovers an immigrant smuggling operation on his farm near Huntingdon.

30 DEC 1971
Sean Connery returns for the final time as Bond in Diamon are Forever.

Twin towers topped out
19th July 1971 The topping out of the South Tower of the new World Trade Center in New York takes place, following the topping-out ceremony for the North Tower six months earlier.

Greenpeace launches
14th October 1971 Greenpeace is founded in Vancouver, Canada, to campaign actively against US plans for nuclear tests in Alaska. As the organization grows its action-based but non-violent opposition to causes such as large-scale whaling, seal hunting and the dumping of nuclear waste at sea brings it into direct conflict with governments.

DO YOU REMEMBER THIS?

Chocolate cigarettes

ENTERTAINMENT

Top deck
The first episode of *Here Come the Double Deckers* is shown on BBC1 on 15th January. A comedy adventure series with a brilliant theme tune, it features a gang of kids - Scooper, Tiger, Brains, Sticks, Doughnut, Spring and Billie - whose HQ is an abandoned double-decker bus in a London junkyard. The Double Deckers get into various scrapes every episode, and most of us wonder where on earth their parents are.

Clackers really knacker
Possibly the worst idea for a toy ever, 'clackers', consisting of two hard acrylic balls on string, are all the rage during the summer of 1971. After several accidents, many schools ban them as a serious hazard.

Kids get a *Look-In*

Look-in is launched as a junior version of the *TV Times*. Jam-packed with comic strips, interviews and pull-out posters focused on ITV's programmes, it also features pop music, cool hobbies like skateboarding and a regular column from radio DJ Ed Stewart called, 'Stewpot's Newsdesk'. Through most of the 1970s, *Look-in* covers are illustrated by Arnaldo Putzo, who also designs posters for films like *Get Carter* and the *Carry On* series.

Elizabeth R

The success of *The Six Wives of Henry VIII* in 1970 encourages the BBC to tackle the story of his daughter next; the first of six 75-minute episodes is shown on 17th February. *Elizabeth R* has Glenda Jackson in imperious form, playing the queen from a fifteen-year-old princess to the aging Gloriana.

A shocking end

Valerie Barlow (Anne Reid) and husband Ken (William Roache) are preparing to leave the Street for a new life in Jamaica in *Coronation Street*'s 27th January edition when she is electrocuted by a faulty hairdryer and killed instantly.

Music for musos

On 21st September, the thinking person's music show, *The Old Grey Whistle Test* airs for the first time. This is the place to hear non-chart music and album tracks through live performances in a pared-back studio setting. *The Old Grey Whistle Test* boasts some special moments in music from Roxy Music in their glam rock pomp performing *Ladytron* to David Bowie on the eve of his 1972 Ziggy Stardust tour, rattling through a blistering performance of *Queen Bitch.*

Playaway on Saturday

Playaway starts on 20th November and becomes a Saturday afternoon refuge for kids away from sports-dominated weekend TV schedules during the 1970s. A older sibling of the weekday programme *Playschool*, its lively variety show format includes songs, bad jokes, sketches, and general tomfoolery. Along with more familiar Playschool alumni like Brian Cant and Floella Benjamin (photo), Jeremy Irons and Tony Robinson both do time as Playaway presenters.

Comedy sitcoms on-screen

Several popular British TV sitcoms capitalise on their success and get a big-screen upgrade this year with *Dad's Army*, *Up Pompeii* and *On the Buses* all made into full-length feature films.

Upstairs, Downstairs

Upstairs, Downstairs, the long-running drama about the aristocratic Bellamy family of 165 Eaton Place, SW1 and their retinue of servants below stairs, is the surprise hit drama of the decade. Originally the idea of actresses Eileen Atkins and Jean Marsh (who would play parlourmaid Rose Buck in the series), the first episode of this period drama is buried by ITV in the ignominious 10:15pm slot on Sunday 10th October, but audience figures quickly increase, eventually soaring to 18 million. Through five series, the lives of the Bellamys and their employees are interwoven with world events such as the suffragette movement and the sinking of the *Titanic*, in a dramatic formula that would be successfully revived four decades later in *Downton Abbey*.

Save us from Sesame Street

British kids have enjoyed American cartoons and comedy series since the 1950s but are introduced to a very different kind of transatlantic offering this year in a show that provokes significant controversy in advance of its broadcast on 29th March on HTV. *Sesame Street* is populated by a cast of brightly coloured puppets (many created by Jim Henson) whose daily lives form the basis of didactic teaching methods. The BBC refuses to air it since it seems specifically tailored to educating American children; ITV does so reluctantly on the understanding it 'should not be construed as endorsement of *Sesame Street* to British children'. The hand wringing of educationalists means little to parents and children, who love characters like Big Bird, Eric and Ernie and The Count (who, you've guessed it, counts!) and find novelty in exotic Americanisms such as trash, zip code and cookies - as gobbled up by Cookie Monster.

And it's goodnight from him

The Two Ronnies appear on BBC1 on 10th April in a show that will run for the next sixteen years. With many sketches based on Ronnie Barker's fondness for word play (and others playfully mocking Ronnie Corbett's short stature), their partnership produces comedy gold from a brain-teasing *Mastermind* spoof to hardware store confusion in 'Four Candles'.

A ticklish tale

The first six books in the *Mr. Men* series by advertising executive and frustrated cartoonist Roger Hargreaves are published on 10th August. The very first character is *Mr. Tickle*, whose unfeasibly long arms cause all sorts of mischief. *Mr. Men* is an instant success and becomes a cartoon series in 1974 (narrated by Arthur Lowe). Hargreaves goes on to create 46 *Mr. Men* and 33 *Little Miss* characters in total. In 2004, his widow sells the rights to *Mr. Men* to Chorion for a cool £28 million.

Beatrix Potter ballet

The Tales of Beatrix Potter, a ballet film featuring various characters created by Potter, danced by the Royal Ballet to choreography by Sir Frederick Ashton, is released in cinemas 30th June. Wayne Sleep dances the part of Squirrel Nutkin; Ashton himself plays Mrs. Tiggywinkle. The costumes by Christine Edzard form an exhibition on board the *QE2* liner this year.

Very persuasive

The pairing of Tony Curtis and Roger Moore as millionaire playboys from different sides of the tracks in *The Persuaders* is intentionally incongruous, with Curtis as the rough and ready New Yorker Danny Wilde, and Moore playing to type as the posh and polished British nobleman, Lord Brett Sinclair. Sporting equally wide sideburns and ties, *The Persuaders* embark on a series of escapades with the help of fast cars, John Barry's seventies synth soundtrack and glamorous co-stars like Susan George, Imogen Hassall and Joan Collins. Curtis, aged 46, personally performs all of his stunts.

On-screen Gangster

A grim and gloomy Newcastle-upon-Tyne is the setting for *Get Carter*, released 10th March, featuring Michael Caine as a brutal London gangster returning to his roots to seek revenge among the Geordie criminal underworld.

MUSIC

Balm for the soul

10th February 1971 After divorce from Gerry Goffin, re-marriage and a move to the Californian hills, top 60s songwriter Carole King is back with an album full of homeliness and good feeling. Including her own versions of *I Feel the Earth Move, You've Got a Friend* and *A Natural Woman*, *Tapestry* is musical balm for the soul in dark times. Over 25 million sales prove it.

Stones get sticky

12th May 1971 Negative headlines surround Mick Jagger's *très chic* wedding to Nicaraguan socialite Bianca Pérez-Mora Macías in St Tropez. The Stones are getting stick in the music press for becoming tax exiles in the south of France but they are on top form with the *Sticky Fingers* album, the first Stones release on their very own record label. Its cover has a real working zip - the work of Andy Warhol's Factory and a nightmare for record store owners the world over.

Glastonbury
20th - 24th June 1971 Worthy Farm owner Michael Eavis times the first Glastonbury Festival proper - after a small event under a different name a year earlier - to coincide with the summer solstice. The lineup includes Traffic, Fairport Convention, a pre-Ziggy Stardust David Bowie and a diehard of 1970s festivals, Hawkwind.

Blue days
22nd June 1971 Joni Mitchell releases *Blue*, the outcome of a year of travelling after her relationship with Graham Nash breaks up. A searingly honest and self-revealing LP, it will dazzle and inspire scores of artists over the next 50 years.

Satchmo passes on
6th July 1971 Louis Armstrong, the cornet-playing father of Dixieland jazz, dies at the age of 71.

Concerts for Bangladesh
1st August 1971 George Harrison organises two Concerts for Bangladesh at Madison Square Garden, New York. Joining him on stage are Eric Clapton, Bob Dylan and sitar virtuoso Ravi Shankar. The concerts and subsequent album raise around $12 million for victims of the Bangladesh catastrophe.

T. Rextasy!
Singing songs about hobbits and goblins in a quavering voice, Marc Bolan of *Tyrannosaurus Rex* was an icon of late 1960s progressive rock. Now former male model Marc has truncated the band's name to T. Rex and is ditching the hippie gear for an androgynous glittery look and a much younger (and female) audience.

Marvin's mission
21st May 1971 Motown superstar Marvin Gaye releases the album *What's Going On*, a huge shift from the punchy dance-driven tracks he is known for. Largely inactive since the death of his singing partner Tammi Terrell and his failing marriage to Berry Gordy's sister Anna, Marvin has set a series of socially conscious songs to a looser, expansive sound. Motown owner Gordy thinks it's commercial suicide but hands him a new deal allowing him creative freedom - at one million dollars, the most lucrative deal yet secured by a black recording artist.

DO YOU REMEMBER THIS?

Rotary dial telephone

Gene Vincent RIP
12th October 1971 Be Bop a Lula legend Gene Vincent dies in California aged 36. Although plagued by a leg injury aggravated by the car crash that killed his friend Eddie Cochran in 1961, he epitomised the rough and greasy sound and look of classic rock'n'roll.

The club of 27

3rd July 1971 Jim Morrison, charismatic leader of California band the Doors, is found dead in his bathtub at his apartment in Paris aged 27. The rest of the group try to carry on but disband at the end of 1972.

Zappa attacked

10th December 1971 Frank Zappa, musical iconoclast and satirist of the pretentious and worthy, receives life-changing injuries when he is pulled off stage by a fan at the Rainbow Theatre, Finsbury Park.

Lennon leaves UK

3rd September 1971 John Lennon leaves the UK for New York with wife Yoko. He will never return. After exploring his primal therapy treatment in *John Lennon and the Plastic Ono Band*, he makes the mellower *Imagine* but can't resist a scoff at Paul McCartney on the track *How Do You Sleep*. He and Yoko end the year by wishing everyone *Happy Xmas (War is Over)* in a Christmas single.

MY FIRST 18 YEARS
TOP10 1971

1. **Maggie May** *Rod Stewart*
2. **Help Me Make it Through ...** *Kris Kristofferson*
3. **Theme from Shaft** *Isaac Hayes*
4. **My Sweet Lord** *George Harrison*
5. **Sweet Caroline** *Neil Diamond*
6. **Gypsies, Tramps and Thieves** *Cher*
7. **Family Affair** *Sly and the Family Stone*
8. **Just My Imagination** *The Temptations*
9. **Coz I Luv You** *Slade*
10. **I'm Still Waiting** *Diana Ross*

Open 🟢 | Search 🔍 | Scan 📷

Hello ELO

October 1971 As the Move call it a day with a final concert tour, Roy Wood and Jeff Lynne launch the Electric Light Orchestra (ELO) with a musical blueprint inspired by the Beatles' cello-laden *I Am the Walrus*. Within a year Wood leaves to form Wizzard and Lynne takes ELO to the next level with plans for a full string section and spectacular stage effects.

SPORT

A league of their own
The Great Britain rugby league team arrive for the World Cup in France as the underdogs, but confound expectations and win the tournament. Great Britain is captained by Clive Sullivan, the first black player to captain a British team at any sport.

Pawns or kings?
11th July 1972 It's the Cold War in miniature: seemingly invincible world chess champion Boris Spassky of the Soviet Union versus mercurial US champion Bobby Fischer in neutral Reykjavik, Iceland. After 21 games, with Fischer leading, Spassky concedes. The final score is 12 ½ to 8 ½. Fischer becomes the first American world chess champion.

Golden girl
33-year-old Mary Peters from Belfast is Britain's Olympic champion in Munich when she triumphs over her rival, the West German Heide Rosendahl, to clinch the gold medal in the pentathlon. Peters wins by just 10 points, setting a world record in the process.

DO YOU REMEMBER THIS?

Platform shoe

Gymnastic wonder
Belarussian gymnast Olga Korbut rewrites the rule book by performing unprecedented moves at the Olympics; a back flip on the beam and what becomes known as the 'Korbut flip' on the asymmetric bars. Korbut's gobsmacking performance is hugely influential and within two years, three million British girls are members of gymnastic clubs.

Women on the ball
It is a freezing afternoon on 18th November, when England and Scotland play the first ever women's football international in the UK at Ravenscraig Stadium, Greenock. England come from 2-0 down to win 3-2.

13 JAN 1972
Royal Navy officer David Bingham is sentenced to 21 years in prison after selling defence secrets to the Soviet Union to pay family debts.

16 FEB 1972
Nine-hour blackouts imposed across the country and householders asked to heat only one room as miners' pay dispute continues.

31 MAR 1972
A revival of the anti-nuclear Aldermaston marches of the 1950s and 1960s takes place, but with just 600 participants.

DOMESTIC
NEWS

Miners and dockers strike

9th January 1972 Members of the National Union of Mineworkers go out on strike for seven weeks, with the fuel shortages and a cold snap leading to the Prime Minister declaring a national state of emergency as blackouts grip the nation. The strike ends in February with a pay agreement, but on 4th August a second state of emergency is declared after dock workers go out on strike following the trial of the Pentonville Five.

Economic trouble

20th January 1972 New figures demonstrate that over 1 million people are unemployed in the UK for the first time since the 1930s. The number has almost doubled in two years, casting doubt on Prime Minister Heath's handling of the economy. In November, the government freezes pay and prices in the hope of countering inflation, which falls slightly in the following months.

Bloody Sunday

30th January 1972 A dark day in British history as troops open fire on unarmed demonstrators in Derry, killing fourteen. The event becomes known as Bloody Sunday and precedes one of the worst years of the Troubles with 497 fatalities across numerous protests, clashes, and bombings. In February, the British Embassy in Dublin is burnt by rioters as days later mounted police charge protesters in London. Bombings in 1972 include explosions at Aldershot Barracks, 'Bloody Friday' bombings in Belfast, and the 'Claudy' bombing or 'Bloody Monday'. In March the British government introduces direct rule over Northern Ireland and enters secret negotiations with the Provisional IRA that prove fruitless.

27 APR 1972

Five Oxford University colleges announce plans to admit up to 100 women students in 1974.

22 MAY 1972

The Dominion of Ceylon becomes the Republic of Sri Lanka but remains within the British Commonwealth.

27 JUN 1972

The Official IRA calls a ceasefire and embarks on secret talks with the British government, but sectarian violence erupts again after two weeks.

Thomas Cook & Son privatised
26th May 1972 Thomas Cook, owned by the government since 1948 as part of the British Transport Commission, is privatised. The business is purchased by a consortium including the Midland bank, which later becomes the sole controller, and continues to provide holidays to the British public well into the 21st century.

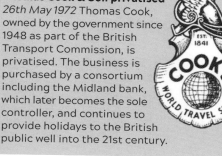

Staines air disaster
18th June 1972 British Airways Flight 548 crashes just outside Staines shortly after take-off from London Heathrow. All 118 people on their way to Brussels are killed, despite at least one person initially surviving the impact. It remains the deadliest air accident in UK history.

Battersea Fun Fair disaster
30th May 1972 The nation is horrified when the Big Dipper rollercoaster at Battersea Fun Fair comes off its rails, killing five children and injuring thirteen. An investigation finds the ride manager and engineer guilty of manslaughter, and despite attempts to reopen with a replacement ride, the park closes in 1974.

Idi Amin expels British Asians
4th August 1972 President of Uganda Idi Amin expels people of South Asian origin from the country in a wave of anti-Indian sentiment. Over the next three months, 27,200 of those who are British passport holders emigrate to the United Kingdom.

School leaving age
1st September 1972 The school leaving age in the UK is raised from 15 to 16 years old, sparking a wave of construction work across the country as schools build new classrooms to cater for the increase in student numbers.

Gay Pride
1st July 1972 The UK's very first Pride march takes place when 2,000 members of London's gay community take to the streets. The date selected is the nearest Saturday to the anniversary of the Stonewall riots in New York in 1969 and sees attendees protesting legislation targeting the gay community and demonstrating their pride in their sexuality.

28 JUL 1972
Nationwide dock strike begins and lasts until 16th August.

31 AUG 1972
American super swimmer Mark Spitz wins seven gold medals at the Munich Olympics, each in a record time.

14 SEP 1972
Death of Geoffrey Francis Fisher, former Archbishop of Canterbury who had presided over the 1953 Coronation.

1972

The Second Cod War

5th September 1972 The Second Cod War between Britain and Iceland breaks out as Iceland seeks to expand its territorial waters to 50 miles off the coast. An altercation between an Icelandic Coast Guard vessel and a British trawler, the *Peter Scott*, results in violence as the crew refuse to identify themselves and instead play *Rule Britannia!* over the radio. In November, the Foreign Secretary announces that British Navy ships will be stationed to defend trawlers in the disputed waters.

Rise of Japanese cars

1972 proves a popular year for Japanese cars, as Honda begins importing vehicles such as its Civic hatchback (photo). Nissan sells over 30,000 cars in Britain, more than three times the previous year's total, and Mazda and Toyota also enjoy success.

Death of Duke of Windsor

The Queen visits her uncle the Duke of Windsor on 18th May during a state visit to France. The former king is too ill to be able to attend a tea provided by the Duchess downstairs, but the Queen spends fifteen minutes with her 'Uncle David' in his first-floor sitting-room. Just ten days later he dies of complications arising from throat cancer. He is laid to rest in the Royal Burial Ground at rogmore, Windsor on 5th June after a funeral service at St. George's Chapel.

Tragedy for the Gloucesters

Thirty-year-old Prince William of Gloucester, elder son of the Duke and Duchess of Gloucester and cousin of the Queen, dies when his Cherokee single-engine aircraft crashes at the Goodyear International Air Trophy at Halfpenny Green near Wolverhampton on 28th August.

ROYALTY & POLITICS

Direct rule for Northern Ireland

On 30th March, the situation in Northern Ireland leads to the suspension of the Parliament of Northern Ireland which is replaced by direct rule by Westminster. William Whitelaw is appointed Secretary of State for Northern Ireland.

DO YOU REMEMBER THIS?

Rolodex

23 OCT 1972
Access credit cards - 'your flexible friend' - introduced as a rival to Barclaycard.

NOV 1972
The PEOPLE party is formed in Coventry, changing its name to the Ecology Party in 1975 and then the Green Party in 1985.

6 DEC 1972
Four members of revolutionar left-wing group The Angry Brigade are each jailed for ten years at the Old Bailey.

FOREIGN
NEWS

Yokoi at peace
24th January 1972
Apparently unaware of his country's surrender at the end of the Second World War, Japanese soldier Shoichi Yokoi is discovered on the Pacific island of Guam after spending 28 years hiding in the jungle.

Nixon on the world stage
21st February 1972 Richard Nixon's popularity is on a high as he becomes the first US President to visit the People's Republic of China. In May, he is the first US President to visit the Soviet Union where he agrees a drastic reduction in nuclear weaponry with Soviet leader Brezhnev.

Tricky Dicky
17th June 1972 Five men are arrested when they break into the Democratic Party headquarters in the Watergate complex in Washington DC. Dogged *Washington Post* reporters Carl Bernstein and Bob Woodward make the link between the burglars and President Nixon's re-election campaign team and uncover a much larger plan of 'dirty tricks' to thwart the Democrat challenge. Nixon defeats Senator George McGovern in a landslide in November but is already slipping towards possible impeachment.

War photo
8th June 1972 After a devastating US napalm bombardment on the Vietnamese village of Trang Bàng, Nick Ut takes the most famous war photo in history. Nine-year-old girl Phan Thi Kim Phúc is running away from her bombed village, naked and crying. The desperate moment is captured by the photographer – who then takes her to hospital. When the photo appears on the front page of the *New York Times*, it prompts a further wave of revulsion against the war.

Pocket calculator
Hewlett-Packard markets the first scientific pocket calculator, consigning the slide rule to history. The HP-35 weighs only 248 grams and measures 15 x 8.1 centimetres. It costs $395. Ultimately, 300,000 are sold.

Massacre at Munich
5th - 6th September 1972 At the Olympic Games in Munich, two members of Israel's Olympic team are killed and nine kidnapped when Arab terrorist faction Black September invades the athletes' village. In an attempt by West German police to free the hostages, eleven Israelis, five terrorists and a policeman are killed. Incredibly, the Games continue.

Andean air disaster
13th October 1972 A Uruguayan plane carrying a rugby union team crashes into a glacier in the Andes on the border between Argentina and Chile. Only sixteen of the 45 passengers survive. They manage to stay alive in freezing conditions for 72 days by eating the flesh of their deceased fellow passengers.

So long Apollo
19th December 1972 With the return of Apollo 17 to Earth, the Apollo programme closes. Astronauts Gene Cernan and Harrison Schmitt are the last men to set foot on the Moon. Planning for the next crewed mission to the Moon will not begin until 2017.

The limits to growth
A new report called *The Limits to Growth* shows that humanity's future is threatened by overpopulation, environmental pollution and depletion of raw materials. Modern phosphate-based detergents are blamed for water pollution, and aerosol cans and old refrigerators spread chlorofluorocarbons (CFCs) that cause the hole in the ozone layer.

ENTERTAINMENT

Fingerbobs
Quite possibly the lowest budget children's programme ever made, *Fingerbobs*, which is first shown on 14th February, features presenter Rick Jones aka Yoffy, who sits making up stories with the help of a random selection of creatures made from gloves and sugar paper - a rodent called Fingermouse, Gulliver the seagull, Scampi the sea creature and a typically slow and steady tortoise called Flash. Simple, charming, homespun fun.

Puppy love
Andrex toilet tissue commercials featuring an adorable yellow Labrador puppy are shown for the first  time this year. With guaranteed 'aah' factor, the puppy becomes the brand's enduring mascot, and helps Andrex build their market share to 30% by the end of the decade.

And...action
On the April, *Clapperboard* begins on ITV. Presented by Chris Kelly, *Clapperboard* offers a fascinating insight into the world of film and television, past and present. It's a fount of knowledge for any budding movie buff.

Here is the news

John Craven's Newsround, explaining serious news in simple terms for kids, is broadcast on 4th April on BBC1. Craven fronts over 3,000 bulletins for *Newsround* until he leaves the programme in 1989. He also becomes resident news specialist on *Multicoloured Swap Shop* and *Saturday Superstore*.

Cosmo girls

The first UK issue of the notoriously racy *Cosmopolitan* magazine is published in March. Alongside articles on fabulous fashion, beauty and careers, *Cosmo* delivers frank advice on sex and relationships. Over in the US, the April issue causes a sensation when it features a naked Burt Reynolds as the first male centrefold. No subject is taboo to the magazine's international editor-in-chief, Helen Gurley-Brown, whose 1962 international bestseller, *Sex and the Single Girl*, sets the tone. Cosmo readers are single career girls; ambitious, glamorous, and sexually adventurous. Can women have it all? Cosmo says 'yes'!

Evel Knievel doll released

Ideal Toys release a six-inch action figure of American stunt motorcyclist Evel Knievel in the same year the real Evel attempts a high-publicised jump across the Snake River Canyon in Idaho (his parachute releases prematurely, ruining the stunt, but he gets away with only minor injuries).

Watership Down

Richard Adams' epic novel about a band of rabbits risking everything to establish a new warren goes on to sell 50 million copies worldwide. The 1978 animation film is an instant classic, fuelled by the Art Garfunkel's song *Bright Eyes*.

Pebble Mill at One

In January, the government lifts the restrictions on the numbers of hours of broadcasting and schedulers begin to look at expanding daytime programming. *Pebble Mill at One*, the magazine programme filmed in the foyer of the BBC's Pebble Mill studios in Birmingham, is first broadcast at 1pm on 2nd October and remains a fixture of daytime television until 1986.

Give us a wave

As the 1970s becomes renowned as the decade of the disaster movie, *The Poseidon Adventure*, about an ailing ocean liner capsized by a tidal wave, vies to be the one filled with the most hysterical screaming. An ensemble cast play a small group of survivors led by Gene Hackman's maverick preacher, taking their chances and dicing with death as they navigate their way out of the topsy-turvy vessel.

I've started so I'll finish

Hopeful quizzers take to the black chair to face questions asked by Magnus Magnusson in *Mastermind*, which is first broadcast on BBC1 late at night on 11th September (it's moved to a primetime slot the following year).

A British *Jesus Christ Superstar*

Andrew Lloyd-Webber and Tim Rice's biblical rock opera *Jesus Christ Superstar* opens at the Palace Theatre on 9th August with Paul Nicholas moving from *Hair* to take on the role of Jesus, Stephen Tate as Judas and Dana Gillespie playing Mary Magdalene. *Jesus Christ Superstar* began as an album before stage musical adaptations on Broadway and in Australia and by the time it opens in London, the timing, the anticipation and the buzz ensure it's a smash hit. *Jesus Christ Superstar* runs for 3,358 performances until 1980, then tours the UK from 1983.

Retail therapy

There's rarely a dull moment at Grace Brothers Department Store, what with Mr Humphries camping it up in his latest outrageous sales promotion costume, or Mrs Slocombe, head of the ladies' department, changing her hair colour and worrying about her pussy. The pilot episode of the retail comedy *Are You Being Served?* is broadcast on 8th September. Famed for its double entendres, a series follows in 1973, with nine more, and a 1977 feature film, produced over the next twelve years.

The Adventures of Black Beauty

The Adventures of Black Beauty begins on ITV on 27th September and although inspired by Anna Sewell's 1877 novel, the action is instead shifted forward to the turn of the twentieth century and places Beauty in the care of widower Dr. James Gordon and his two children Vicky and the very un-Edwardian-sounding Kevin. Featured in ITV's family-friendly Sunday teatime slot, the uplifting *Black Beauty* theme tune, Denis King's *Galloping Home*, becomes more famous than the series itself, ingrained in the memory of every 1970s kid.

The Godfather

'A bloody good story, or a good bloody story' is how Derek Malcolm describes *The Godfather* in his *Guardian* review. Francis Ford Coppola's monumental gangster film based on Mario Puzo's novel about the Corleone family is released in the UK on 24th August. Conflict over casting decisions had dogged the early stages of production, with Coppola digging in his heels to cast Marlon Brando as Vito Corleone and Al Pacino as his son and heir, Michael; Brando wins an Oscar and *The Godfather* becomes the highest-grossing film of 1972.

Birth of Pong

The video game revolution begins in America with the release of the Pong arcade game on 29th November. Three years later, the simple table-tennis game is adapted for play on a console connected to a television allowing early gamers to pong and ping to their heart's content from the comfort of their armchair.

MUSIC

Paul spreads his Wings
8th February 1972 Paul and Linda McCartney hit the road with their new band Wings. They make their live debut at Nottingham University when they turn up unannounced and offer to do a lunchtime gig. Tickets are just 40 pence.

American Pie
15th January 1972 Don McLean was inspired to write his seven minute-epic *American Pie*, now at No. 1 in the US, by the death of his idol Buddy Holly in 1959. It tells the story of rock music with biblical imagery and cloaked allusions to Dylan, the Beatles, the Rolling Stones, Janis Joplin and others.

Far from plain
21st January 1972 A session on John Peel's Radio 1 evening show introduces Roxy Music, who don't even have a record deal yet. The band is an art-cum-music project fronted by Bryan Ferry, whose strangled diction makes for a sneering vocal style. Musically and visually they mix Hollywood cool with futuristic sonic wizardry and costumes to match. A dazzlingly inventive debut album is followed by the single *Virginia Plain*, its rococo lyrics referencing everything from Fred Astaire movies to casinos and chic American cars.

Heartbreak tale
11th March 1972 At No. 1 in the UK is one of the most affecting heartbreak ballads ever, *Without You* by Harry Nilsson, who is best known for singing *Everybody's Talkin'* over the *Midnight Cowboy* credits. Written by Pete Ham and Tom Evans of Badfinger, its sales are so huge that the two young songwriters should be set up for life. Instead, disputes over royalties lead to the suicides of both men, in 1975 and 1983 respectively.

Bowie breakthrough
16th June 1972 After years as one of UK rock's fringe figures, David Bowie makes a huge breakthrough with *The Rise and Fall of Ziggy Stardust and the Spiders from Mars*. On the album he assumes the role of an androgynous rock star who soars to fame as the Earth awaits an apocalypse. The Bowie look and style defines glam rock at its most serious and sexually questioning, underpinned by Mick Ronson's searing guitar.

Bagpipe blast
15th April 1972 Over the years the record chart has featured singing nuns, chickens, dogs and even ventriloquists, but never bagpipe bands. Standing proudly at No. 1 are the Pipes and Drums and Military Band of the Royal Scots Dragoon Guards with the eighteenth-century hymn *Amazing Grace*. Its million-selling success is generally credited to (or blamed on) Radio 1 DJ Tony Blackburn. A vocal-only version by folk singer Judy Collins is also one of the year's top sellers.

1972

School's Out!

29th July 1972 As schools break for summer, never has a record release been better timed than *School's Out* by Alice Cooper. Alice and his horror movie-derived stage show, his pet snake, garage band sound and all-American sweetheart name are calculated to appal parents and delight adolescents.

MY FIRST 18 YEARS
TOP 10 — 1972

1. **Let's Stay Together** *Al Green*
2. **All the Young Dudes** *Mott the Hoople*
3. **Sylvia's Mother** *Dr Hook and the Medicine Show*
4. **Me and Mrs Jones** *Billy Paul*
5. **Starman** *David Bowie*
6. **Mama Weer All Crazee Now** *Slade*
7. **Rocket Man** *Elton John*
8. **Ain't No Sunshine** *Michael Jackson*
9. **I Can See Clearly Now** *Johnny Nash*
10. **Guitar Man** *Bread*

Open | Search | Scan

Osmonds everywhere

Osmondmania grips the country. Twelve year-old Donny revives *Puppy Love* and *Too Young* and joins his Mormon brothers on a string of Top Tenners before his younger brother Jimmy - just nine years old - bags the Christmas No. 1 with *Long Haired Lover from Liverpool*. Waiting in the wings is sister Marie, soon to top the chart with *Paper Roses*.

The Philly sound

Challenging Motown's grip on making precision-tuned radio-friendly soul music are producers Kenny Gamble and Leon Huff at the Philadelphia International label. The 'Philly sound' they have perfected matches great rhythm tracks to sweet orchestral backings on hits for Harold Melvin, Billy Paul and the O'Jays. Another Philly producer, Thom Bell, is behind the hits of the Stylistics while Barry White gives the template a twist with his vocal group Love Unlimited.

All crazee now

While glam rock avatars T. Rex are beginning to stutter, Wolverhampton band Slade's raucous and cheeky brand of updated rock'n'roll reaches out to the guys as well as the girls. Their trademarks are hits with deliberately misspelt song titles like *Take Me Bak 'Ome* and *Mama Weer All Crazee Now*, while guitarist Dave Hill's platform boots and singer Noddy Holder's mutton-chop sideburns make the Clockwork Orange-influenced look the height of teen fashion.

SPORT

Football's FA Cup Fairytale

When Second Division side Sunderland arrive at Wembley on 5th May for their FA Cup final match against Leeds, few people fancy their chances against a tough team who are the 1972 Cup winners and have dominated First Division football over the past couple of seasons. But in one of the most spectacular examples of giant-killing football, the Black Cats win 1-0, with Ian Porterfield's goal coming in the thirty-second minute, and several outstanding saves from the Wearsiders' goalie Jimmy Montgomery to keep them ahead. When the final whistle goes and Sunderland's manager Bob Stokoe runs onto the pitch, it's a fairytale ending for a team whose fanbase is as loyal as it is large.

Flying Scot quits at the top

Following the death of his Tyrrell-Ford team-mate Francois Cevert in a practice race at Watkins Glen on 6th October, three-times world F1 champion, Jackie Stewart announces his retirement.

Hunt the Shunt hits F1

James Hunt makes his debut in Formula One racing as a driver for Hesketh; his highest position is second in the US Grand Prix. The RAC award him with the Campbell trophy at the end of the season for best British driver.

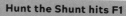

Battle of the Sexes

In the year the US Open pays equal prize money to male and female players, a tennis match between 55-year-old Bobby Riggs and 29-year-old Billie Jean King takes place on 20th September. Billed as the 'Battle of the Sexes' the contest had arisen due to Riggs's public declarations about the inferiority of the women's game. After a $100,000 prize is offered, King agrees to take up the challenge. Watched by a global television audience of 90 million, King wins 6-4, 6-4, 6-3, a significant point scored in King's long-running battle for equality in the sport.

7 JAN 1973

British Darts Organisation is founded.

5 FEB 1973

The Wombles begins on BBC1, narrated by Bernard Cribbins and with music by Mike Batt.

27 MAR 1973

The first women traders are admitted onto the floor of the London Stock Exchange.

The Sunshine Showdown

Number-one-ranked heavyweight boxer George Foreman and heavyweight champion Joe Frazier slug it out on 22nd January in Kingston, Jamaica in a bid to become WBA, WBC and The Ring champion. Foreman overpowers Frazier who hits the canvas six times in just two rounds before the match is stopped and Foreman declared the winner.

DOMESTIC NEWS

IRA bombs England

1973 sees the trouble in Northern Ireland spread to London and Manchester, with a series of bombings taking place across the country. Thirteen bombs are planted in the capital, ten of which detonate. These include bombs at Whitehall and the Old Bailey, and in stations such as Victoria, King's Cross and Euston, injuring over 60 people. In March, a referendum on sovereignty in Northern Ireland sees 98.9% of voters choose to remain within the UK, although turn-out for Catholics is less than 1%.

European Economic Community

1st January 1973 Britain enters the EEC alongside fellow new members Ireland and Denmark.

Everton shelled by Iceland

26 May 1973 British Trawler Everton refuses to follow instructions from the Icelandic Coast Guard and is shelled as it flees to the protection of British Navy ship HMS Jupiter. This latest incident in the Second Cod War precedes a number of escalations and collisions throughout the year before an agreement is signed in November bringing the conflict to an end.

London Bridge opens

17th March 1973 The newly completed London Bridge, at least the fourth to stand on the site, is opened by Her Majesty the Queen. Traffic flows over the newly widened bridge, reducing the congestion that has been prevalent in the city since the old bridge was dismantled in 1968.

Secondary banking crisis

The country's economic problems continues in 1973, as the end of the year witnesses the start of the secondary banking crisis, which would last into 1974. The sharp drop in property prices and an increase in interest rates threatens many secondary lending banks with bankruptcy.

8 APR 1973

Jackie Stewart wins the BRDC International Trophy at Silverstone.

18 MAY 1973

Soviet party leader Leonid Brezhnev visits West Germany.

24 JUN 1973

90-year-old Eamon de Valera, the world's oldest head of state, resigns as President of Ireland.

New radio stations

8th October 1973 The London Broadcasting Company (photo David Jessel) begins broadcasting and becomes the first commercial independent radio station to operate legally within the UK. LBC's talk radio content is followed eight days later by the launch of Capital Radio, which focuses on music programming.

Value added tax

1st April 1973 Value added tax replaces purchase tax in the UK. Unlike its predecessor, VAT is applied at the point of sale, not at the point of manufacture, and is fixed at 10%. Purchase tax had varied based on the perceived luxuriousness of the goods in question, from 13% for small items, up to 55% for purchases such as motor vehicles.

Oil crisis

4th November 1973 Angered by western support for Israel in the Yom Kippur War, the Organization of the Petroleum Exporting Countries (OPEC) hits back by raising prices and reducing supplies, triggering an oil crisis with huge consequences for all western economies, forcing the introduction of petrol rationing by some and pushing up material and transport costs.

Pizza Hut opens

American restaurant chain Pizza Hut opens its first UK branch in Islington, London. Pizza Hut expands to offer a variety of branches, from diner-style restaurants to take-away premises, and quickly becomes a firm high street favourite.

ROYALTY & POLITICS

Princess Anne marries at the Abbey

On 14th November, the same day as her brother Prince Charles turns twenty-five, Princess Anne marries Captain Mark Phillips at Westminster Abbey wearing a medieval-style gown and Queen Mary's fringe tiara.

Queen opens Opera House of Oz

During a tour of Australia, on 20th October, the Queen opens the Sydney Opera House.

Tory sex scandals

Government ministers Lord Lambton and Earl Jellicoe both resign this year after the secret service discover their associations with prostitutes. The story breaks when photographs of Lambton are sold to the papers.

1 JUL 1973

A merger of the British Museum Library and the National Lending Library for Science & Technology at Boston Spa, creates the British Library.

15 AUG 1973

Sitcom *Man About the House* starring Richard O'Sullivan begins on ITV.

3 SEP 1973

Death of J. R. R. Tolkien, scholarly creator of 'Lord of the Rings'.

1973

FOREIGN NEWS

LBJ dies
22nd January 1973 Lyndon Baines Johnson, 36th President of the US, dies at his Texas home aged 64.

'Peace with honour'
27th January 1973 US President Richard Nixon signs the Paris Peace Accords. The historic agreement with the governments of North and South Vietnam ensures a temporary ceasefire, after which US troops will withdraw.

Skylab
14th May 1973 Skylab, the US space station, is launched. Three extended manned missions are completed aboard the station by the end of November.

Watergate rumbles on
16th July 1973 The revelation that President Nixon has been secretly recording conversations in the Oval Office opens a whole new avenue of investigation into the Watergate burglary and whether he knew of it or approved it. The newly convened US Senate Watergate Committee demands access to the tapes and Nixon refuses.

Mobile calling
3rd April 1973 Inventor Martin Cooper makes the very first cell phone call with a prototype of the Motorola DynaTAC, a 2.5lb cordless phone connected to an antenna on the roof of the hotel across the street. Cheekily, Cooper calls a major competitor to report that Motorola has succeeded in making mobile phone calls.

WOULD YOU BUY A USED CAR FROM HIM?

Yom Kippur War
6th October 1973 On Israel's holiest day, Yom Kippur, Egypt and Syria launch a surprise attack to recapture the territories lost in the Six-Day War in 1967. Egyptian troops cross the Suez Canal and enter the Sinai Desert as Syria retakes the Golan Heights. Israel launches a counter-offensive and pushes the Egyptians back across the Suez Canal. On 24th October, when Israeli troops are within one hundred kilometres of Cairo, the US presses Israel to sign an armistice.

Picasso
8th April 1973 Pablo Picasso dies at the age of 91. He was the founder of cubism and creator of masterpieces such as *Guernica*, depicting the German-Italian bombardment of the city during the Spanish Civil War.

17 OCT 1973
The price of oil increases by 70% leading to rocketing petrol prices and pressure on the UK economy.

1 NOV 1973
Final issue of the underground, counterculture magazine *Oz* is published.

5 DEC 1973
50mph speed limits put in place on UK roads in a bid to save fuel.

Dictator Pinochet

11th September 1973 With CIA support, General Augusto Pinochet stages a military coup against Chile's socialist President Salvador Allende. The object is to ensure that the country will not be the next domino to fall to communism. During the coup, the presidential palace is bombed and Allende is killed. Pinochet's tenure as President is vicious and uncompromising.

High, wide and handsome

It's a giddy year for architecture as dazzling new structures are unveiled in different parts of the world. The Sears Tower in Chicago becomes the world's tallest building at 442 metres. The iconic Sydney Opera House is opened by Queen Elizabeth II. In Istanbul, the Bosphorus Bridge connects Europe and Asia for the first time across the Bosphorus Strait. But the new buildings of most long-term significance are the twin towers of the new World Trade Center: construction has taken ten years and final costs are estimated at $900 million.

ETA attacks

20th December 1973 Luis Carrero Blanco, General Franco's (photo) Prime Minister and right-hand man, is killed in a bomb attack by the Basque separatist movement ETA.

Kissinger controversy

10th December 1973 The most surprising and controversial award in the history of the Nobel Prize is made as US Secretary of State Henry Kissinger and North Vietnamese negotiator Le Duc Tho are jointly awarded the Nobel Prize for Peace. Kissinger is widely seen as a power broker who has acted with a consistent disregard for democracy and human rights. Tho declines the prize but Kissinger accepts.

DO YOU REMEMBER THIS?

Fisher Price Tree-house

1973

ENTERTAINMENT

Delia's Debut
After appearing in the cookery slot on East Anglia Television's *Look East* programme, Delia Smith fronts her own BBC1 programme, *Family Fare*, which is first broadcast on 15th May. She writes several successful cookbooks this decade including 1978's best-selling *Complete Cookery Course* and is rapidly on track to become the doyenne of British food writers and television cooks.

Teddy Edward
Based on the books by Mollie and Patrick Edward, *Teddy Edward* is a gentle tale of a toy bear and his friends, told through still photographs and narrated by Richard Baker. It begins on BBC1 on 5th January.

Game of the Year
The game Mastermind, which pits code-maker against code-breaker, with the help of a series of coloured, plastic pegs, is announced as Game of the Year. First launched in 1970, Mastermind has huge international success selling 30 million during the decade.

Big biba
Biba moves into the old seven-storey Derry and Tom's store in Kensington High Street. 'Big' Biba is a phenomenon, offering the complete Biba lifestyle and becoming London's second-biggest tourist attraction after the Tower of London.

Let's do the time warp
Richard O'Brien's musical fantasy, *The Rocky Horror Show*, opens at the 63-seat performance space, Royal Court Theatre Upstairs on 19th June. Made on a shoe-string budget, with costumes begged, borrowed and adapted, *The Rocky Horror Show* takes inspiration from old Hollywood sci-fi B-movies, goth horror and burlesque and blends it with a witty and knowingly camp celebration of seventies sexual fluidity. The production later moves to the King's Road Theatre where it continues until 1979. With the release of a 1975 film, *The Rocky Horror Picture Show*, this wickedly wacky musical gains a loyal, global following cementing Rocky Horror's status as a cult classic.

Charley says...
Kids in 1973 are kept safe from daily hazards with the help of Tony and his pet cat Charley, whose feline wisdom warns against going off with strangers or playing with matches. Charley's meowed advice is in fact the voice of radio DJ Kenny Everett.

The Wicker Man

A folk horror about paganism and sacrifice, *The Wicker Man*, released 6th December, is British film-making at its most weird and inventive. The sacrificial target in question is Edward Woodward, playing a devoutly Christian police officer who travels to a remote Scottish island in search of a missing girl, only to discover the inhabitants are fully-fledged pagans under the patriarchal leadership of Christopher Lee's fiendish Lord Summerisle. The film's horrifying climax goes on to have a wide-ranging cultural impact.

Wheely, wheely funny

Half man, half walking disaster, Frank Spencer, of *Some Mothers Do 'Ave 'Em*, goes to a roller disco and finds himself accidentally flying through the exit doors and dodging the traffic of Edmonton in the episode 'Fathers' Clinic' which airs on 20th December. Michael Crawford, who plays the luckless, neurotic but ultimately adorable Spencer (ably supported by Michele Dotrice as wife Betty), performs all his own stunts in the series.

Lizzie Dripping

In East Midlands dialect, 'Lizzie Dripping' is a term for a girl with an overly active imagination and a tendency to tell fibs. Prolific children's author Helen Cresswell uses this as the premise for a children's drama serial, which begins on BBC1 on 13th March. Cresswell's main character, Penelope Arbuckle, is a typical 'Lizzie Dripping' who discovers a mischievous witch in her village. Of course, only Lizzie can see her. Tina Heath who plays Lizzie goes on to become *Blue Peter*'s tenth presenter in 1979.

Away you go!

We Are the Champions, presented by Ron Pickering, begins on BBC1 on 13th June - an inter-school competition which is 70% school sports day and 30% *It's a Knockout*. The highlight of every episode comes after the swimming races when Pickering shouts, 'Away you go!' and the kids forget their savage rivalry and dive bomb into the pool en masse. Joyful chaos.

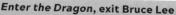

Enter the Dragon, exit Bruce Lee

On 20th July, Bruce Lee, legendary martial arts expert and actor, is found dead in his Hong Kong hotel room of cerebral edema. He is just 32. Lee's last film, *Enter the Dragon*, acquires almost mythological status when it is released a month after his death, becoming the highest-grossing martial arts film of all time.

Petrifying puppets

The hallowed halls of children's TV puppetry welcome a number of strange new arrivals this year. *Pipkins* (photo) introduces attention-seeking Hartley Hare along with a motley selection of animal friends all of whom have a different regional accent. Pig is a Brummie, Mrs Penguin a Geordie and the blank-eyed, frankly petrifying Topov the Monkey is a Cockney. If the *Pipkins* posse wasn't odd enough, then over at *Hickory House*, which first broadcasts on 12th March, there is sleepy, banana-guzzling Humphrey the Cushion, and a red-nosed, obsessively houseproud kitchen mop called Dusty Mop!

Wholegrain nostalgia

Ridley Scott directs a TV commercial for Hovis bread that strikes a chord with nostalgic Brits. Showing a boy pushing a bike up a cobbled hill (the famously picturesque Gold Hill in Shaftesbury) to the strains of Dvorak's *New World Symphony* played with mournful tones by the Ashington Colliery Brass Band, the tune will forever more be known as 'the Hovis tune' and the advert is later voted the UK's favourite of all time in a 2006 poll.

Pucker up

The lip balm revolution begins when skincare company Bonne Bell develop a special balm to help protect skiers' lips. Before long the balm is sold in a range of sickly flavours for the teen market under the name Lip Smackers.

Why Don't You?

Why don't you just switch off television set and go out and do something less boring instead? That is the rather ironic question posed by the opening credits of *Why Don't You*, which becomes a fixture of morning telly through the school summer holidays as of 20th August 1973.

 MUSIC

Guess the subject

January 1973 Peaking at No. 3 in the UK, Carly Simon's *You're So Vain* has everybody guessing who she has in mind. The betting is on infamous womaniser Warren Beatty but could it be Mick Jagger, who can be heard on backing vocals?

On the dark side

1st March 1973 Pink Floyd release *The Dark Side of the Moon*, an album exploring the theme of madness that has taken over a year to record and fine-tune. Their most emotional work, it propels them into the big league of British bands in the US, where it spends over 730 weeks in the LP chart.

Tubular Bells

25th May 1973 The first release from Richard Branson's new Virgin record label is Mike Oldfield's *Tubular Bells*. It's a mesmeric, slow-building 50-minute work featuring scores of overdubs by Oldfield playing different instruments and narration by Viv Stanshall of the Bonzo Dog Doo Dah Band. The album is not only a surprise hit, its main theme is heard in *The Exorcist*.

Second time unlucky

7th April 1973 Ever hopeful, Cliff Richard has another go at winning Eurovision with *Power to All Our Friends*. He comes third. Anne Marie David wins it for Luxembourg with *Wonderful Dream*.

Join the love train!

24th March 1973 Philadelphia soulsters the O'Jays invite the people of every nation to join hands and form a *Love Train*. The song's mentions of Egypt, Israel, Russia and China catalogue the enmities that characterise global politics in 1973. Hopelessly idealistic, *Love Train* makes the world seem just a little more jolly.

Yellow ribbons

21st April 1973 At No. 1 in the UK is the year's biggest-selling global hit. Dawn's *Tie A Yellow Ribbon Round The Old Oak Tree* is a story song that resonates with returning servicemen from prison camps in Vietnam who really are welcomed home by yellow ribbons.

Rhymin' Simon

6th May 1973 Paul Simon starts his first solo tour since splitting with Art Garfunkel to promote *There Goes Rhymin' Simon*, an album embracing gospel, reggae and doo-wop styles and including his comment on Watergate malaise, *American Tune*.

Bowie and Reed

3rd July 1973 David Bowie announces his retirement from live performing but his real aim is to abandon his alter ego stage creations, Ziggy Stardust and Aladdin Sane. His skills as a producer benefit Velvet Underground founder Lou Reed, whose *Transformer* takes him from cult figure to major star. Amazingly, iconic track *Walk on the Wild Side* is added to the Radio 1 playlist, despite clear references to cross-dressing, drugs and oral sex.

Suzi Q

Under the Chinnichap banner, songwriting team Nicky Chinn and Mike Chapman and veteran producer Mickie Most deliver hit after hit for Sweet, Mud, Suzi Quatro and more. Suzi is a leather-clad, bass-playing rock'n'roller from Detroit whose sound is pared-down and punky. It's no wonder that she'll be chosen to play streetwise Leather Truscadero in the 1950s-set US TV comedy *Happy Days*.

Stevie feels the sunshine

6th August 1973 Stevie Wonder lies in a coma for four days after a car accident in North Carolina but returns to live performing within weeks. Having won full creative freedom from Motown, his albums retain the soulful accessibility of earlier records but are now explorative, innovatory and deeply philosophical. When asked by an interviewer how he can write *You Are the Sunshine of My Life* when he has never seen the Sun, he explains 'but I can feel it, man'.

MY FIRST 18 YEARS
TOP10 1973

1. **Superstition** *Stevie Wonder*
2. **Stuck in the Middle with You** *Stealers Wheel*
3. **Nutbush City Limits** *Ike and Tina Turner*
4. **Loving and Free** *Kiki Dee*
5. **Like Sister and Brother** *The Drifters*
6. **Goodbye Yellow Brick Road** *Elton John*
7. **Live and Let Die** *Paul McCartney and Wings*
8. **Roll Away the Stone** *Mott the Hoople*
9. **See My Baby Jive** *Wizzard*
10. **Reelin' in the Years** *Steely Dan*

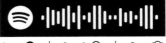

Open | Search | Scan

Slade stalled

4th July 1973 With a US tour beckoning, Slade drummer Don Powell is seriously injured in a car crash that kills his girl-friend. The band opt to stay in the UK and help him learn to play the drums again. They return to form in December with the song that Noddy Holder will call his pension because it is released year after year - *Merry Xmas Everybody*. Recorded during a New York heatwave, it brings much-needed hope and fun to a nation about to knuckle down to a three-day week.

Golden oldies

7th July 1973 As the Carpenters proclaim it's *Yesterday Once More*, the hits of 1973 prove their point. There are revivals and comebacks galore, by Neil Sedaka, the Drifters, Perry Como, Ike and Tina Turner and many more, while TV-advertised compilations of past hits clog the album charts and 'golden oldie' radio explodes in the US. Roy Wood's new band Wizzard bring back the Phil Spector wall of sound, 10cc recall the Beach Boys on *The Dean and I*, while David Essex stars as a would-be early 1960s rock star in the film *That'll Be The Day* and storms the chart with *Rock On*, which name-checks James Dean and blue suede shoes.

Walrus of Love

After working for years as an arranger and producer, the rotund Barry White has become an unlikely superstar and sex icon. His every record is soaked in lush orchestrations and bass rhythms as belly-deep as his voice.

SPORT

Sunday league

In 1974, Sundays are still viewed as a day of rest. But an energy crisis caused by spiralling oil costs and a strike by the National Union of Mineworkers is the catalyst for the introduction of Sunday football league matches this year. With Edward Heath's three-day week affecting the UK in the first two months of the year, energy saving measures are crucial, including daytime matches that require no floodlights. The first Sunday match is played between Millwall and Fulham at The Den at 11:30am on 20th January. Millwall wins 1-0.

Rumble in the Jungle

The long-awaited and much-hyped fight between champion heavyweight George Foreman and Muhammad Ali takes place in Kinshasa, Zaire on 30th October. Foreman's heft and power is more than matched by Ali's clever tactics, including his dope-and-rope technique, and after eight rounds, Foreman is floored by a straight punch to the face from Ali. The fight attracts an estimated global audience of one billion and is considered one of the greatest sporting moments of all time.

DO YOU REMEMBER THIS?

Monchichi monkey

Nude interruption

A streaker makes the front pages after he runs onto the pitch stark naked at Twickenham on 20th April during a friendly rugby international between England and France. The man had made the streak for a £10 bet after drinking several pints of lager. The police officers who catch up with him cover his genitals with a helmet before carting him off to Twickenham magistrates' court (where his £10 bet is immediately handed over as a fine for 'insulting behaviour'). He returns to the ground as one of the founding fathers of a streaking craze which continues throughout the 70s and beyond.

1 JAN 1974

News Year's Day becomes a public holiday for the first time.

1 FEB 1974

Ronnie Biggs, one of the perpetrators of the Great Train Robbery is arrested in Brazil.

6 MAR 1974

Miners' strike ends after a 35% wage increase is agreed and two days later, the UK returns to a five-day working week.

Love match

There is romance in the air at Wimbledon this year when American golden couple Jimmy Connors and Chris Evert arrive at the tournament engaged to be married. When they each win the singles title, it seems like the perfect outcome. At the Wimbledon Champions' Dinner the pair dance to 'The Girl That I Marry' but in October, they break off their engagement, deciding that tennis must come before love.

Conteh the champion

Liverpudlian John Conteh becomes WBC World Light Heavyweight Champion after defeating Jorge Ahumada at the Empire Pool, London on 1st October. It's an excellent year for Conteh, who not only has an episode of *This Is Your Life* dedicated to him, but also wins the second series of masters of sport TV competition *Superstars*.

Flixborough Disaster

1st June 1974 The chemical industry reels as news breaks of an explosion at a chemical plant near the village of Flixborough, North Lincolnshire. Faulty, modified equipment leads to a large cloud of hydrogen leaking and igniting, killing 28 people and injuring 36 more. There is a national outcry over the event, which occurs as a new Health and Safety at Work Act is passed through Parliament.

DOMESTIC NEWS

Three-day week

1st January 1974 Coal shortages caused by industrial action lead to a reduction in the generation of electricity, with Prime Minister Edward Heath introducing the three-day working week. Businesses are limited to three consecutive days of electricity consumption in a seven-day period. It lasts until 7th March.

First McDonald's

13th November 1974 Britain gets its first McDonald's restaurant, in Woolwich, southeast London. Soon the restaurant chain begins to compete with established brands like Wimpy, and the so-called 'Golden Arches' become a familiar site on British high streets.

Oil embargo ends

18th March 1974 The Organisation of Arab Petroleum Exporting Countries finally lift their embargo on oil exports to the United Kingdom, relieving the pressure on the fuel shortages felt across the country.

2 APR 1974

Tatum O'Neil, aged 10, becomes youngest recipient of an Academy Award for Best Supporting Actress.

6 MAY 1974

Chancellor Willy Brandt resigns amidst controversy over his aide's ties with the Stasi.

13 JUN 1974

Prince Charles makes his maiden speech in the House of Lords.

Red Lion Square
15th June 1974 Members of the National Front marching through London clash with counter-protesters in Red Lion Square. Individuals representing the International Marxist Group charge a police cordon separating them from the marchers, and riots break out. In the melee twenty-year-old student Kevin Gately is killed.

Ceefax launched
23rd September 1974 The BBC launches Ceefax, a pun on the words 'see facts', as the first teletext service in the world. Starting with 30 pages, viewers can use their television remotes to type in a page number before viewing useful information on a variety of topics

Economic trouble
Economic trouble for the UK continues throughout 1974. Aside from the strikes and the three-day week implemented in January, figures launched at the beginning of the year show the country had entered its first post-war recession at the end of 1973. Inflation reaches a 34 year high of 17.2%.

Lord Lucan disappears!
7th November 1974 London is rocked by the disappearance of Lord Lucan, following the murder of the children's nanny. Lucan's wife is found injured, claiming that her husband has attacked her and murdered the nanny. Lucan's car is found abandoned and stained with blood, and the peer disappears, never to be heard from again.

The Birmingham Six
21st November 1974 The bombing of two pubs in Birmingham kills 21 people and is the single most deadly attack on the country since the end of the Second World War. Six Irish men are arrested almost immediately amid concerns the IRA is to blame and undergo brutal treatment at the hands of the police. Their conviction, on flawed evidence, becomes one of the country's most famous miscarriages of justice.

The Troubles
Trouble in Northern Ireland continues as the collapse of the Sunnydale agreement leads to the re-establishment of direct rule. 1974 sees many bombings across the country, including the M62 massacre which kills 12 people. Bombs in the summer detonate in Dublin and Monaghan planted by the Ulster Volunteer Force, and in London at the Houses of Parliament and the Tower of London by the IRA. October brings the Guildford pub bombings, killing five, and an attack on Brook's club in London. Sports Minister Denis Howell's family survive a car bomb, and the home of Edward Heath is targeted.

3 JUL 1974
Long-standing Leeds United coach Don Revie accepts £200,000 to become the new England manager.

29 AUG 1974
Hippies and police clash when the latter try to close down the illegal, Windsor Free Festival.

14 SEP 1974
Giant pandas Chia-Chia and Ching-Ching arrive at London Zoo, the result of a diplomatic deal with China brokered by Edward Heath.

ROYALTY & POLITICS

The balance of power
Juggling several crises and locked in a battle with trade unions, a beleaguered Edward Heath calls a General Election for 28th February to secure a new mandate for his policies. His gamble backfires and he resigns, and Harold Wilson returns as Labour Prime Minister. Labour wins a second election on 11th October with a tiny majority of just three seats. It is the first time since 1910 that two general elections have been held in one year.

Attempted kidnapping
20th March 1974 Princess Anne narrowly escapes a kidnapping as she and husband Captain Mark Philips wrestle with attacker Ian Bail. Bail stops the Princess's car and shoots her driver and protection officer, before attempting to drag her from the vehicle. He is foiled by intervening citizens and the timely arrival of the police, despite shooting a police officer and a member of the public. No one is killed, and Bail is detained under the Mental Health Act.

Death of the Duke of Gloucester
Henry, Duke of Gloucester, uncle to the Queen and the last surviving son of George V, dies on 10th June at his home, Barnwell Manor, following a period of ill health.

Hover bother
During his General Election campaign, Liberal leader Jeremy Thorpe tours the coastal towns of south-west Britain via hovercraft, the transport mode of the moment.

FOREIGN NEWS

Worst air disaster
3rd March 1974 The highest fatalities to date in an air disaster occur when the rear cargo hatch of a DC-10 of Turkish Airlines Flight 981 flies open over Meaux, France. The sudden pressure difference causes the hull to burst and all 340 passengers and crew are killed instantly.

Terracotta Army
29th March 1974 A magnificently preserved Terracotta Army of life-size figures is discovered at Xi'an in China. The sculptures date from 210-209 BC and were buried with the body of Emperor Qin Shi Huang to protect him in the afterlife. The three pits in which they are found contain more than 8,000 soldiers, 130 chariots with 520 horses, and 150 cavalry horses.

16 OCT 1974
Riots break out at the Maze prison in Belfast.

27 NOV 1974
The Prevention of Terrorism Act is passed giving police special powers when they suspect terrorism.

22 DEC 1974
The London home of Conservative party leader and ex-PM Edward Heath is bombed by the Provisional IRA.

Golf launch
30th March 1974 A worthy successor to the immensely popular but outdated Beetle rolls off the Volkswagen production line at Wolfsburg. An affordable small family hatchback, the first Golf model sells around thirty million.

Four billion
1st April 1974 The US Census Bureau calculates that for the first time there are more than four billion people on the planet - a doubling of the world's population since 1930.

Pompidou est mort, Brandt tritt zurück
April - May 1974 Within a month, Europe loses two of its most effective political leaders. French President Georges Pompidou dies aged 62 having initiated the large-scale industrialisation of France. On 6th May, West German Chancellor Willy Brandt resigns with his secretary revealed as an East German spy and the oil crisis threatening his social reforms.

Rubik's cube
19th May 1974 Hungarian mathematician Ernő Rubik has a question: 'How can I make part of an object move without the whole object falling apart?' He builds a cube to answer that question and shows it to his students. Put into mass production, it becomes one of the biggest fads of the 1970s and 1980s.

Nixon resigns
9th August 1974 Facing impeachment over his role in the Watergate burglary and subsequent cover-up, President Richard Nixon announces his resignation. The final straw was the US Supreme Court decision the day before to order the release of tapes of Oval Office conversations. He is succeeded by his Vice President Gerald Ford, who pardons Nixon for any federal offences he might have committed. Nixon is the first US President to resign from office.

Haile Selassie deposed
12th September 1974 After more than 700 years, the Ethiopian Empire comes to an end. Plagued by famine and economic malaise, citizens strike in protest against Emperor Haile Selassie. The army and police seize their opportunity, place Haile Selassie under house arrest and take power.

Perón dead
1st July 1974 General Perón, stripped of power by a coup in 1955, returns to Argentina from exile with his wife Isabel and is elected President for the third time. Two days later, he suffers a fatal heart attack and Isabel assumes the presidency.

PLO recognized

1st October 1974 The Palestine Liberation Organisation is recognised by the UN and the Arab League as the representative of the Palestinian people. PLO leader Yasser Arafat addresses the UN: 'Today I came with an olive branch and the weapon of the freedom fighter. Don't let the olive branch fall from my hands.'

Lucy in the ground

24th November 1974 Bones of a 3.2 million year old hominid are found in Ethiopia. The fossil is named Lucy, after the Beatles song *Lucy in the Sky with Diamonds*. Lucy, probably 1.10 metres tall and weighing 29 kilos when alive, is the oldest two-legged animal ever recovered and one of the most important excavations in history.

ENTERTAINMENT

Paint the whole world with a rainbow

Geoffrey Hughes, who has been a jobbing actor in dramas like *Z Cars* and *Dixon of Dock Green*, joins the Thames Television children's programme *Rainbow* this year and now spends his days with a large, absent-minded bear called Bungle, a sheepish pink hippo called George, and Zippy, a talkative orange creature of indistinct species. Over the next eighteen years, Geff-wee (as George pronounces it) takes on the role of teacher, parent, and peacekeeper to his furry, fuzzy colleagues.

The Flake girl

Since the 1960s, the TV commercials for Cadbury's Flake have focused on the sensual, languorous pleasure of solo chocolate consumption, with a succession of Flake girls showing us how it's done.

'Just an old, saggy cloth cat'

Bagpuss, is first shown on BBC1 on 12th February. Full of gentle, old-world charm, the inhabitants of a Victorian shop run by a little girl called Emily, come to life whenever she brings a new thing to be repaired. It's Bagpuss, a plump, quizzical-looking pink and white striped cat who is the catalyst for the others to wake; a woodpecker bookend called Professor Yaffle, Madeleine the doll, Gabriel the toad and his banjo, and an army of industrious little mice. A 1999 poll votes *Bagpuss* the UK's favourite children's programme.

Tiswas - Saturday morning mayhem

Saturday mornings are never the same again after *Tiswas* begins on 5th January on ITV. *Tiswas*, which comes from ATV's Birmingham studios, is chaotic, subversive and a bit rebellious with a gaggle of hyperactive presenters including Chris Tarrant and Sally James, who embrace the custard pies and slapstick, the buckets of water, mischief and mayhem. Bad jokes and impressions are provided by Bob Carolgees and Spit the dog and local comedian Lenny Henry, while Spike Milligan and Jasper Carrot are two more names who often pop up to join in the anarchic fun.

Goodnight, John Boy

Already a huge hit in America, *The Waltons* comes to the UK this year, airing on BBC2 on 18th February. The Waltons - seven siblings, Ma and Pa, Grandma and Grandpa - live in Depression-era Virginia, run a sawmill, wear mainly denim dungarees and every night insist on calling goodnight to each other as they turn out their lights. It's an unapologetic slice of very sweet American apple pie and Britain adores it.

Kubrick withdraws *Clockwork Orange*

When Stanley Kubrick's *A Clockwork Orange* was re-leased in cinemas in 1971, the film's controversial themes and 'ultraviolence' divided opinion. But following a spate of re-al-life crimes which some argue are strongly influenced by the rapes and murders depicted in the film, Kubrick and his family begin to receive death threats. In an unprecedented example of self-censorship, he insists Warner Broth-ers withdraw the film from circulation in the UK. *A Clockwork Orange* remains an underground cult movie until it is once again permitted general release in 2000, a year after Kubrick's death.

Roobarb (and Custard)

Roobarb bounces onto television screens for the first time on 21st October on BBC1 in a cartoon perfectly capturing the uni-versally recognised differences between cats and dogs. Roobarb is an exuberant green dog, and his rival, the laid-back Custard, is a puce-coloured cat who spends most his days calculating how to get the better of Roobarb.

Opportunity Knocks for Lena

Diminutive Italian-Scottish singing sensa-tion Lena Zavaroni, aged ten, appears on Hughie Green's talent show, *Opportunity Knocks* and becomes the only contestant to win five weeks in a row. Her version of 'Ma - He's Making Eyes at Me' becomes a chart hit for her at the age of thirteen.

Baker Who?

Doctor Who number four is intro-duced to audiences for the first time on 28th December in an episode called 'Robot'. Tom Baker's Doctor wears a floppy hat, an unfeasibly long stripey scarf, has a penetrating gaze and seems quite excitable. It doesn't take long to win viewers round and for many, Baker remains the definitive Doctor Who, delighting many middle-aged fans when he appears in the show's 50th anniversary special, 'Day of the Doctor' in 2014.

Miss Pears turns 21

Pears Soap celebrates the 21st birthday of its famous Miss Pears competition by inviting all the past winners to a special party. Since 1958, hopeful parents around the country submit photographs of their offspring each year for this highly-pub-licised contest in which one little girl is chosen to be the face and brand ambas-sador for the classic glycerine soap.

Hysteria and tragedy at Cassidy concert

26th May 1974 Fourteen-year old Bernadette Whelan dies in a hysterical stampede at a David Cassidy concert at White City Stadium in London. The incident has a profound effect on the singer, who quits live performing and his *Partridge Family TV show*.

Smash hit

Instant mash brand Smash score a smash hit with a TV advertising campaign created by ad agency BMP DDB, featuring metallic aliens chortling over the primitive and labour-intensive way in which earthlings peel and boil their potatoes. 'Get Mash, Get Smash' is the advertising jingle on everyone's lips and the Smash Aliens go on to be voted among the top UK advertisements of all time by the public and advertising industry alike.

Bedsits and Beckinsale

September treats TV viewers to the launch of not one but two winning sitcoms. ITV's *Rising Damp* starts on 2nd September, with Leonard Rossiter playing Rigsby, the miserly landlord of a creaking Victorian townhouse, whose bedsits are occupied by Richard Beckinsale's medical student, a suave Don Warrington and Frances de la Tour as the romantic spinster Miss Jones, with whom Rigsby is besotted. On BBC1 on 5th September, Beckinsale appears a second time this week as Lennie Godber, the cell mate of Ronnie Barker's Norman Stanley Fletcher ('Fletch') in prison comedy *Porridge*.

Good clean fun?

Robin Askwith puts on his best cheeky chappie persona as he takes on the role of disaster-prone window cleaner, Timothy Lea, who spends more time in bed with his customers than he does actually cleaning their windows. *Confessions of a Window Cleaner*, releaed 16th August, treads a fine line between sauce and soft porn but the promise of lewd slapstick, full frontal female nudity, and constant views of Askwith's derrière somehow compels people to see it.

Head-swivelling horror

When William Friedkin's film *The Exorcist* is released in UK cinemas on 14th March, its reputation precedes it, with reports of American audiences suffering shock, fainting and vomiting after witnessing the terrifying demonic possession of twelve-year-old Regan MacNeil, played by Linda Blair. There has never been a horror like *The Exorcist*; seeing it becomes a test of bravery and endurance.

MUSIC

Streets of London

30th January 1974 Singer-songwriter Ralph McTell packs London's Royal Albert Hall on his first headlining appearance. Croydon-born Ralph is best known for the contemporary folk standard *Streets of London*, which he wrote in 1968. He has a surprise hit with the song over Christmas 1974 when its no-room-at-the-inn sentiments strike a chord with a broader audience.

Queen on tour

1st March 1974 Queen headline their first UK tour. Initially regarded as yet another glam-rock outfit, they are starting to make a big impact as an album band thanks to Freddie Mercury's charismatic vocals and the uniquely sonorous, melody-driven guitar style of former astronomy student Brian May.

Dolly's debut year

21st April 1974 Country singer-songwriter Dolly Parton says goodbye to her long-time singing partner Porter Wagoner with the heartfelt *I Will Always Love You*. In her first solo year, Dolly tops the US country chart with this, *Jolene* and *Love is Like a Butterfly*.

Abba win Eurovision

6th April 1974 A landmark day in pop music as the Eurovision Song Contest - hosted by the UK at the Brighton Dome - introduces the world to Abba. Comprising two wonderfully costumed Swedish couples who sing in English, they win with *Waterloo*, written by members Bjorn Ulvaeus and Benny Andersson with producer Stig Anderson. It's the start of an incredible six years for the group who will be the world's leading singles act by 1980.

Northern soul

In industrial Lancashire, 'northern soul' rules. Fans and disc jockeys hunt out the best 1960s soul records from the US - the more obscure the better - and dance to them at 'all nighters' at venues such as Wigan Casino. It's now common for the tracks to be turned into national hits by radio play, as happens with R. Dean Taylor's *There's a Ghost in My House* and Robert Knight's *Love on a Mountaintop*.

Lennon's lost weekend

March 1974 Having parted from Yoko Ono and with the threat of deportation from the US hanging over him, a drunken John Lennon is thrown out of the Troubadour in Los Angeles. He is in the middle of what he will later call his 'lost weekend'; reconciliation with Yoko follows a Thanksgiving Night concert in New York in at which Lennon joins Elton John on stage.

Cass Elliot dies

29th July 1974 Aged just 32, the ebullient, wise-cracking Cass Elliot of the Mamas and the Papas dies in her sleep at Harry Nilsson's London flat, where she has been staying during an exhausting two-week spot at the London Palladium.

Reggae for it now

26th October 1974 Thanks to names like Desmond Dekker and Jimmy Cliff, Jamaican reggae is no stranger to the UK charts. A No. 1 is a rarity, however. *Everything I Own* by Kingston's Ken Boothe is a reggae version of a song by David Gates of Bread who wrote it as a tribute to his late father.

A song for Annie

12th October 1974 Best known for writing *Take Me Home Country Roads* and *Leavin' on a Jet Plane*, country-folk singer John Denver has his only UK chart hit - a No. 1 - with *Annie's Song*, dedicated to his wife of seven years.

Wailers 'too good'

Having been famously fired from supporting Sly and the Family Stone on tour for being too good, Bob Marley and the Wailers continue to nurture the US and UK markets with their reggae-rock fusion. Eric Clapton's chart-topping US cover of Marley's *I Shot the Sheriff* raises the band's profile despite the departures of key men Peter Tosh and Bunny Wailer.

MY FIRST 18 YEARS
TOP 10   1974

1. **Tiger Feet** *Mud*
2. **Jolene** *Dolly Parton*
3. **Rock Your Baby** *George McCrae*
4. **The Air That I Breathe** *The Hollies*
5. **Band on the Run** *Wings*
6. **Raised on Robbery** *Joni Mitchell*
7. **I Know What I Like (In Your Wardrobe)** *Genesis*
8. **Midnight at the Oasis** *Maria Muldaur*
9. **When Will I See You Again?** *The Three Degrees*
10. **Spiders and Snakes** *Jim Stafford*

Open 🟢 | Search 🔍 | Scan 📷

King of clubs

21st September 1974 Reaching the UK Top Ten is the runaway dance hit of the year, *Queen Of Clubs* by Miami-based showband KC and the Sunshine Band. KC (Howie Casey) is the man behind the airy production sound of the TK label, which has just sold a million with the slinky, sensuous *Rock Your Baby* by George McCrae (photo).

Wombled out

Bizarrely, the UK's leading chart act of 1974 is not a real group at all but the Wombles, who are songwriter Mike Batt and chums dressed in furry clothing. They follow up *The Wombling Song* with further variations on the wombling theme like *Remember You're A Womble*, *Wombling White Tie And Tails* and *Wombling Merry Christmas*.

SPORT

Fitness guru gets royal recognition

Fitness pioneer Eileen Fowler, who has inspired the nation to keep fit since the 1950s with her exercise programmes on radio, records, and TV, is awarded an MBE. Fowler continues to evangelise about the benefits of exercise and even after moving into a retirement home in her nineties, encourages other residents to join her in a daily fitness routine.

The Thrilla in Manila

In a decade defined by epic boxing confrontations, the Thrilla in Manila, between Muhammad Ali and Joe Frazier on 1st October, is perhaps the biggest and the most brutal. It's a gruelling, forty-two-minute marathon with temperatures reaching a muggy 49 degrees, as the two heavyweights slug it out in what is their third meeting. Ali prevails when Frazier's team stop the fight in the fourteenth round, the victory cementing his status as 'The Greatest'.

A

Terror on the terraces

Football hooliganism is rampant by the mid-1970s and has serious consequences for Leeds United who are defeated by Bayern Munich in the European Cup Final. Riots by Leeds fans break out during the match, triggered by a disallowed Peter Lorimer goal. The club is handed a four-year ban from European football which is reduced to two years after an appeal. Two years later, Liverpool is also banned from Europe after riots at a Cup Winners' Cup game against St. Etienne. The so-called 'English disease' will overshadow football for the next decade.

Arthur Ashe conquers Wimbledon

It's an all-American affair for the men's singles final at Wimbledon on 5th July as defending champion and favourite Jimmy Connors meets Arthur Ashe in the final. Ashe plays a perfect, tactical match, and when he beats Connors in four sets, he becomes (and remains) the only black man to win the Wimbledon as well as the US and Australian Open titles.

World Cup cricket

The cricket World Cup takes place in England from 7th to 21st June, the first major tournament in the history of one-day international cricket. The West Indies under Clive Lloyd emerge the victors.

2 JAN 1975

It is announced Charlie Chaplin will receive a knighthood in the New Year Honours.

26 FEB 1975

Off-duty Metropolitan Police officer Stephen Tibble, aged 22, is shot and killed at point blank range while pursuing a member of the Provisional IRA.

15 MAR 1975

The Army is drafted in to clear 70,000 tonnes of rubbish accumulated during a nine-week binmen's strike in Glasgow.

1975

New start for Martina in the States
Czech player and rising tennis star Martina Navratilova announces her defection from Czechoslovakia to the US.

Sobers becomes Sir
On 19th February, during her Commonwealth tour of the West Indies, the Queen knights cricket hero Gary Sobers at Bridgetown racecourse, in front of a crowd of 10,000 cheering Barbadians.

DOMESTIC
NEWS

WHERE IS THIS GIRL?

LESLEY WHITTLE
Born 3-6-57

Black Panther
14th January 1975
Headlines are dominated by the kidnapping of 17-year-old Leslie Whittle, an heiress taken from her home in Bridgnorth, Shropshire. The kidnapper demands a £50,000 ransom, but confusion regarding the kidnapper's instructions means it is never delivered. On 7th March her body is discovered, and the killer identified as the 'Black Panther', a serial burglar and murderer. Newspapers cover the investigation until Donald Nielson is arrested in December. He spends the rest of his life in prison.

Moorgate tube crash
28th February 1975
London is left reeling when a train entering its final stop at Moorgate underground station fails to slow down and collides with the end of the tunnel. 43 people are killed and 74 injured, prompting the introduction of an automatic system to slow speeding trains on the network, known as the 'Moorgate' protection.

MOORGATE

Local government in Scotland
16th May 1975 Following major changes to the administrative map in England the previous year, Scotland's local government areas are redrawn leading to the creation of nine new regions and a two-tier system of regions and districts.

DO YOU REMEMBER THIS?

Cassette carousel

Dibbles Bridge coach crash
27th May 1975 Tragedy strikes as the brakes fail on a coach carrying 45 female pensioners on a day trip to Grassington. The bus plunges off a bridge near Hebden, North Yorkshire, killing 33 and injuring everyone else on board.

International Women's Year
15th January 1975 The United Nations declares 1975 'International Women's Year' in the hope of prompting nations to examine inequality. In November, the UK introduces the Employment Protection Act, which establishes the provision of paid maternity leave, and in December the Sex Discrimination Act 1975 and Equal Pay Act 1970 come into force.

UNITED NATIONS 1975
INTERNATIONAL WOMENS YEAR

23 APR 1975
As South Vietnam falls to the Communists, the British Embassy in Saigon is closed and staff evacuated.

22 MAY 1975
One of Britain's leading sculptors, Barbara Hepworth, is killed in a fire at her St. Ives studio.

19 JUN 1975
Striking stable-boys march around the course at Royal Ascot on Gold Cup Day. They accept a 19% pay rise in July.

European Space Agency
31st May 1975 The UK becomes one of the ten founding members of the European Space Agency, which launches its first mission later in the year. The Cos-B space probe is launched to study sources of gamma radiation in the cosmos.

Snow in June
2nd June 1975 England is stunned when June brings unexpected snow showers. The brief flurries fall as far south as London, the first time the capital has seen snow in June in almost 200 years.

EEC referendum
5th June 1975 The country goes to the polls for a referendum on membership of the European Economic Community, which would later become the European Union. The 'Yes' vote is successful with 67% choosing to remain within the community.

The Spaghetti House siege
28th September 1975 The Spaghetti House restaurant in Knightsbridge, London, is robbed by three gunmen who take the staff hostage when the police are called. On the advice of psychologists, police allow the siege to continue for six days in the hope that the gunmen will feel sympathy for their hostages. Eventually, the gunmen release the staff and surrender.

Balcombe Street siege
6th December 1975 A year of continuing violence regarding Northern Ireland culminates with the Balcombe Street siege. After months of bombings in London, police give chase to four Provisional IRA operatives who had fired shots into a Mayfair restaurant. The chase ends with the operatives breaking into a flat and taking the two occupants hostage for six days, before eventually surrendering. Events are broadcast live on television across the country. Two of the operatives, Harry Duggan and Hugh Doherty, had been responsible for the assassination of Guinness Book of Records founder Ross McWhirter in November, after he had offered a reward for information about their activities.

First Ripper victim
30th October 1975 The murder of 28-year-old Wilma McCann in Leeds is the first in a string of killings committed by the so-called 'Yorkshire Ripper' Peter Sutcliffe. The search for the Yorkshire Ripper becomes one of the decades' biggest news stories.

18 JUL 1975
British racing driver Graham Hill announces his retirement from the sport. He is killed in an air crash on 29th November.

7 AUG 1975
Temperatures soar to 32 degrees centigrade in London, the highest recorded in 35 years.

19 SEP 1975
British Forces Broadcasting Services broadcasts television programmes for the first time from the Trenchard Barracks, Celle, near Hanover.

1975

ROYALTY & POLITICS

Thatcher becomes Tory leader
On 11th February, Margaret Thatcher, becomes the first woman leader of a British political party when she defeats four other (male) candidates with 146 out of 215 votes. 'I beat four chaps. Now let's get down to work,' says the 49-year-old mother of twins.

Politics on the radio
The idea of broadcasting Parliamentary proceedings has been resisted for some time but on 24th February, a Commons vote approves the presence of microphones in the chamber and in June, during a month-long experiment, Radio 4 listeners can hear for the first time what is debated in Westminster; Labour minister Tony Benn is the first MP to be heard. Permanent radio coverage of Parliament is introduced in 1978, but television must wait until November 1989.

Queen visits Japan
Thirty years after the end of the Second World War, the Queen makes the first state visit to Japan as the guest of Emperor Hirohito. She and the Duke of Edinburgh attend a welcome banquet on 7th May and they experience plenty of Japanese culture and tradition during the visit.

Order of the Bath anniversary
Prince Charles, sporting a moustache, is installed as Great Master of the Most Honourable Order of the Bath at Westminster Abbey on 25th May, in a service marking the 250th anniversary of the founding of the order by George I.

FOREIGN NEWS

Digital watches
Too expensive and out of reach for the average consumer, digital LED watches start to take off when Texas Instruments starts mass production in a plastic housing. These watches sell for $20 and cost half the price a year later.

Microsoft launch
4th April 1975 After developing an operating system called an interpreter for the Altair 8800, which makes the microcomputer interesting for hobby programmers, childhood friends Bill Gates and Paul Allen launch their own company. Allen coins the name 'Micro-Soft', short for 'microcomputer software'.

---

30 OCT 1975
A report is published stating that 6.5 million elm trees have been destroyed due to Dutch elm disease.

27 NOV 1975
Ross McWhirter, co-founder of the Guinness Book of World Records with his twin Norris, is shot and killed by the Provisional IRA.

25 DEC 1975
Heavy metal band Iron Maiden are formed in east London by bassist Steve Harris.

Fall of Saigon

30th April 1975 After nearly twenty years of fighting, North Vietnamese forces penetrate Saigon and 'liberate' the capital of South Vietnam. Without the support of the US, South Vietnam is lost. News cameras capture the mass panic of the final moments in the fall of Saigon, as desperate civilians mass around US helicopters sent to rescue the remaining American Embassy staff.

Khmer Rouge

17th April 1975 Despite three years of bombing by the US, the Khmer Rouge emerge victorious in the Cambodian civil war. On 17th April, their forces enter the capital Phnom Penh, where they expel the rulers and install dictator Pol Pot as leader. The stage set is set for one of the most brutal regimes in human history.

Carlos the Jackal

21st December 1975 With five accomplices, Venezuelan terrorist Ilich Ramírez Sánchez, nicknamed Carlos and called 'the Jackal' by the press, kidnaps delegates to the ministerial conference of the Organization of the Petroleum Exporting Countries (OPEC) in Vienna. They capture 60 and kill three. A day later, the hostage takers are given a free exit by plane to Algiers and Tripoli, where the hostages are freed in return for a ransom of more than $20 million.

Franco is dead

20th November 1975 After a three-week-long coma, Spain's fascist dictator General Francisco Franco dies. Two days after his death, the monarchy returns, as he had wished. But against expectations, King Juan Carlos pushes for reconciliation with the socialists, a return to democracy and more freedom for regions such as Catalonia and the Basque Country.

ENTERTAINMENT

High-rise horrors

'A night of blazing suspense' is perhaps an understatement for *The Towering Inferno*, a collaboration between Warner Bros. and Twentieth Century Fox based on two separate books about a skyscraper uncontrollably ablaze. This is the disaster movie to end all disaster movies and when it's released in the UK on 29th January, audiences flock to see not only the scorching special effects but an A-list cast who must find a way to escape as the flames lick at their heels. Who will survive, and who will get roasted? *The Towering Inferno* is 165 minutes of catastrophic, nail-biting conflagration and becomes the year's biggest box-office hit.

Six Million Dollar toys

The Six Million Dollar Man action figure is launched in the UK, based on the hit US TV series starring Lee Majors as NASA astronaut Steve Austin who is rebuilt with bionic body parts following a deadly crash. Now kids can have their own thirteen-inch-high Steve Austin, who comes wearing a natty red NASA tracksuit and sneakers. Steve can show off his power by lifting a car engine, you can look through his bionic eye via a hole in his head, and his rubber skin peels back to reveal those $6,000,000 bionics.

Shark attack

Jaws may be one of Stephen Spielberg's earliest films but his ability to keep the tension taut, and to play on audiences' fear of the unseen, turns it into a major movie event in the US this summer before it has its UK film premiere on Christmas Day. Roy Scheider, Richard Dreyfus and Robert Shaw do battle with an underwater menace terrorising the East Coast resort of Amity Island before it picks off any more of its swimmers for a mid-morning snack. The suspense is intensified by John Williams's menacing music, and brilliant lines like, 'We're gonna need a bigger boat.' *Jaws* becomes an instant classic.

Little House on the Prairie

Following on from the success of *The Waltons*, the next historical family drama from America to hit these shores (on 25th February) is *Little House on the Prairie*. Loosely based on the books by Laura Ingalls Wilder about growing up in the nineteenth-century Mid-West as a child of pioneer settlers, *Little House on the Prairie* isn't afraid to tackle some thorny subjects from racism to disability and has no qualms about tugging at viewers' heartstrings - many were moved to tears when Mary Ingalls wakes up to discover she has gone blind. It also fuels a growing taste for prairie style as frilled floral maxi dresses, patchwork bed covers and characters such as Hollie Hobbie gain in popularity.

Tune in to Doonican

Irish crooner Val Doonican, known for his easy manner, cosy cardigans, and relaxing rocking chair performances, returns to BBC1 on 24th May with *The Val Doonican Show* after several years at ATV (ITV). A regular on British TV screens since 1963, Doonican is comfortable with his uncool status, having sold millions of records including the completely unthreatening *Val Doonican Rocks, But Gently* in 1967.

Toffee transformation

Chewy sweets Toff-o-Lux are rebranded as Toffos this year, and if that wasn't enough to rattle toffee fans, they are also launched in a fruit-flavoured version featuring strawberry and banana toffees.

Music hall for the masses
The Good Old Days, a recreation for television of the late Victorian and Edwardian music hall, presented with great flourish by Leonard Sachs, and with songs and sketches performed in the style of greats like Marie Lloyd or Harry Lauder, began way back in 1953 and continues to enjoy a loyal following throughout its long, thirty-year run. The live audience is encouraged to dress up in costume and sing along at the end to 'The Old Bull and Bush'. During the 1970s, the waiting list to be part of that audience is 24,000.

The Good Life
The Good Life appears on our screens for the first time on 4th April, with Richard Briers and Felicity Kendal as Surbiton's ever-optimistic pioneers of suburban self-sufficiency, Tom and Barbara Good. The Good Life taps into – and encourages –a resurgence in growing your own vegetables, jam making and experimenting with homemade wine, but we tune in just as much to laugh at the barely suppressed snobbery and bemusement of socially mobile, kaftan-wearing neighbour Margo Leadbetter (a magnificent Penelope Keith) and her long-suffering husband Jerry (Paul Eddington).

Chop Phooey
'Who IS the superhero? Sarge? No. Rosemary? The telephone operator? No. Penry? The mild-mannered janitor? Could be!' Hong Kong Phooey karate chops his way onto British TV screens on 17th March, a canine crime-fighter full of enthusiasm but with ambitions far beyond his capabilities. He regularly has to stop to consult the 'Hong Kong Book of Kung Fu', and even his transformation into superhero is marred by getting stuck in a filing cabinet drawer. Thank goodness for Spot the cat (who is actually striped) who covers for his friend's incompetence with casual efficiency.

TV cops get tough
The Sweeney airs on ITV on 2nd January and introduces a whole new side of policing to the British public. This is no cosy drama along the lines of Dixon of Dock Green. Taking its title from Sweeney Todd, the Cockney rhyming slang for the Flying Squad, Detective Inspector Jack Regan (John Thaw) and Detective Sergeant George Carter (Dennis Waterman) tackle violent crime head on, frequently throwing out the rule book to bring hardened criminals to heel. Police slang terms are revealed (a 'snout' is an informer, a 'stoppo' is a getaway car), and with so much filming done on location around London, this is drama with a heavy dose of reality.

Trainspotting
Trainspotters and rail enthusiasts assemble as the National Railway Museum is opened in York this year. The first national museum outside of the capital, the National Railway Museum welcomes 2 million visitors in the first twelve months.

1975

Faultlessly Fawlty

In 1967, the Monty Python team stay at the Gleneagles Hotel in Torquay and are amused and fascinated by the hotel owner who John Cleese describes as 'the rudest man I have ever come across in my life'. That hotelier becomes the inspiration for Basil Fawlty, the misanthropic owner of *Fawlty Towers*, which begins on BBC2. Written by Cleese and his then-wife Connie Booth (who plays maid Polly), the pair spend weeks writing and fine tuning the script for each episode, and then more weeks editing, during which time Cleese appears in several TV commercials to earn income. The show first airs on 19th September, with Cleese as Basil, Prunella Scales as his domineering wife Sybil and Andrew Sachs as Manuel, the hapless Spanish waiter whose mix-ups and accidents are always because, 'He's from Barcelona'. Just twelve episodes of Fawlty Towers are made, divided into two series. But it's quality not quantity and Cleese and Booth's pursuit of perfection pays off. In 2000, *Fawlty Towers* is voted first out of the 100 best British television programmes of all time by the British Film Institute.

How we used to live

Queen Elizabeth, the Queen Mother, visits Beamish Museum near Stanley, Co. Durham on 17th July. Beamish is an open-air museum and pioneer of living history, preserving north-east heritage by authentically recreating typical communities and industries of the area in the late nineteenth and early twentieth centuries.

Runaround

Cockney geezer Mike Reid is the MC of ITV's kids' quiz show *Runaround*, which airs for the first time on 2nd September. It's high energy fun with teams zooming around the studio when Reid asks a question and shouts, 'G-g-g-g-g-GO!' jumping in front of what they think is the correct answer. The elusive yellow ball – and two extra points – goes to any brainbox who selects the right answer when nobody else does.

Bod

Bod first appears on the BBC in 1974 in a story read on *Playschool*. The BBC decide to bring Bod to life on screen and the resulting animation airs on 23rd December, narrated by John Le Mesurier with a jazzy theme tune by *Playschool* and *Playaway* regular Derek Griffiths. *Bod* is quite odd; a bald little figure of indeterminate gender in a yellow smock and with a circle of acquaintances limited to a policeman, a farmer, a postman and his aunt Flo.

Comedy's Holy Grail

'Sets the film industry back 900 years!' and 'Makes Ben Hur look like an epic' are just some of tongue-in-cheek slogans across the film poster for *Monty Python and the Holy Grail*, which opens in the UK on 3rd April. A farcical retelling of the Arthurian legend with non-stop jokes and silliness, it's a film crammed with memorable (and quotable) moments from the ridiculous Knights of 'Ni' to the gory duel where the Dark Knight insists 'Tis only a scratch' as Graham Chapman's King Arthur systematically dismembers him.

Big potato

Mr Potato Head, first launched in 1952, expands in size this year making him safe for small children to play with too.

A right royal drama

ITV's historical royal drama *Edward the Seventh* begins on 1st April, and traces the life and eventual reign of Edward VII, whose older self is played by Timothy West, with Annette Crosbie as his mother, Queen Victoria. Through the years we witness the appearance of figures both central and peripheral to European history, played by an eclectic cast.

One Flew Over the Cuckoo's Nest

When Randle P. McMurphy (Jack Nicholson) claims insanity so he can get himself transferred to a state psychiatric hospital in order to avoid hard labour, he doesn't factor in a formidable foe in the form of sadistic Nurse Ratched (Louise Fletcher). Produced by Michael Douglas, whose father Kirk owned the film rights to Ken Kesey's best-selling novel about his experiences working in a Californian Veterans Hospital, *One Flew Over the Cuckoo's Nest* wins five Oscars including Best Actor for Nicholson and Best Actress for Fletcher.

Galileo, Galileo

31st October 1975 Queen close out the year with one of the records of the decade. *Bohemian Rhapsody* is a six minute-long multi-layered five-part mini-opera that takes three weeks to record. The band also make their own film for television stations to play when they can't appear live - effectively the first promotional video of the kind that will become commonplace in the 1980s. *Bohemian Rhapsody* stays at No. 1 in the UK for nine weeks.

Ch-Changes

March 1975 David Bowie changes style again. As he prepares for filming *The Man Who Fell to Earth*, his *Young Americans* album reveals a new soul-based direction. *Fame*, a collaboration with John Lennon and Carlos Alomar, gives him his first US No. 1.

Rollermania!

22nd March 1975 'Rollermania' explodes as the Bay City Rollers spend five weeks at No. 1 with an old Four Seasons tune, *Bye Bye Baby*. From the Glasgow area, they appeal most to teenage and pre-teenage girls with a tinny and clanky sound that's deliberately under-produced to underline their ingenuousness. In the charts and on teen magazine covers, it is difficult to escape the tartan-covered quintet during 1975. The Rollers offer a final blast of pop hysteria before punk rock and disco take hold.

MUSIC

Mac additions

1st January 1975 US rock duo Lindsey Buckingham and Stevie Nicks join Fleetwood Mac, setting the once all-British blues band on a whole new course.

Voulez-vous coucher?
23rd March 1975 One of the cheekiest lines in songwriting history - *'Voulez vous couchez avec moi, ce soir?'* - is heard in *Lady Marmalade* by Labelle, now No. 1 in the US. Fronted by Patti Labelle, Labelle is an all-female trio whose space-age stage suits and in-your-face attitude put them light years ahead of previous all-female outfits like the Supremes.

Gabriel leaves
28th May 1975 Peter Gabriel leaves Genesis (photo), the art rock band he formed with fellow Charterhouse public schoolboys Mike Rutherford and Tony Banks in 1967. Stepping up as vocalist is Phil Collins, drummer with the band since 1970, who once played the Artful Dodger in *Oliver!* in the West End. Far from jeopardising the band's future, as some suggest, the switch gives the band a more mainstream direction and a new lease of life.

MY FIRST (18) YEARS
TOP 10   1975

1. **I'm Not in Love** *10cc*
2. **Lovin' You** *Minnie Riperton*
3. **This Old Heart of Mine** *Rod Stewart*
4. **Jive Talkin'** *The Bee Gees*
5. **At Seventeen** *Janis Ian*
6. **Cat's in the Cradle -** *Harry Chapin*
7. **You Ain't Seen Nothing Yet** *Bachman-Turner...*
8. **December '63** *The Four Seasons*
9. **No Woman No Cry** *Bob Marley*
10. **Mamma Mia** *Abba*

Open 🟢 | Search 🔍 | Scan 📷

Zeppelin in exile
May - June 1975 Now the biggest band in the world in terms of earnings, Led Zeppelin enter tax exile in Switzerland after playing a series of four hour shows at Earl's Court. Their first release on their own SwanSong label, *Physical Graffiti,* is an instant chart-topping album in the US and UK.

Rod goes west
As Rod Stewart admits he is considering US citizenship, his debut album for Warner Brothers has the appropriate title of *Atlantic Crossing*. Meanwhile Rod's private life goes public as he begins an affair with actress Britt Ekland.

Lennon can stay
7th October 1975 With John Lennon and Yoko Ono now reconciled, son Sean is born two days after Lennon's deportation order is rescinded. He receives his Green Card allowing him permanent residence in the US nine months later.

SPORT

Ice gold perfection

On 11th February, at the Winter Olympics in Stockholm, Birmingham's John Curry wins the gold medal in the men's figure skating. Curry's early ambitions to be a ballet dancer were quashed by his father but there is a balletic quality to his performance, which combines grace with athleticism.

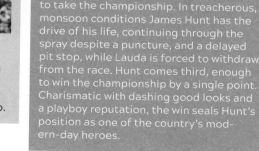

Life in the fast lane

Marlboro Maclaren's chances of victory in this year's Formula One Championship rest on the final race at the Fuji Speedway track in Japan, and the ability of their British driver, James Hunt, to secure a place in the top four. Hunt has been chasing his Austrian rival, Niki Lauda, all season and when they line up on the grid on 24th October, he needs just three points to take the championship. In treacherous, monsoon conditions James Hunt has the drive of his life, continuing through the spray despite a puncture, and a delayed pit stop, while Lauda is forced to withdraw from the race. Hunt comes third, enough to win the championship by a single point. Charismatic with dashing good looks and a playboy reputation, the win seals Hunt's position as one of the country's modern-day heroes.

Borg begins

On 3rd July, cool, calm and collected Swede Bjorn Borg defeats Ile Nastase in the men's singles final at Wimbledon in three sets and secures the first of five consecutive titles at the All England club.

Seven times Derby winner

Lester Piggott becomes the most successful jockey ever in the Derby when he wins the race for the seventh time on Empery on 2nd June. Piggott's seven titles put him ahead of the six wins of both Jim Robinson in the 1830s, and the legendary Steve Donoghue. He will go on to consolidate his achievement, winning the race twice more, in 1977 and 1983.

13 JAN 1976

Queen of crime writing Agatha Christie dies at the age of 85.

2 FEB 1976

The Queen opens the huge National Exhibition Centre (NEC) in Birmingham.

20 MAR 1976

The speedy Oxford crew win the Boat Race in 16 minutes, 58 seconds; a record for the event.

Montreal Olympics

One of Britain's three gold medals is thanks to swimmer David Wilkie who sets a new world record of 2:15:11 in the men's 200 metre breaststroke.

Montréal 1976

It is the first Olympic gold swimming medal for Great Britain in 68 years. Elsewhere, sporting history is made by Romanian gymnast Nadia Comaneci who is awarded the first ever 10.0 score on the asymmetric bars in the team competition, followed by six more perfect scores in individual events on her way to winning three gold medals

Concorde arrives!

21st January 1976 Supersonic jet Concorde makes its first commercial flight between London and Bahrain, launching the era of supersonic passenger flights. Concorde becomes an icon of luxury and modernity but suffers with sales thanks to its high cost and the difficulties flying it over land thanks to its sonic boom.

DOMESTIC
NEWS

Britain's Buddhist temple

Britain gets its very first purpose-built Buddhist temple. Following the Thai style of Buddhism, the Wat Buddhapadipa opens in Wimbledon following a move from its original location on a residential street in East Sheen.

Northern Ireland

5th January 1976 A year of continuing violence in Northern Ireland begins with the Kingsmill Massacre in South Armagh, in which ten protestant men are killed by members of the Provisional IRA. Twelve bombs strike the West End of London later in the month, and in July Christopher Ewart-Biggs, the UK's ambassador to Ireland, is assassinated by landmine. The year also brings large peace demonstrations, with 10,000 Protestant and Catholic women marching in August, and a Derry Peace March attracting 25,000 people in September. The same year the Guildford Four and the Maguire Seven are wrongly convicted for the Guildford pub bombings, their convictions overturned in 1989 and 1991.

DO YOU REMEMBER THIS?

Marbles

Third Cod War

1st June 1976 Iceland and the UK finally agree an end to the Third Cod War, with the UK accepting Iceland's definition of its territorial waters. The eleven-month conflict has resulted in 55 separate incidents, mostly involving the aggressive ramming of ships on both sides.

26 APR 1976

Comedy actor and *Carry On* star Sid James dies after suffering a heart attack on stage at the Sunderland Empire.

10 MAY 1976

Embroiled in scandal, Jeremy Thorpe resigns as leader of the Liberal Party.

22 JUN 1976

The sizzling 'summer of '76' begins with a heatwave that will be remembered for decades to come.

Ford Fiesta launches

14th July 1976 Nation's favourite the Fiesta is launched by Ford, due to be manufactured at the company's Dagenham plant in Essex. The three-door hatchback is the smallest car Ford has produced so far and becomes popular as a 'run-around' vehicle and especially with learner drivers, making it one of the best-selling cars of the next 40 years.

Ford Fiesta wins award for reducing your motoring costs!

Art fraud exposed

16th July 1976 A series of articles published in *The Times* begin to unravel the story of prolific forger Tom Keating. Convinced dealers are interested only in big names and not the artistic value of a work, Keating has been saturating the market with hundreds of fakes since the 1950s. He is convicted in 1979 and goes on to lead a successful Channel 4 documentary about painting in the 1980s.

Big Ben clock stops

5th August 1976 After more than 100 years of use, the chiming mechanism in the Great Clock of Westminster breaks. The mechanism is badly damaged and is shut down for 26 days while repair is made, the longest break in service since its construction. Westminster feels eerily quiet without its familiar tolls.

Riots at Notting Hill

30th August 1976 The Notting Hill Carnival descends into chaos as mounted police officers attempt to break up the 150,000-strong crowd. Whilst arresting pickpockets at the event, tension had risen between the police and young black attendees who felt unfairly targeted. Violence breaks out and 100 police officers and 60 carnival attendees are injured.

Hull Prison riot

1st September 1976 A three-day long riot breaks out at HM Prison Hull. Protesting against alleged prison guard brutality, 100 prisoners take over the prison, destroying two-thirds of the compound. The riot ends peacefully, but the prison closes for a year to allow for the £3 million worth of repairs.

Renee MacRae disappearance

12th November 1976 36-year-old mother Renee MacRae disappears with her three-year-old son Andrew in what becomes the country's longest-running missing persons case. In 2022, MacRae's lover, and Andrew's father, William MacDowell is found guilty of their murders, although their bodies are never found.

MISSING PERSONS
WHERE ARE THEY NOW?
HAVE YOU SEEN THEM?

14 JUL 1976

Drought Bill introduced to tackle the country's worst drought in 250 years.

1 AUG 1976

Grand Prix champion Niki Lauda suffers severe burns in an accident during the German Grand Prix.

29 SEP 1976

With the pound falling to $1.64, Britain applies to borrow £2.3 billion from the IMF.

1976

Bank of America robbery

16th November 1976 The perpetrators of what is believed to be the world's largest bank heist are sentenced to a total of 100 years in prison. The seven men are responsible for a robbery at the Mayfair branch of the Bank of America last year, in which safety deposit boxes worth £8 million were stolen, and only £500,000 of the loot is ever recovered.

International Monetary Fund loan

15th December 1976 Chancellor of the Exchequer, Denis Healey, announces an agreed £2,300,000,000 loan from the International Monetary Fund to ease the country's financial woes. The loan comes on the condition that public spending be cut and is received against a backdrop of pay freezes and inflation at 16.5%, one of the highest levels since records began.

Extreme weather

1976 brings extreme weather to the United Kingdom. In January, the Gale of 1976 sees hurricane-force winds of 105 miles per hour. In June and July, an extreme heat wave sees fifteen consecutive days of temperatures over 26.7°C. The temperature reaches a peak of 35.9°C before August and September bring drought.

ROYALTY & POLITICS

Hot property

The Queen buys the 730-acre Gatcombe Park estate in Gloucestershire for Princess Anne and Captain Phillips at a reported cost of £300,000, leading to criticism by several Labour MPs.

Callaghan takes over at No. 10

On 16th March, Prime Minister Harold Wilson announces his resignation and recommends Foreign Secretary and former Home Secretary James Callaghan (photo) as his successor. Callaghan, aged 64, becomes Prime Minister on 5th April. Wilson's departure triggers controversy when he includes some questionable individuals in his resignation honours list.

Divorce in the Firm

A statement from Kensington Palace on 19th March announces that Princess Margaret and Lord Snowdon have mutually agreed to live apart. Although the statement goes on to say 'There are no plans for divorce proceedings' the couple do indeed divorce two years later.

FOREIGN NEWS

Dirty War

24th March 1976 In Argentina, President Isabel Perón is kidnapped and deposed by the military, and replaced by Lieutenant General Jorge Videla. Under the name 'Dirty War', the Videla junta is responsible for the disappearance of tens of thousands of trade union workers, students and other left-wing activists.

4 OCT 1976

British Rail launch the new Intercity 125 train which initially runs out of Paddington to Bristol and South Wales.

27 NOV 1976

The Mini continues to be a popular choice of motor. The four millionth rolls off the assembly line this month.

10 DEC 1976

Mairead Corrigan and Betty Williams, founders of the Ulst Peace Movement, are awarde the Nobel Peace Prize.

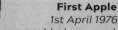

First Apple

1st April 1976 Having built a prototype of an assembled personal computer with Steve Jobs in 1975, Steve Wozniak offers the design to his employer HP and to game console manufacturer Atari, but neither party is interested. Wozniak and Jobs then decide to market their computer themselves. Jobs, who follows a fruit diet, comes up with the name: Apple Computer Company. From 11th April, the Apple I is on sale for $666.66.

Judgement of Paris

1st May 1976 In a blind wine tasting soon to be known as 'the judgement of Paris', an eleven-member jury of nine connoisseurs from France, the UK and US chooses both the white chardonnay and the red cabernet sauvignon from California over the French chardonnay and Bordeaux - a serious blow to the French ego. The so-called 'new wines' are conquering the world.

Soweto uprising

16th June 1976 In South Africa, the apartheid regime comes under further pressure when police in Soweto open fire on students demonstrating against the introduction of Afrikaans as the dominant language of education. Several hundred demonstrators are killed. A photo of the shot twelve-year-old student Hector Pieterson being carried away shocks the world.

CN Tower opened

26th June 1976 The Canadian National (CN) Tower is opened in Toronto, Canada, at this point the highest free-standing structure on the planet at 553 metres.

Operation Entebbe

27th June 1976 Palestinian militants hijack an Air France plane in Greece and fly it to Entebbe in Uganda, where they are welcomed by dictator Idi Amin. They demand the release of militants imprisoned in Israel and other countries in return for the hostages. 148 non-Jewish hostages are released over the next two days but an Israeli force of 100 commandos mounts a rescue of the remaining hostages on 4th July. Three hostages are killed but 102 are brought to safety, while all the hijackers and 45 Ugandan soldiers are killed. The rescuers' sole fatality is Yonatan Netanyahu, brother of future Israeli Prime Minister Benjamim Netanyahu.

Red planet

20th July 1976 In the search for life on other planets, NASA sent an unmanned space mission to Mars on 20th August 1975. Now Viking 1 becomes the first spacecraft in history to successfully soft land on the red planet. The probe soon transmits the first images of Mars to Mother Earth.

Robbery of the century

16th - 17th July 1976 Six robbers spend four months drilling their way through the sewer system to the vaults of the Société Générale bank in Nice. During the weekend after the 14th July national holiday, the robbers strike: 337 safes are emptied containing almost 50 million French francs. Before they leave, the thieves leave a message: 'Without weapons, without hatred and without violence.' Not a single franc from the loot is ever recovered.

Mao is dead

9th September 1976 The architect of Chinese communism and one of the dominant political figures of the 20th century, Chairman Mao Zedong of the People's Republic of China dies in Beijing aged 82.

Carter is President

2nd November 1976 Jimmy Carter (photo right) wins the US presidential election, defeating incumbent Gerald Ford in a close race. He is the first candidate from the southern states to become President since the American Civil War.

ENTERTAINMENT

Emu attacks Parky

On 27th November, Rod Hull and Emu are invited onto chat show *Parkinson* but Emu takes a marked dislike to host Michael Parkinson, rips up his notes and eventually attacks and unseats him. Rod, meanwhile, is powerless to stop him.

Roy of the Rovers scores

Roy Race of Melchester Rovers, aka Roy of the Rovers, first made an appearance in *Tiger* comic back in 1954, but 22 years later, his continuing popularity means he's promoted to the first division and gets to headline his own comic with the first issue on 25th September. With guest appearances by real-life players and even the former England manager Alf Ramsey popping up, plus dramatic storylines including a worrying number of kidnappings, at its peak *Roy of the Rovers* sells an extremely respectable 450,000 copies.

Carry On Budgie

Budgerigars have been popular pets since the Victorian era but in the 1970s, it seems as if every home has a cage hanging in the corner with a gaudy plastic cover. Riding on the crest of the budgerigar wave is *World of Budgerigars*, a short film on how to care for your feathered friends, starring, unexpectedly, Sid James, who listens attentively to the advice delivered with deadpan solemnity by budgie expert Philip Marsden.

Green Cross Code for roads

Since the 1950s, children have been schooled in crossing the road safely by Tufty the Squirrel. Tufty appears as a puppet in public information films and is the face of the Tufty Club which by the early 1970s has two million members. But there is a new road safety kid on the block by this year, with special superpowers. The Green Cross man extols the importance of the Green Cross Code's essential rules of Stop, Look, Listen, Think and, if he spots anyone ignoring this advice, can teleport in an instant to intervene and save kids getting squashed by an Austin Allegro. The Central Office of Information engages 6 ft 6 in bodybuilder, weightlifter and actor David Prowse, who dons the special green and white suit in his quest to rid the world of road accidents.

Open All Hours

Ronnie Barker creates another sitcom anti-hero in the form of Albert Arkwright, the penny-pinching, stuttering shopkeeper of a Doncaster corner shop, assisted by his luckless nephew Granville (David Jason) as he tries to charm Lynda Baron's Nurse Gladys and avoid injury by a temperamental cash register. Barker's comic timing and knack for verbal acrobatics, not to mention the on-screen chemistry with Jason, guarantees *Open All Hours* - which opens on BBC1 on 20th February - is a comedy classic.

High spirits

They've got spooks and ghouls and freaks and fools at *Rentaghost*, an agency run by ghosts for all your haunting needs. Unfortunately, the three ghosts available - Mr Timothy Claypole, a Tudor jester, a fey Victorian gent called Hubert Davenport, and the more recently deceased Fred Mumford - were all failures in life and are equally hopeless in death. The first series of *Rentaghost* begins on BBC1 on 6th January.

Starsky and Hutch

Some of TV's most successful crime-busting duos are based on a personality balance of yin and yang. That's the case with Starsky & Hutch, who first appear on British TV screens on 23rd April. Starsky is a streetwise, ex-US Army veteran from Brooklyn, prone to moodiness and fond of shawl-collars. His partner Hutch is a more reserved, cerebral type with Nordic good looks. Together they tear around the streets of Bay City, California in a red and white striped Ford Gran Torina, on the hunt for drug dealers, pimps and other lowlifes, often tipped off by their friend, fly guy and bar owner Huggy Bear.

Saturday *Swap Shop*

Swapping things is the basic premise for the BBC's new Saturday morning show, the *Multi-Coloured Swap Shop* which opens for business on BBC1 at 9:30am on 2nd October, hosted by Noel Edmonds. Kids can phone in to swap their action man for a Stylograph; their stamp albums for a Viewmaster, while out in the field, perpetually excited Keith Chegwin supervises outdoor 'swaporamas' at various venues around the country. Interspersed with the swapping are interviews with celebrity guests, news segments courtesy of John Craven, interactions with Posh Paws (Edmonds' prehistoric, purple sidekick), music performances and videos.

I, Claudius

Showered with BAFTA awards and still considered a taboo-breaking landmark in historical television drama, *I, Claudius* begins on BBC1 on 20th September. Based on the novels of Robert Graves, the adaptation by Jack Pulman does a fine job at leading the viewer through the complicated web of corruption, debauchery, power struggles, treachery and murder marking the early days of Imperial Rome, with Derek Jacobi, as the Emperor Claudius, unravelling the story as narrator. The huge cast includes Sian Phillips as the scheming Livia (never far from a vial of poison), John Hurt as Caligula and Brian Blessed, in booming form, as Augustus.

Muppetry

The Muppet Show is Jim Henson's move away from *Sesame Street* to a puppet show with a broader appeal. *The Muppet Show* is made at Elstree Studios and airs on ITV on 5th September with a vivid cast of hundreds including a skinny green frog called Kermit who acts as MC; temperamental diva, Miss Piggy; a struggling stand-up called Fozzie Bear, a groovy house band - Dr. Teeth and the Electric Mayhem (with a lunatic, Keith Moon-style drummer called Animal); Gonzo, Rowlf, and many more.

Happy Days

16th October 1976 The show's central character, Arthur 'Fonzie' Fonzarelli, played by Henry Winkler, is a global phenomenon. Kids everywhere try to channel The Fonz's cool, impersonating the click of his fingers, the thumbs up and the drawled, 'He-ey'. Fonzie appears on magazine covers, annuals, posters, bubblegum packets and there is, of course, a play figure. Goofy teen Richie Cunningham is played by Ron Howard, who goes on to become a successful Hollywood film director.

MUSIC

Patti's in town

16th March 1976 Punk rock may come to be seen as a very British phenomenon but its roots are on the US east coast with Iggy and the Stooges, the New York Dolls and Television. Another big influence is the Ramones, whose buzzsaw sound is what every punk band wants to emulate. Now rock journalist and poet Patti Smith adds another dimension with the stunningly unadorned and daring debut album *Horses*, produced by Velvet Underground's John Cale.

Eurovision win

3rd April 1976 This year's Eurovision Song Contest, held in the Hague, sees Brotherhood of Man represent the UK with *Save Your Kisses For Me*. And what do you know, the UK has a winner for only the third time in Eurovision history. A cutesy love song from a father to his three-year-old, it gives the group a whole new lease of life after a couple of hits in the early 70s.

On a dark desert highway

As ego clashes and general excess start to pull the Eagles apart, they peak with an album that articulates all that's enervating and vacuous about the cocaine-fuelled Californian rock lifestyle. *Hotel California* has elements of the country rock they once championed on *Desperado* and *Take It Easy* but it's a self-loathing set that nevertheless becomes the sixth best selling album of the whole decade.

Frampton live

8th April 1976 Peter Frampton achieves platinum status for sales of his double album *Frampton Comes Alive!*, which includes the hit *Show Me The Way*. Recorded at San Francisco's Winterland Ballroom, it's a stunning comeback for a guitarist whose career stalled after leaving Humble Pie.

Forever Demis

17th July 1976 Sitting atop the singles chart is the long-haired, kaftan-clad Demis Roussos, whose distinctive high trill once adorned the progressive rock band Aphrodite's Child. He has a huge fanbase among British holidaymakers who first heard his music in the tavernas and discotheques of the Greek islands. The single is made up of four tracks and titled *Roussos Phenomenon*, with most radio airplay going to the dreamy *Forever And Ever*.

Elton and Kiki

24th July 1976 The big hit of the long, hot drought-ridden summer of 1976 is Elton John's duet with Kiki Dee, *Don't Go Breaking My Heart*. Oddly, they don't actually record the track together: Elton makes his vocal in Canada and ex-Motown artist Kiki adds hers in London. It is Elton's first UK No. 1.

Here comes Summer

Clubs and disco-
theques playing
black-originated
dance music have
been part of the New
York scene since the
late 60s. Now disco music becomes a
truly global phenomenon as producers
Giorgio Moroder and Pete Bellotte and
former *Hair* performer Donna Summer
begin collaborating at the Musicland studios in Munich. On *Love to Love You Baby*,
over a looping part-synthesised backing
track, Summer adds moans of ecstasy
as if approaching climax. Released as a
seventeen-minute twelve-inch single, it
causes a sensation in the discos and clubs
of Europe. By the time Summer makes the
even more orgasmic *I Feel Love* in 1977,
they have established the blueprint for
what becomes known as 'Eurodisco'.

MY FIRST 18 YEARS

TOP10   1976

1. **The Boys are Back in Town** *Thin Lizzy*
2. **This Masquerade** *George Benson*
3. **If You Leave Me Now** *Chicago*
4. **You to Me are Everything** *The Real Thing*
5. **Let's Stick Together** *Bryan Ferry*
6. **Beautiful Noise** *Neil Diamond*
7. **All By Myself** *Eric Carmen*
8. **Blitzkrieg Bop** *The Ramones*
9. **Free** *Deniece Williams*
10. **Golden Years** *David Bowie*

Open 🟢 | Search 🔍 | Scan 📷

Abba go regal

4th September 1976 A triumphant year
for Abba brings no fewer than three No.
1s including their majestic contribution to
the growing disco boom, *Dancing Queen*.
It is quintessential Abba: soaring, heart
touching and an instant dancefloor filler.

Punk grabs the headlines

1st December 1976 Punk rock has been
making waves in the press all year. Now
comes the moment when its notoriety goes
national. On the TV programme *Today*,
the Sex Pistols scoff and swear their way
through a live interview with unamused
host Bill Grundy. Even though they haven't
played a note, suddenly they are every
stroppy and disaffected kid's dream. With
their *Anarchy in the UK* tour about to start,
sixteen of the nineteen planned gigs are
cancelled on local authority orders.

10cc split

27th November 1976 Founder members Lol Creme and Kevin Godley leave 10cc to pursue
other projects, including a new guitar-attachable gadget called a 'Gizmo'. Graham Gould-
man and Eric Stewart - the creators of No. 1s *I'm Not in Love* and *Dreadlock Holiday* - will
carry on as a duo under the 10cc banner.

SPORT

Red Rum hat trick

Despite doubters claiming that at twelve years old he is too old, Red Rum, ridden by Tommy Stack, wins the Grand National at Aintree on 2nd April, his third victory in the event, making him the only horse to win the race three times.

Liverpool conquer Europe

Liverpool FC win their first European Cup title, beating Borussia Monchengladbach in the final. It begins a golden age of European Cup football for the club as they reach five finals in nine years, winning the title four times in total.

Boycott's Ashes century

On 11th August, England's opening batsman, Geoffrey Boycott, scores 191 against Australia in the 4th Test match of the summer Ashes series in front of a full house at his home ground of Headingley; the first cricketer to score his one hundredth first-class century in a Test match. Never afraid to court controversy, when his cricket career ends, Boycott goes on to commentate on radio and television and is notorious for his outspoken views on modern players' techniques.

Wade wins Wimbledon

British player Virginia Wade is a veteran of Wimbledon, having played there for sixteen years yet never having reached the final; until now. She beats Chris Evert in the semi-final to face the Netherlands' Betty Stove in the final and wins in three sets. The timing is perfect. Not only does 1977 mark the centenary of the founding of the Wimbledon Championships but it is the Queen's Silver Jubilee year and Wade's victory is played in front of Her Majesty, attending the tournament for the first time since 1962.

Bras ban bounce

The first sports bra, the 'Jockbra', later renamed the 'JogBra', is invented this year by Lisa Lindahl, a student at the University of Vermont, in collaboration with theatre costume designer Polly Smith and her assistant, Hinda Schreiber.

DO YOU REMEMBER THIS?

Flash cubes

29 JAN 1977

Seven IRA bombs explode in Oxford Street and surrounding area, damaging buildings, and causing fire at Selfridge's department store.

18 FEB 1977

Rock band KISS play their first concert in New York.

28 MAR 1977

Yorkshire and Tyne Tees television conduct a nine-week experiment in breakfast television.

DOMESTIC
NEWS

Two-inch TV launched
10th January 1977 A new two-inch screen television is launched by Sinclair Radionics as an update to their 1966 world-leading design. Able to fit in your pocket, with a pull-out aerial, the television is more portable than ever.

Dounreay explosion
10th May 1977 At the Dounreay nuclear facility in Caithness, a shaft containing radioactive waste, sodium and potassium is flooded with seawater, leading to an explosion. The lids of the shaft are dislodged, and radioactive particles enter the surrounding area.

British cars in trouble
15th March 1977 Under threat of government withdrawal, part-nationalised car manufacturer British Leyland announce the termination of 40,000 workers who have gone on strike, after industrial action costs the company £10 million a week. Car industry figures released in September show that foreign-made cars are outselling British cars for the first time, although companies like Vauxhall are still the market leaders. Vauxhall launches the Luton-made Cavalier in August.

Queen visits Northern Ireland
10th August 1977 Under tight security, the Queen visits Northern Ireland, as part of a tour celebrating her Silver Jubilee. For the first time in her reign, she travels by helicopter in order to avoid ambush, and no one without a pass is allowed within a mile of her.

Economic trouble continues
29th March 1977 The government announces that they are cutting income tax from 35 pence in the pound to 33 pence on the condition that trade unions agree to a third year of wage restraints. Government figures launched earlier in the month reveal that rampant inflation has led to prices rising 70% since 1973.

11 APR 1977
London Transport launch a special series of AEC Routemaster buses to mark the Queen's Silver Jubilee.

29 MAY 1977
11-year-old Nigel Short becomes the youngest player to qualify for the national chess championship.

6 JUN 1977
Beacons are lit across the country to mark the Silver Jubilee, sparking a week of festivities.

Battle of Lewisham

13th August 1977 A march by 500 members of the far-right National Front is confronted en route from New Cross to Lewisham by around 4,000 counter-protesters. Protestors block streets and throw bottles and bricks at the marchers. Mounted police deploy smoke bombs and enter the crowd, and the march is diverted after protesters occupy Lewisham town centre. 111 people are injured in the violence and over 200 arrested. Days later riots break out in Birmingham during further National Front demonstrations.

Laker launches Skytrain

26th September 1977 Laker Airlines launches its 'Skytrain' flights from London Gatwick to New York's JFK, ushering in the era of budget travel. It is the first airline in the UK to offer international travel at such affordable rates.

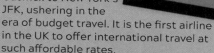

Jeremy Thorpe allegations

27th October 1977 Former leader of the Liberal Party, Jeremy Thorpe, denies allegations made by airline pilot Andrew Newton that he had paid him to kill his former lover, Norman Scott. The allegations are

printed in London's *Evening News* and cause a sensation, with the case going to trial in 1979. Thorpe is found innocent, but the scandal contributes to the decline of the Liberal Party.

Yorkshire Ripper hunt continues

28th October 1977 The police appeal to the public for help in finding and identifying the so-called Yorkshire Ripper, who they believe has attacked five women already this year, killing four of them. Another woman would be injured before the year is out.

Firefighters strike

14th November 1977 The first ever national strike of firefighters is called as they negotiate for a 30% wage increase. The strike lasts nine weeks, into January of 1978, and sees so-called 'Green Goddess' fire engines take to the streets, operated by the British Army. Despite attempts by the army to fill the firefighters' shoes, 119 people die in fires across the country before the year is out. In January the strike is settled with a 10% pay rise.

ROYALTY & POLITICS

One is a grandmother

Princess Anne gives birth to a baby boy, Peter Phillips, on 15th November. The Queen receives a message about the safe arrival of her first grandchild just before an investiture ceremony at Buckingham Palace. Arriving ten minutes late, she tells those waiting the good news, adding proudly, 'I am now a grandmother.'

JUL 1977

The average house price in London and the south-east is now £16,731.

23 AUG 1977

New, smaller pound notes are introduced.

8 SEP 1977

Jimmy McCulloch leaves Wings, leading to another reshuffle for Paul McCartney's band.

Shops go Jubilee crazy

The Silver Jubilee, the first major royal event since the 1953 Coronation, sees shops flooded with Jubilee memorabilia. There are the expected t-shirts, mugs, hats and flags, but even food manufacturers jump on the Jubilee bandwagon. Shoppers can buy Silver Jubilee ice cream, ice lollies and frozen mousse, Silver Jubilee margarine and cans of strawberry flavoured 'Jubilade' from the Co-op!

Roy Jenkins becomes head of EEC

Home Secretary Roy Jenkins resigns from both the Cabinet and his parliamentary seat on 3rd January to become president of the EEC commission in Brussels. Disillusioned about the Labour Party's views on Common Market membership, the position suits the Europhile Jenkins. It is speculated that he will return to form an alternative party in the near future.

Death of Anthony Eden

Former Prime Minister Sir Anthony Eden dies at his home, Alvediston Manor, Wiltshire, on 14th January at the age of 79.

FOREIGN NEWS

Chinese New Year disaster

18th February 1977 A huge fire in Khorgas, China, claims 694 lives at a military-run agricultural colony. The fire starts when a firecracker ignites wreaths to the late Mao Zedong during a Chinese New Year celebration.

Tenerife plane crash

27th March 1977 Dense fog, miscommunication and inadequate equipment combine to cause the worst air disaster in history, though neither of the planes involved are airborne at the time. A KLM jumbo jet collides with a Pan Am Boeing at Tenerife Airport, resulting in 583 fatalities.

Blackout!

13th July 1977 Much of New York City suffers an electricity blackout lasting 24 hours following a lightning strike on a Hudson River substation. There is widespread looting and arson, LaGuardia and Kennedy airports are closed down for eight hours and most television stations are forced off air during the hottest week of the year.

2 OCT 1977

Niki Lauda wins his second Formula 1 World Drivers' Championship.

4 NOV 1977

The tv series *The Incredible Hulk* with body builder Lou Ferrigo premieres.

25 DEC 1977

British-born comic screen legend Charlie Chaplin dies aged 88.

To the North Pole
17th August 1977 Ships have been trying to reach the North Pole for decades. Now the Soviet vessel *Arktika* succeeds for the first time. The nuclear icebreaker is powered by two nuclear reactors that provide power via four steam turbines. The ship makes its way between ice floes up to three metres thick.

Biko killed
12th September 1977 Prominent anti-apartheid activist Steve Biko is tortured, beaten and left for dead by South African police. He is taken to hospital but dies of a brain haemorrhage, causing international outrage.

Milk elected
8th November 1977 Harvey Milk becomes the first openly gay man to be elected to any government post in the US when he is voted San Francsico's City Supervisor. He becomes an icon to the US gay community during his tenure, which is cut short by his assassination just over a year later.

📺 ENTERTAINMENT

Abigail's Party
Mike Leigh's *Abigail's Party* opens at Hampstead Theatre on 18th April, and is such a hit it has a second run before becoming a BBC *Play for Today*. On 1st November, the nation is introduced to Beverly as she and her husband Laurence entertain their new neighbours in an evening that slowly reveals, by way of chilled Beaujolais and Demis Roussos, the petty prejudices, middle-class aspirations and compelling need to keep up appearances in 1970s suburban Britain.

All Aboard the SkylArk
Grange Calveley, the creator of *Roobarb and Custard*, is behind a new BBC children's animation, *Noah and Nelly in...SkylArk*. Captain Nutty Noah, and champion knitter Nelly, equipped for wet weather in their yellow sou'westers, travel to fantastical places with an ark full of strange animals, each with two heads - a happy one at one end, a grumpier one at the other.

First steps to peace
19th November 1977 Egyptian President Anwar Sadat lands at Ben-Gurion Airport in Tel-Aviv and becomes the first Arab leader to make an official visit to Israel. His historic speech in the Israeli Knesset marks a turning point in Middle East geopolitics and paves the way to peace between Egypt and Israel after 30 years of tension and war.

Putty in Hart's hands
Morph, a little man made from plasticine, joins Tony Hart's popular art programme, *Take Hart* on BBC1, making his first appearance on 15th February. Created by stop-animation specialists Aardman Animations, Morph shape-shifts, speaks in (very expressive) gibberish, sleeps in a wooden box, and provides a comic foil to Hart's calm, industrious presence. Later, Morph is joined by Chas, who is naughtier with a dirty laugh, and sometimes tests the patience of the serene Mr. Hart.

Christ alive
Beginning 3rd April, Robert Powell stars as the main man in the Biblical mini-series, *Jesus of Nazareth* directed by Franco Zefferelli. Powell's appearance, with his penetrating gaze and wavy locks, bears an eerie resemblance to traditionally accepted depictions of Christ from the Turin shroud onwards. A supporting cast of acting royalty, including Laurence Olivier, James Mason, Anne Bancroft and Olivia Hussey, make this an essential piece of Easter viewing.

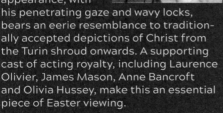

Charlie's Angels
The Glamo-meter is dialled up to the max when the much-anticipated *Charlie's Angels* airs for the first time on UK television on 3rd January. Flicked hair, boob tubes and lip gloss share just as much screen time as the handguns as Kelly, Jill and Sabrina chase down criminals at the behest of the unseen Charlie.

Poldark - Ross Rides Again
The 1975 series of *Poldark*, the eighteenth-century Cornish saga based on Winston Graham's novels, has been a smash hit success, with average UK audiences of 15 million gripped by the sex, scandal and smuggling among the tin mines. On 20th November, Ross Poldark returns to screens for a new season, using three more of Graham's novels for the storylines. Poldark's producers would like to make a third series, but Graham cannot write fast enough to keep up with demand. His later books are instead incorporated into a 2015 adaptation when the Poldarks captivate a whole new generation. Fans of the 1970s original are delighted to spot the first Ross, Robin Ellis, taking on a cameo role as Judge Hayter.

Tapping in
1st December 1977 As part of the TV special, *All Star Record Breakers*, multi-talented Roy Castle, host of *Record Breakers*, joins a mass tap-dancing world record at BBC Television Centre as 500 dancers tap their way around the centre's famous central, circular 'doughnut'. Castle was already a tap-dancing world record holder having recorded the fastest tap dance in 1973, achieving an astonishing 1,440 taps per minute.

Generation gap

Bruce Forsyth has been the host of *The Generation Game*, television's most successful Saturday night show, since 1971. He's on hand with quips and guidance as pairs of contestants (who are always related) attempt various skilful tasks like potter's wheels, Highland dancing or icing a cake in order to score enough points and win a chance to recall all the prizes that pass before them on a conveyor, including the ubiquitous 'cuddly toy'. But Forsyth decides to leave this year, lured over to ITV to front *The Big Night*, and presents his last *Generation Game* on 31st December. He's replaced by Larry Grayson in 1978 who, assisted by 'the lovely Isla St. Clair' brings his own brand of high camp to a show that continues to enjoy huge popularity on his watch.

Roots

Based on Alex Haley's 1976 novel, *Roots - The Saga of an American Family*, the American miniseries *Roots* begins on BBC1 on 8th April after winning critical acclaim in America. A sprawling story that tells of the struggles of successive generations from the capture and enslavement of Kunta Kinte in eighteenth-century Gambia to the eventual liberation of his descendants from the brutal inhumanity of slavery, *Roots* is powerful, thought-provoking, necessary television - a historical drama that has everyone talking, and one that still ranks as one of the most-watched television events of all time.

The Flumps

The Flumps, a family of furry, bobble hat-wearing creatures with Yorkshire accents, who live at the bottom of an abandoned garden, arrive on BBC1 on 14th February.

Brain AND brawn

The ultimate test in physical and mental prowess, *The Krypton Factor*, named after Superman's home planet, is the TV contest that puts other quiz shows in the shade. Hosted by Gordon Burns, participants must face a series of tough challenges every heat in order to reach the final and the possibility of being crowned British Super Person of the Year. Their mental dexterity and spatial awareness are tested with fiendish puzzles, they scramble through an Army assault course to prove their fitness, take an observation test, and answer general knowledge questions.

Poems for the populace

After appearing on *Opportunity Knocks* in 1975, Pam Ayres has become a favourite TV personality; audiences adore her comic poems about the trivial and everyday, delivered in her slow Oxfordshire burr, with the occasional smirk suggesting she might corpse on-air. She is given her own ITV show, *The World of Pam Ayres,* which first broadcasts on 2nd September.

Bye bye Bing

On 11th September, Bing Crosby and David Bowie record *Peace on Earth/ The Little Drummer Boy* at ATV's Elstree Studios as part of Crosby's *Merrie Olde Christmas Special*. The pair perfect the duet in just three takes and afterwards, Crosby compliments Bowie as 'a clean-cut kid and a real fine asset to the show'. Just over a month later, Crosby dies suddenly on 14th October while in Spain, suffering a massive heart attack. When the Christmas Special is broadcast on Christmas Eve, there is a particular poignancy in seeing these two musical icons, each from a different generation, performing together.

Star Wars and other mega movies

1977 is a bumper movie year with something for everyone. Aliens really do exist according to Stephen Spielberg's *Close Encounters of the Third Kind*, while boxing epic *Rocky*, with its thumping theme song *Eye of the Tiger* makes its slurring star Sylvester Stallone a household name. S*aturday Night Fever* presents hip-wiggling John Travolta to audiences and disco music to the masses with a multi-million selling soundtrack. And on 25th May, the words, 'A long time ago, in a galaxy far, far away, introduce UK audiences to *Star Wars*. Director George Lucas's intergalactic saga combines pioneering special effects and memorable characters with old-fashioned, compelling storytelling. The force is strong in this film and Lucas's creation goes on to form the foundation of the world's most successful film franchise.

Atari 2600

The Atari 2600, is launched on 11th September, 1977. Unlike the first generation of game consoles, which only allow for one game on the device (boring!), Atari 2600 comes with a full complement of nine cartridge games including *Outlaw*, *Space War* and *Breakout*. Gamers can simply switch cartridges to their heart's content. It sells a staggering 30 million consoles around the world.

♪ MUSIC

Sex Pistols dropped

6th January 1977 Under pressure from shareholders and the press, EMI drops the Sex Pistols, who replace Glen Matlock with Sid Vicious and they sign with Virgin.

Rumours

4th February 1977 Released today, Fleetwood Mac's *Rumours* turns the emotional lives of the band into public property. Written and recorded when band relationships were breaking down, new ones were forming and members were barely talking to one another, the album nevertheless evolves into the quintessential bitter-sweet California rock record. As Stevie Nicks puts it, 'We created the best music in the worst shape.'

Disco milestone

26th April 1977 Studio 54, soon to be the most famous and exclusive discotheque in the world, opens in Manhattan. Cementing the perception of disco as flamboyant, escapist and sexually free, it comes at the perfect time, just as the Bee Gees' *Saturday Night Fever* soundtrack is sweeping the globe and making a style that was associated strongly with the gay community into something accessible to gay and straight alike.

Supremes disband
12th June 1977 As Diana Ross begins filming the Motown-financed movie *The Wiz*, her former group the Supremes call it quits with an emotional concert at London's Theatre Royal Drury Lane.

Lynyrd Skynyrd
20th September 1977 Steve Gaines and Ronnie Van Zant of southern rock band Lynyrd Skynyrd are killed with four others when their plane crashes in Mississippi. The band are best known for *Sweet Home Alabama*, a riposte to Neil Young's redneck-baiting *Southern Man*.

Billy's movin' out
29th September 1977 After six years as a solo artist, Billy Joel enters the big league of singer-songwriters with breakthrough album *The Stranger* and a trio of hit singles - *Movin' Out*, *Just the Way You Are* and *She's Always a Woman*.

Elvis is dead
16th August 1977 The king of rock dies of heart failure at 42. Elvis Presley is found by his girlfriend Ginger Alden in his bathroom at Graceland. Two days later, 75,000 gather for his funeral. His death renews mass interest in his music and *Way Down*, recorded just days before, becomes the first of many posthumous hits.

Bat Out of Hell
21st October 1977 The surprise hit album of the year is *Bat Out of Hell*. Conceived and performed by giant-voiced Meat Loaf and Jim Steinman, it's a piece of Gothic rock theatre in *Rocky Horror Show* vein, with grandiose power ballads and Springsteen-like production values. The seventh biggest selling LP in history, it shifts over 43 million worldwide.

Bolan killed
16th September 1977 Glam rock pioneer Marc Bolan is killed when a car driven by his wife Gloria hits a tree on Barnes Common. He was 29 years old and always feared that he would die before reaching 30.

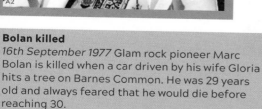

From punk to new wave

While Sex Pistols-inspired punk rock isn't exactly all over the charts in 1977, it marks a sea change in music. Young bands are forming and making music with just three chords, as punk fanzine *Sniffin' Glue* tells them to do. The Clash debut with *White Riot*, John Peel

invites punk bands to play radio sessions, Siouxsie and the Banshees (photo) get record deals and the Damned, Buzzcocks, Angelic Upstarts and Big in Japan are not far behind. Though much older, the Stranglers pass for punk and deliver the right punk attitude on *No More Heroes*. Most significantly, punk opens the door to fringe musicians with more than a touch of anger and insolence, like Elvis Costello and Ian Dury. The industry prefers the term 'new wave', which sticks. Suddenly established bands from Pink Floyd to ELO are sounding like dinosaurs.

MY FIRST 18 YEARS
TOP 10   1977

1. **Chanson d'amour** *Manhattan Transfer*
2. **Holidays in the Sun** *The Sex Pistols*
3. **Sex and Drugs and Rock'n'roll** *Ian Dury*
4. **Go Your Own Way** *Fleetwood Mac*
5. **Roadrunner** *Jonathan Richman*
6. **No More Heroes** *The Stranglers*
7. **I Feel Love** *Donna Summer*
8. **Knowing Me Knowing You** *Abba*
9. **Show Some Emotion** *Joan Armatrading*
10. **Sir Duke** *Stevie Wonder*

Open 🟢 | Search 🔍 | Scan 📷

Mull of Kintyre

3rd December 1977 Complete with bagpipes, Paul McCartney's wistful tribute to his Scottish bolt hole, *Mull of Kintyre*, monopolises the No. 1 spot for nine weeks. With domestic sales alone topping two million, it is the biggest selling single in the UK to date.

Iggy and Bowie

No longer fronting the Stooges, godfather of punk Iggy Pop is invited on tour by David Bowie, who also produces Iggy's two solo albums, *The Idiot* and *Lust for Life*. Iggy's *The Passenger* from the latter becomes his best-known song and is still being used in television commercials 45 years later.

SPORT

Prince of sails
Windsurfing, or sail boarding, introduced at the beginning of the decade, is all the rage. In August, 'Action Man' Prince Charles is photographed windsurfing in Australia and the image is published around the world, fuelling interest further.

Tractor Boys lift the Cup
Bobby Robson's Ipswich Town face Arsenal in the FA Cup final on the 6th May. It's the East Anglian club's first time in the FA Cup final against a team who have won four times. Ipswich dominate the match with several chances at the goal before Roger Osborne scores in the 77th minute to secure the cup for his team.

Martina wins at Wimbledon
Martina Navratilova wins her first Wimbledon ladies' singles title (and her first Grand Slam title), beating no. 1 seed Chris Evert in the final, 2-6, 6-3, 7-5. Elsewhere the Great Britain team enjoy a strong run in the Davis Cup. They eventually lose in the final to a US team inspired by tennis 'superbrat' John McEnroe.

World Cup woes
Argentina win the World Cup, beating the Netherlands 3-1 in extra time in the final on 25th June. It is a controversial tournament. Argentina has recently become a military dictatorship and the World Cup is seen as an opportunity to legitimise the regime and bolster national pride. Argentina's win is overshadowed by allegations of match fixing, intimidation, and scheduling of matches to favour the home side. England fail to qualify for the tournament and the only home side to do so, Scotland, are knocked out in the group stages.

DOMESTIC NEWS

North Sea storm surge
11th January 1978 A huge storm surge in the North Sea sees damage done to coastal areas as floods affect the coastline from the Humber to the Thames. Pleasure piers in Herne Bay, Margate, Hunstanton and Skegness are severely damaged, with some never recovering.

1 JAN 1978

The otter becomes a protected species in Britain, bringing otter hunting to an end.

17 FEB 1978

Twelve people are killed when La Mon restaurant in Belfast is bombed.

25 MAR 1978

Oxford win the Boat Race after Cambridge sink a mile from the finish line.

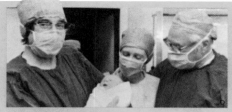

First 'Test tube' baby
25th July 1978 The first success from pi-oneering new fertility treatment 'in vitro fertilisation' results in the birth of Louise Brown in Oldham. The new treatment gives hope to millions worldwide who struggle to conceive.

El Al bus shooting
20th August 1978 Gunmen from the Pop-ular Front for the Liberation of Palestine open fire on a bus in Grosvenor Square, London, in broad daylight. The bus carries staff from the Israeli airline El Al, and the terrorists use guns and grenades to carry out their attack. Nine people are injured, and one flight attendant is killed.

Murder by umbrella
7th September 1978
Georgi Markov, a Bulgarian dissident, dissenter, and BBC journalist, collapses at work at after being stabbed by a poisoned umbrella as he crosses Waterloo Bridge. He dies in hospital four days later in what was widely considered to be an assassination by the Bulgarian Secret Service and the KGB.

Flipping amazing
Constructed in pressurised concrete, the UK's first permanent skateboard park opens in Hornchurch, East London. It's a sign of the growing popularity of a hobby-sport that started in the 1960s in California. Armed with boards customised in street art style and dressed in a uniform of baseball caps, baggy pants and Vans shoes, skateboarders are now showing off a dazzling repertoire of heelflips, kick turns and tail slides.

West Brom/Nuneaton shootings
26th - 28th October 1978 Foundry worker Barry Williams kills five people and wounds four more in a rampage that begins in West Bromwich and ends in Nuneaton. He is arrested by police after a high-speed chase and is convicted of manslaughter on grounds of diminished responsibility.

DO YOU REMEMBER THIS?

VHS video cassettes

Bridgewater murder
19th September 1978 The nation is gripped as police investigate the murder of thirteen-year-old newspaper boy Carl Bridgewater, who is shot dead whilst disturbing a burglary at a West Midlands farmhouse. Four men are arrested and tried in December for the murder, but their convictions are quashed in 1997 and the murder remains unsolved.

3 APR 1978
Vanessa Redgrave wins an Oscar and makes a speech condemning those who had threatened her for making a documentary about Palestine.

1 MAY 1978
The nation enjoys its first early May Bank Holiday.

27 JUN 1978
Oil output from the North Sea exceeds one million barrels a day making Britain the world's 16th biggest oil producer.

Bakeries ration bread
4th November 1978
After strikes in bakeries across the country, the nation is gripped by a surge of panic-buying, forcing bakeries to ration the sale of bread. The shortages last until 10th November, when bakers go back to work and calm resumes.

British Embassy burned
5th November 1978 Students from the University of Tehran take to the streets, attacking Western symbols such as hotels and cinemas. The British Embassy is burned and vandalised as the country moves closer to full-scale revolution.

Concrete cows
Milton Keynes unveils the iconic 'Concrete Cows' by American artist Liz Leyh, her parting gift to the city. Over the years the sculptures become the subject of a lot of local fun, including amusing graffiti, interesting paint jobs, the addition of a papier-mâché bull, and even a calf kidnapping as part of a university fundraising stunt.

ROYALTY & POLITICS

Prince Michael of Kent weds
Prince Michael of Kent, younger brother of the Duke of Kent and cousin of the Queen, marries Baroness Marie-Christine von Reibnitz, Vienna on 30th June. Marie-Christine is a Roman Catholic and therefore Prince Michael loses his place in the order of succession.

Tories get boost from ad men
A little-known advertising agency, Saatchi & Saatchi, run by brothers Maurice and Charles Saatchi, is appointed by the Conservatives in March and tasked with creating a campaign to hammer home the Tory message in the run-up to a General Election. Their poster 'Labour Isn't Working' showing a dole queue snaking out of an employment office, becomes a landmark piece of political campaigning, and catapults Saatchi & Saatchi into the major league.

17 JUL 1978
Protestors, led by the Bangladeshi community, demonstrate in the Brick Lane area of east London against the National Front.

3 AUG 1978
The 11th Commonwealth Games opens in Edmonton, Canada.

23 SEP 1978
Government announces plans to replace O-level and CSE examinations with a single exam. The GCSE finally comes into effect in 1988.

FOREIGN
NEWS

Aldo Moro kidnapped
16th March 1978
Terrorists from the Red Brigades kidnap former Italian Prime Minister Aldo Moro and kill his five bodyguards. Mass demonstrations follow throughout

Italy and normal life comes to a halt while the government refuses to give into the kidnappers' demands. His body is found in the boot of a red Renault 4 on 9th May.

Amoco Cadiz oil spill
17th March 1978 The mammoth tanker *Amoco Cadiz* is en route to Rotterdam with a cargo of 1.6 million barrels of crude oil when it encounters heavy weather off the Brittany coast and runs aground. The next morning the ship breaks in two. This causes the largest oil spill in history as 220,000 tons of oil leak into the sea. The coast is smeared with oil for hundreds of kilometres, and dead birds and sea creatures are still washing ashore many months later.

Three Popes in one year
6th August 1978 Pope Paul VI dies after a heart attack. After a short conclave, Albino Luciani is elected the new Pope John Paul I. But the 'laughing Pope' does not have long to live himself. He dies on 28th September. After the second conclave in three months, Poland's Karol Józef Wojtyła is elected as the first non-Italian pope since Adrian VI in 1522. Taking the title of Pope John Paul II, his reign proves one of the most active and far reaching of any Holy Father in history.

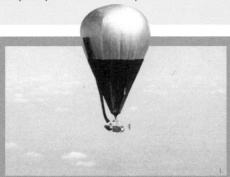

A ballooning first
12th August 1978 Three Americans - Ben Abruzzo, Maxie Anderson and Larry Newman - are the first to cross the Atlantic by gas balloon on Double Eagle II. The 5,001-kilometre journey takes 136 hours and six minutes.

30 OCT 1978

Following a dispute between management and unions, publication of *The Times* and *Sunday Times* is suspended.

4 NOV 1978

France performs nuclear test at Mururoa atoll.

17 DEC 1978

Police increase security as the IRA embark on a Christmas bombing campaign.

Camp David

17th September 1978 Egyptian President Sadat and Israeli Prime Minister Begin conclude the Camp David Accords, in which Egypt recognises Israel's right to exist and Israel returns the Sinai desert to Egypt after eleven years. Both receive criticism from their own supporters and the United Nations rejects large parts of the agreement. The historic progress they have made is enough to secure Sadat and Begin a joint award of the Nobel Peace Prize.

Jonestown massacre

18th November 1978 People's Temple cult leader Jim Jones orders a mass murder-suicide at the community of Jonestown that he has established in Guyana. Over 900 lose their lives including 270 children. The massacre is triggered by the shooting of Congressman Leo G. Ryan, who was visiting Jonestown to investigate claims that people were being held against their will.

China after Mao

1st December 1978 After the death of Mao Zedong, his critics gain the upper hand in the Communist Party of China. In December, the rehabilitated moderate Vice Prime Minister Deng presents his 'open-door policy' as de facto leader of the People's Republic of China and states that revolutionary 'capitalism with socialist features' will be the turning point in China's modern history. Deng breaks definitively with Mao's ideas and makes possible enormous economic reforms, development and growth by opening the nation to foreign trade and diplomacy.

ENTERTAINMENT

Grease is the Word

The release of the original soundtrack album of 1950s high school musical, *Grease*, two months before that of the film itself is a canny move. The singles *You're The One That I Want* and *Summer Nights* are the sound of summer this year, spending nine and seven weeks respectively at No. 1 in the UK music charts, while three more tracks are top ten hits. By the time the film opens on 14th September, cinema audiences know every single word and are up and dancing in the aisles. *Grease* cements the star status of the leads, John Travolta and Olivia Newton John as Danny and Sandy, and rakes in £14.7 million at the UK box office. Britain, it seems, is hopelessly devoted to *Grease*.

Space Invaders

Arcade game *Space Invaders* is launched this year. The game, where players have to move a shooter across the bottom of the screen to evaporate approaching aliens, becomes an instant classic and the highest-grossing video game of all time.

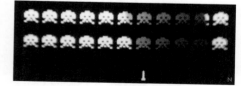

Golda Meir dies

8th December 1978 Golda Meir, the Ukraine-born Prime Minister of Israel who led her country during the Yom Kippur War, dies in Jerusalem at the age of 80.

Spain's new constitution

29th December 1978 Following the death of Franco in 1975 and elections in 1977, democratic government is restored to Spain by the passing into law of the Spanish Constitution.

1978

Skool dayz

A new BBC children's drama, *Grange Hill*, begins on 8th February. Set in a typical North London comprehensive, *Grange Hill*'s creator, Phil Redmond, doesn't flinch from showing the grittier side of school life, and storylines on bullying, racism, shoplifting, teenage sex, pregnancy and, by the 1980s, drug abuse, all contribute to the show's controversial reputation. Kids love it; life at Grange Hill is relatable and educational (although not, perhaps in the way, school should be). It continues to be a regular fixture on the BBC for the next 30 years.

The Water Babies

Starring James Mason, Bernard Cribbins and Billie Whitelaw, *The Water Babies* blends live action with animation (the latter created in Poland) to retell Charles Kingsley's morality story of Tom the Chimney Sweep. The cartoons are crude, but it has a certain charm and the film is redeemed by some toe-tapping tunes including the catchy *High Cockalurum*.

Simon says

Blinking and beeping electronic game Simon, named after the Simple Simon copying party game, is launched this year by Milton Bradley. It's a circular device requiring players to copy light sequences; simple at first, and then increasingly, panic-inducingly complex, until you make a mistake and Simon makes his displeasure known.

Cheggers Plays Pop

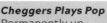

Permanently upbeat Keith 'Cheggers' Chegwin, having found fame via *Multi-Coloured Swap Shop*, hosts his own quiz show for kids, in which two teams (the Reds and the Yellows) supported by their screaming supporters compete in a variety of challenges, races and quizzes based on their pop music knowledge. Team captains are harvested from the current crop of music celebrities. Throughout, Cheggers' enthusiasm is as sparkling as his wardrobe of glam rock-inspired bomber jackets.

Don't Cry For Me

The Andrew Lloyd Webber and Tim Rice musical *Evita*, telling the life story of the divisive Argentine leader Eva Perón, opens in London's West End on 21st June. The concept album *Evita* has already been released in 1976, with the single *Don't Cry For Me, Argentina*, reaching no. 1 in the UK music charts. With everyone already humming tunes from the album, and rave reviews in the press for the show, *Evita* is a resounding success and runs in London until 1986.

Superhero saviours

You can't move for superheroes in 1978. DC Comics' *Superman* comes to the big screen, opening in the UK on 14th December. Christopher Reeve is perfectly cast as the hunky, caped Krypton native who masquerades as mild-mannered, short-sighted *Daily Planet* reporter Clark Kent, in between wooing Lois Lane and single-handedly saving the planet. The not-so-jolly green giant, *The Incredible Hulk* (a role admirably grunted by Lou Ferrigno), the alter ego of Dr. David Banner (Bill Bixby), started as a Marvel comic strip and debuts on ITV on 26th May.

Watership Down

Often remembered as the film that traumatised a generation of children, *Watership Down*, the feature-length animation, is released on 19th. It is given a 'U' classification by the British Board of Film Censors, which claims, 'Animation removes the realistic gory horror in the occasional scene of violence and bloodshed, and we felt that, while the film may move children emotionally during the film's duration, it could not seriously trouble them once the spell of the story is broken.' Parents who have to deal with children having nightmares about a warren of bunnies being murdered disagree and in 2022, the film is finally re-classifed as a PG (Parental Guidance).

Wedded bliss?

Barbados-born singer Janice Hoyte, becomes the UK's first West Indian game show hostess when she joins Alan Taylor on ITV's *Mr and Mrs*. The show tests married couples on their knowledge of each other with often cringeworthy results.

Doings of the Ewings

Dallas, Aaron Spelling's long-running drama about the family feuds, sibling rivalries, shady deals and bed-hopping antics of the oil barons of Texas airs on BBC1 for the first time on 5th September. There is never a dull moment in this soapiest of soaps as the dysfunctional millionaire Ewings of South Fork ranch provide British viewers with quite a contrast to the cobbles of *Coronation Street*, but also prove that money can't necessarily buy you happiness.

Five go on television

Enid Blyton's intrepid quintet, the *Famous Five*, are given a 1970s revamp for TV, with mystery-solving cousins Julian, Dick, Ann and George sporting flares and sneakers, rather than shorts and sandals. Toddy, a border collie, plays the fifth member, Timmy the dog. The series begins on ITV on 3rd July and inspires a range of merchandise, re-packaged editions of Blyton's books featuring the actors and even a release of the theme tune. Sadly, two series of half-hour episodes use up all 21 of the Famous Five adventures, and the estate refuses permission for any more to be written.

Paint Along with Nancy

Paint Along with Nancy debuts, a daytime ITV programme that encourages viewers to create their own artistic masterpiece by following the step-by-step advice of Nancy Kominsky, as she dollops paint on to a canvas with what appears to be a kitchen knife.

All Creatures Great and Small

The popular stories of life as a Yorkshire vet by Alf Wright, writing under the pen name of James Herriott, have already been made into two feature films. Now James Herriott is adapted for television with Christopher Timothy as James, Robert Hardy as the ebullient Siegfried Farnon and Peter Davidson as his younger brother, Tristan. First broadcast on 8th January, the combination of authentic veterinary scenes, colourful local characters, Tricki Woo the pampered Pekingese, and the glorious North Yorkshire scenery, introduced in the opening credits to the tune of *Piano Parchment* composed by Johnny Pearson, combine to make this nostalgic series one of the BBC's greatest successes.

The Kenny Everett Video Show

Mischievous and multi-talented Radio 1 DJ Kenny Everett gets his own Thames Television comedy sketch show beginning 3rd July, featuring characters such as Sid Snot, Captain Kremmen and Marcel Wave. He defects back to the BBC in 1982 and creates a new set of characters including General Cheeseburger, agony aunt Verity Treacle and the fabulous, pneumatic blonde actress Cupid Stunt (Everett in drag) who would end each gossipy monologue by extravagantly crossing her legs, revealing racy red underwear, and declaring, 'It's all done in the best POSSI-BLE taste'.

Win or Dusty Bin?

ITV game show *3-2-1* begins on 29th July hosted by Ted Rogers, whose blink-and-you'll-miss-it hand gesture showing 3, 2, 1 fingers, has kids around the country trying to replicate it. The show is renowned for its extravagant and often rather unusual prizes with contestants being offered all kinds from a St. Bernard dog to a year's supply of fish. The booby prize is a dustbin, represented by Ted's sidekick, Dusty Bin.

MUSIC

Pistols down
18th January 1978 At the close of a chaotic US tour, Johnny Rotten announces the end of the Sex Pistols. In October, Sid Vicious is arrested for the fatal stabbing of his girlfriend Nancy Spungen in a New York hotel room.

Here's Harry
18th February 1978 Making their UK chart debut with *Denis* are Blondie, a New York band who play hard-driving, punkish pop with echoes of the 60s girl group sound. Knowing, sexy and fronted by the fabulously photogenic Debbie Harry, Blondie are set to be the biggest band of the post-punk era despite being virtually unknown in their native US.

Sandy Denny is dead
21st April 1978 Singer-songwriter Sandy Denny, former Fairport Convention member and in many ways the first lady of UK folk music, dies aged 31 of head injuries sustained in a fall at her home in Surrey.

Jamming for Jamaica
22nd April 1978 Flying high with his *Exodus* album and the singles *Jamming* and *Is This Love*, Bob Marley brings warring factions together in Jamaica at a 'One Love Peace Concert' in Kingston.

At the close, he joins hands with political rivals Michael Manley and Edward Seaga in a show of unity.

Wayne's War
9th June 1978 Producer-composer Jeff Wayne unveils his *War of the Worlds* concept album, based on the H. G. Wells novel. Written in rock opera style, the double LP set features David Essex, Justin Hayward, Phil Lynott of Thin Lizzy and actor Richard Burton as narrator.

Bush heights

11th March 1978 At No. 1 in the UK is a major new artist. *Wuthering Heights* features the strange, ethereal voice of its composer, eighteen-year-old Kate Bush, and has all the atmosphere and mystery of the Emily Brontë novel that inspired it. Not only is her singing a revelation, she has a stunningly choreographed stage act to match it. Backing her on *Wuthering Heights* is Pink Floyd guitarist Dave Gilmour, who first brought her to the attention of EMI Records.

Keith Moon dies

7th September 1978 The Who's drummer Keith Moon dies aged 32 after taking an overdose of prescription drugs. He is found dead at the same London flat in which Cass Elliott died in 1974.

B2

MY FIRST 18 YEARS

TOP 10 — 1978

1. **Three Times a Lady** *The Commodores*
2. **FM (No Static at All)** *Steely Dan*
3. **Baker Street** *Gerry Rafferty*
4. **Because the Night** *The Patti Smith Group*
5. **Up Town Top Ranking** *Althia and Donna*
6. **Blame it on the Boogie** *The Jacksons*
7. **More Than a Woman** *Tavares*
8. **Pump it Up** *Elvis Costello*
9. **Teenage Kicks** *The Undertones*
10. **Mr Blue Sky** *Electric Light Orchestra*

Open 🟢 | Search 🔍 | Scan 📷

Ra-ra-Rasputin

18th October 1978 History teachers despair as *Rasputin* by Boney M begins its chart rise: calling mad monk Rasputin 'lover of the Russian queen' isn't historically accurate. Boney M is the creation of German producer Frank Farian, who matched together Maizie Williams, Bobby Farrell, Liz Mitchell and Marcia Barrett in 1976. With their singalong vocals and Bobby's engagingly gangly dancing, they are now the biggest pop act in Europe.

C2

Under a groove

9th December 1978 Scornful of disco's purloining of black music, George Clinton has reinvented funk-soul with his bands Parliament and Funkadelic. Now in London with an elaborate space age stage show starring both bands and ex-James Brown sideman Bootsy Collins, he closes the year with one of the greatest dance anthems ever, *One Nation Under the Groove* for Funkadelic.

D2

Weller at Wembley

29th November 1978 The Jam headline the Great British Music Festival at Wembley Arena. Having come through the first wave of punk rock looking and sounding like a throwback to the 1960s mod era, the three-man Jam are now becoming hugely influential. Leader Paul Weller's songs have fiercely political themes and an edgy, biting quality that matches the group's dour demeanour. Their latest single is *Down In The Tube Station At Midnight* from the band's new *All Mod Cons* album.

SPORT

Bat out of hell
Viv Richards hits one of the most memorable innings ever witnessed at Lord's, when he scores an unbeaten 138 runs in a victory for the West Indies over England in the Cricket World Cup final, held in England from 9th to 23rd June.

Go Coe go

On 15th August, Sebastian Coe achieves a world record for the 1500 metres at the Weltklasse meeting in Zurich, his time, 3:32:1 shaving a tenth of a second off the record set five years earlier. Coe had already set new world records for the 800 metres and the mile at a meeting in Oslo a month earlier, therefore smashing three world records in the space of just 41 days.

Superhero Capes
The inaugural *Britain's Strongest Man* competition takes place in Woking and is broadcast on ITV in a show hosted by Derek Hobson and bubbly Barbara Windsor in front of a mainly juvenile audience. Field athlete Geoff Capes wins the title and is invited in 1980 to take part in Europe's Strongest Man and then World's Strongest Man in New Jersey where he finishes third.

CHiPs boosts BMX
ITV shows the US cops programme *CHiPs* this year, which features a storyline involving a kids' bicycle motorcross team, therefore introducing BMX racing to the British public. The following year, the first BMX track is opened at Landseer Park in Ipswich, and sales of BMX bikes soar.

The one-million-pound man
First Division champions, Nottingham Forest under Brian Clough, sign Birmingham City forward Trevor Francis for the sum of £1,000,000, the first British football club to pay a seven-figure fee for a player. Francis repays the investment on 30th May when he heads a goal to secure victory for Forest against Malmo in the final of the European Cup.

16 JAN 1979
BBC's landmark nature programme, *Life on Earth*, begins, presented by David Attenborough.

18 FEB 1979
Snow falls in Sahara Desert.

3 MAR 1979
The Deer Hunter opens in UK cinemas, the first of a string of Vietnam War films over the next decade.

1979

Seve saves the day

On 20th July, Seve Ballesteros becomes only the second European to win the British Open at Lytham St. Annes, where despite hitting his tee shot into a car park on the sixteenth hole, he still makes a birdie, and eventually triumphs by three strokes to lift the claret jug.

Anti-Nazi protester killed

23rd April 1979 Blair Peach, an Anti-Nazi League protester is killed during an anti-National Front demonstration in Southall. Peach, a teacher from New Zealand, receives a blow to the head as violence breaks out between police and protesters. Anger regarding Peach's death motivates a number of riots and demonstrations into the 1980s.

DOMESTIC
NEWS

'The Winter of Discontent'

The strikes and pay disputes that had characterised the end of 1978 blossom as 1979 begins into the so-called 'Winter of Discontent'. In January lorry drivers go on strike, leading to huge shortages of food and heating oil. Ten days later they are joined by rail workers, and by January 22nd tens of thousands of public sector employees take industrial action too. The strike is accompanied by cold weather, freezing rain, and snow, adding to the country's misery. In February the weather and fuel shortages lead to over a thousand schools closing before an agreement is eventually struck at the end of the month.

Devolution referendum

1st March 1979 Scotland and Wales hold major referendums on the devolution of government powers, and the creation of separate Welsh and Scottish assemblies. In Wales, voters reject devolution with 79.7% against the idea, and in Scotland, whilst a majority vote for devolution, they represent less than 40% of the electorate, so the act is repealed.

Jubilee Line opens

1st May 1979 London's newest tube line, the Jubilee Line is opened by Prince Charles, who poses for photographs at the helm of one of the new trains. Connecting Stanmore to Charing Cross, the line is named in honour of the Queen's silver jubilee two years previously but opens late due to problems installing the escalators.

Privatisation

21st May 1979 The government announces its proposals to begin a wide-sweeping programme of privatisation across the nation, with

the selling of various nationalised industries. The programme begins with British Petroleum, which the government starts to disinvest from later in the year.

---

17 APR 1979

A remote-controlled 1,000-pound bomb, detonated by the Provisional IRA, kills four police officers at Bessbrook, Co. Armagh.

27 MAY 1979

With a drop in oil production in the wake of the Iranian Revolution, queues form at petrol stations as motorists panic buy.

26 JUN 1979

Muhammad Ali announces his retirement from boxing.

Thorpe Park
24th May 1979 Thorpe Park in Surrey opens for the first time as a leisure and water sports facility. Attractions include a replica Stone Age cave and Norman castle, which delight visitors. In the 1980s it is redeveloped as a theme park with rides, becoming one of the most popular in the country.

Isle of Man millennium
5th July 1979 The Isle of Man celebrates 1,000 years of its parliament, the High Court of Tynwald, in festivities attended by the Queen. 1979 is chosen arbitrarily as the year to celebrate, as although the parliament is believed to be over 1,000 years old, no official first meeting date is recorded.

Fastnet Yacht Race storm
14th August 1979 The 303 yachts competing in the Fastnet Yacht Race meet with disaster as a storm in the Irish Sea decimates the competition. Force 11 gusts capsize 75 boats and nineteen people are killed, including four spectators.

Lord Mountbatten assassinated
27th August 1979 The Queen's beloved cousin Lord Mountbatten of Burma, his fifteen-year-old nephew, a boat boy of the same age, and the Dowager Lady Brabourne, are killed when the Provisional IRA plants a bomb onboard the family's fishing boat. The same day, eighteen British soldiers are killed at Warrenpoint in an ambush, in a year that has already seen the British ambassador to the Netherlands shot dead, and a bomb killing one person in the House of Commons car park.

Harrier jets hit house
21st September 1979 Two RAF Harrier jets collide in mid-air over Wisbech in Cambridgeshire, with one plane ploughing into several semi-detached houses. The pilots eject safely, but two men and a young boy are killed on the ground, leading the RAF to raise its minimum height for training exercises from 5,000 to 8,000 feet.

J D Wetherspoons opens
The very first J D Wetherspoon pub opens in Muswell Hill. The brainchild of Sir Tim Martin, 'Wetherspoons' or simply 'Spoons' as they become known, prove popular for their cheap but cheerful fare. Martin names his pubs after 'JD', a character from *the Dukes of Hazzard*, and the surname of a teacher, Mr Wetherspoon, who had told Martin he wouldn't amount to much.

Fourth man revealed
15th November 1979 The 'fourth man' in the Cambridge Five spy ring scandal of the 1950s is revealed as Anthony Blunt, the art historian in charge of the Queen's Collection.

5 JUL 1979
The Isle of Man celebrates the 1,000th anniversary of its Parliament ('Tynwald') with a ceremony attended by the Queen.

AUG 1979
Picture puzzle book *Masquerade* by Kit Williams is published and sparks a nationwide treasure hunt.

1 SEP 1979
U2 release their first record, an EP titled *U2-3*, only available in Ireland.

145

ROYALTY &
POLITICS

FOREIGN
NEWS

'Crisis? What crisis?'

On 10th January, Prime Minister Jim Callaghan returns from sun-drenched Guadeloupe where he has been attending a summit of world leaders, and interviewed by the press at Heathrow, denies the country is in a state of mounting chaos. *The Sun* newspaper paraphrases his comments with a front page headline, 'Crisis? What Crisis?' Meanwhile, Tory leader Margaret Thatcher makes a televised party political broadcast to acknowledge the gravity of the situation.

DO YOU REMEMBER THIS?

Walkie Talkies

Maggie gets to No. 10

The country goes to the polls on 3rd May, electing its first woman Prime Minister (and the first female head of government in Europe) as the Tories win with a majority of 44 seats, marking the start of what will be eighteen years of Conservative government.

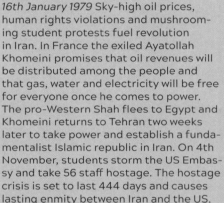

Revolution in Iran

16th January 1979 Sky-high oil prices, human rights violations and mushrooming student protests fuel revolution in Iran. In France the exiled Ayatollah Khomeini promises that oil revenues will be distributed among the people and that gas, water and electricity will be free for everyone once he comes to power. The pro-Western Shah flees to Egypt and Khomeini returns to Tehran two weeks later to take power and establish a fundamentalist Islamic republic in Iran. On 4th November, students storm the US Embassy and take 56 staff hostage. The hostage crisis is set to last 444 days and causes lasting enmity between Iran and the US.

Dictators gone

1979 is a bad year for dictators. The Shah is expelled from Iran, guerrilla fighters put an end to the Somoza family's reign of terror in Nicaragua, rebels oust General Romero's junta in El Salvador and a democratic government comes to power for the first time in Ecuador. In Africa, the continent's cruellest dictator, Idi Amin, is deposed. Dictator Bokassa's fairy tale in the CAR also comes to an end when France supports his cousin's coup.

12 OCT 1979

Following the success of the radio series, *The Hitchhiker's Guide to the Galaxy* by Douglas Adams is published.

22 NOV 1979

Building societies increase mortgage rates to an all-time high of 15%.

19 DEC 1979

Francis Ford Coppola's *Apocalypse Now* is released in UK cinemas.

Three Mile Island
28th March 1979 What nuclear energy sceptics have feared for years is happening: a meltdown at the Three Mile Island nuclear power plant in Harrisburg, Pennsylvania. An explosion is avoided but the disaster galvanises opponents of nuclear energy to organise large-scale protests around the world.

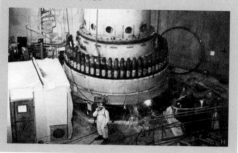

European elections
10th June 1979 Polling stations open throughout the European Union for three days. For the first time, citizens of the nine Member States elect their representatives to the European Parliament.

Happy Meal
15th June 1979 McDonald's aims a major campaign at children with a secret weapon called the Happy Meal. A colourful cardboard box contains a special children's menu with a hamburger, a small portion of fries and a drink, plus a small plastic toy.

Communist kiss
5th October 1979 A remarkable sight at the 30th anniversary celebrations of the German Democratic Republic: Chief of State Erich Honecker welcomes Soviet leader Leonid Brezhnev with a traditional socialist brotherly kiss on the mouth.

Mother Teresa
December 1979 In the 1970s, Mother Teresa's congregation has grown to encompass almost a hundred monastic homes across the world. Now she receives the Nobel Peace Prize for her work with the vulnerable and impoverished.

DO YOU REMEMBER THIS?

Telephone flip up index

One-child policy
In China, Mao's successor Deng Xiaoping announces a drastic scheme to slow down population growth: in future, parents will be allowed to have only one child.

📺 ENTERTAINMENT

Blankety Blank
Terry Wogan, armed with a unique, wand-like microphone, hosts *Blankety Blank*, a new game show starting 18th January in which six celebrities try to help contestants fill in the blanks. The amiable Wogan never takes things too seriously, wryly raising an eyebrow at blundering answers and good-naturedly mocking the prizes - miserly in comparison to those on rival channel ITV. The winner of the first episode of *Blankety Blank* takes home a fridge freezer. We almost hope contestants will instead leave with the underwhelming and yet strangely iconic consolation prize, the *Blankety Blank* cheque book and pen.

Kids give up smoking
The government launch a national anti-smoking campaign aimed at school children where Superman fights his enemy Nick O'teen and asks kids to sign an 'I'm against smoking' pledge. In tandem with this, sweet cigarettes, which come in miniature boxes and mimic real cigarettes, are renamed 'candy sticks'.

Cash in the attic
Antiques Roadshow begins on BBC1 on 18th February. Arthur Negus leads a team of ten experts as they assess various treasures brought

along by members of the public. It's a format that changes little through the years, and although it occupies the cosy early evening slot on Sundays, there is always a frisson of tension as everyone awaits the valuation of each item.

Sony Walkman launched
1st July 1979 The Sony Walkman Is a simple yet revolutionary idea: a battery-operated cassette tape-playing machine with earphones, small and lightweight enough to take anywhere. Now consumers can hear the music of their choice wherever they go. It's the first step in the reorientation of audio from communal to personalised listening.

Tricks on TV
'You'll like this. Not a lot, but you'll like it.' Middlesbrough conjurer Paul Daniels becomes the UK's magical top dog with *The Paul Daniels Magic Show* which begins on 9th June. Soon accompanied by his assistant, 'the lovely Debbie McGee', Daniels blends sleight of hand tricks with larger set pieces, invites celebrity guests to become part of his illusions, and debunks magic myths in the 'Bunco Booth'. *The Paul Daniels Magic Show* continues until 1994.

Nanu nanu

Mork (Robin Williams) comes from the planet Ork and is sent to Earth, where humour is forbidden, to observe human behaviour; Mindy (Pam Dawber) be-friends him, invites him to live with her and teaches him about the American way of life. *Mork and Mindy* begins on ITV in December 1978 but by 1979, everyone is adopting the typical Orkan greeting, 'Nanu nanu'.

Is *Life of Brian* blasphemous?

'He's not the Messiah. He's a very naugh-ty boy!' The Pythons unite for another smash-hit film, this time with a contro-versial parody of the New Testament di-rected by Terry Jones. Graham Chapman is Brian, who, through a case of mistaken identity, is proclaimed the Messiah, in a story that pokes fun at organised religion and factious radical politics. Nervous about its potential to offend, EMI Films pulls the plug on finance, but the produc-tion is saved by George Harrison who sets up Handmade Films in order to fund it. Italy, Ireland and Norway bans it (allowing the Pythons to gleefully print 'So funny they banned it in Norway' on the film posters for Sweden) as do several town councils around the UK.

Sapphire and Steel

The lack of any budget for special effects in *Sapphire and Steel*, which starts on ITV on 10th July, forces the show's creator, Peter J. Hammond, to be inventive with locations, lighting, and sound effects. The result is a surprisingly tense and claustrophobic sci-fi drama in which Joanna Lumley as Sapphire and ex-*Man from U.N.C.L.E.* David McCullum as Steel investigate strange events and anomalies in time and space.

G-Force – Guardians of the Galaxy

Battle of the Planets, which is first shown in the UK on 3rd September, is an Amer-ican adaptation of the Japanese anima-tion, *Science Ninja Team Gatchaman*. The series is not only dubbed in English but is edited to remove scenes of violence and any profanities. The group of five protect Earth from attacks by the planet Spectra and its evil mastermind, Zoltar.

Stone Age superhero

'Set free by the Teen Angels from his prehistoric block of glacial ice, comes the world's first superhero... Captain Caaaaaaaavve-ma-aa-aaaaaan!' Cavey, a walking ball of hair with a club that propels him through the air, and transforms into various gadgets, first appears on BBC1 on 28th June. He's the secret weapon of the Teen Angels, whenever Dee Dee, Brenda and Taffy are on a mystery-solving mission.

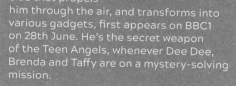

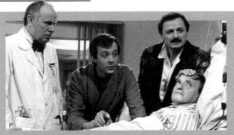

Laughter is the best medicine

In *Only When I Laugh*, which is shown for the first time on ITV on 29th October, Roy Figgis (James Bolam), Archie Glover (Peter Bowles) and Norman Binns (Christopher Strauli) are the in-patients of a men's hospital ward, under the care of sardonic surgical consultant Mr Thorpe (Richard Wilson). Its popularity leads to three more series. Very much of its time, the patients in *Only When I Laugh* regularly puff away on cigarettes.

Flambards

K. M. Peyton's trilogy of novels, set before and during the First World War, are the basis for this thirteen-part series in which an orphaned heiress, Christina Parsons, goes to live with her uncle and his two sons at their crumbling country pile, Flambards. It's a picture-perfect Edwardian family saga, with love affairs, class division and war shaping the characters' destinies.

Moonraker

The Star Wars effect leads Bond producers to send 007 into space in *Moonraker*, the eleventh Bond film, and fourth featuring Roger Moore. The production budget is double that of 1977's *The Spy Who Loved Me* with the special effects nominated for an Academy Award. Opening at the Odeon Leicester Square on 26th June, *Moonraker* becomes the most financially successful Bond escapade to date.

Mod-ern times

The Mod movement of the mid-1960s is recreated in *Quadrophenia*, released on 29th October and based on the Who's 1973 rock opera album. Phil Daniels dons a parka and hops on his scooter, supported by a cast that includes Phil Davis, Lesley Ash, Sting and Toyah. *Quadrophenia* captures the rebellious mood and tribalism of 1960s youth, while a carefully curated selection of additional songs on the soundtrack such as *Louie Louie* by The Kingsmen and *Green Onions* by Booker T and the M.G.s further enhance the period atmosphere.

Rock on Tommy

Two ex-welders from Oldham, comedy duo Tommy Cannon and the impish Bobby Ball, appear on various variety programmes until this year, they get their own ITV show, which begins on 28th July. Tommy is the straight man, and Bobby, with his catchphrase, 'Rock on, Tommy!' accompanied by a twanging of his braces, is cheeky and excitable. It's a combination made for family viewing, and they become a staple of Saturday night entertainment as the show runs for the next nine years.

MUSIC

Oh so Chic
1st January 1979 Bass-driven dance track sensation *Le Freak* tops the US chart for Chic, the band formed by producers Nile Rodgers and Bernard Edwards. Replacing mechanised disco rhythms with sumptuous guitar and bass riffs, they end the decade as the most in-demand producers around.

Monday blues
29th January 1979 In San Diego, California, teenager Brenda Spencer goes on a shooting spree in her school playground. Asked why, she explains 'I don't like Mondays'. The incident leads Bob Geldof of Irish new wavers the Boomtown Rats to write *I Don't Like Mondays*, a UK No. 1 in late July that many US radio stations decline to play.

Vicious death
2nd February 1979 Former Sex Pistol Sid Vicious is found dead from an overdose in New York, having been released on bail the day before ahead of his trial for the murder of girlfriend Nancy Spungen.

Punk meets disco
3rd February 1979 Having brought sex, glamour and catchy tunes to punk rock, Blondie and producer Mike Chapman - one of the godfathers of glam-rock in the early 70s - ally it to the synthesised dance rhythms heard on disco tracks. Acquiring a Roland drum machine, they create *Heart Of Glass* - a brilliant first-time marriage of new wave sensibility with disco that shapes the electro-pop of the 1980s.

Village People
6th January 1979 The first ever openly gay group to top the UK chart are the Village People, four men from New York City brought together by Moroccan Jacques Morali and launched with the irresistible disco track *YMCA*. After they introduce the famous hand gestures spelling out the letters on TV's *American Bandstand*, the *YMCA* dance becomes an overnight sensation.

Earth, Wind and Fire
9th January 1979 Starring at the Music for UNICEF concert at the UN in New York is the fabulous multi-member Earth, Wind and Fire, whose eye-popping costumes reflect leader Maurice White's passion for Egyptology and mysticism. They close their set with *Boogie Wonderland*.

She will survive

17th March 1979 No. 1 on both sides of the Atlantic is a true feminist-cum-gay anthem - *I Will Survive* by New Jersey singer Gloria Gaynor. As a song of resilience, it's the exact opposite in sentiment to Gloria's previous big seller, *Never Can Say Goodbye*. Originally intended only as a B-side, the song was 'flipped' at Gloria's insistence.

Music with a message

3rd April 1979 The 2 Tone label, bearing the distinctive black and white logo designed by owner Jerry Dammers, is launched in Coventry as a vehicle for his multi-racial, seven-man group the Special AKA (known to all as the Specials). Debuting with *Gangsters*, they deliver anti-racist and anti-authority lyrics to a classic 1960s ska backing. They're the ultimate dance band with a message.

A brick for Christmas

15th December 1979 The most unlikely of all Christmas No. 1s is *Another Brick in the Wall* from progressive rock royalty Pink Floyd, who usually never bother to release singles. It's from their latest album *The Wall* and features a choir of children from Islington Green School.

MY FIRST 18 YEARS
TOP10 · 1979

1. **Hit Me with Your Rhythm Stick** *Ian Dury*
2. **Sunday Girl** *Blondie*
3. **Message in a Bottle** *The Police*
4. **Gangsters** *The Special AKA*
5. **Good Times** *Chic*
6. **I'm Every Woman** *Chaka Khan*
7. **Oliver's Army** *Elvis Costello & The Attractions*
8. **Sultans of Swing** *Dire Straits*
9. **Off the Wall** *Michael Jackson*
10. **London Calling** *The Clash*

Open ⬤ | Search 🔍 | Scan 📷

Off the Wall

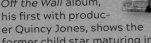

10th August 1979 Michael Jackson has been a hitmaker for nine years but his new *Off the Wall* album, his first with producer Quincy Jones, shows the former child star maturing into one of the most creative and free-thinking musicians in contemporary music.

Rap in the chart

1st December 1979 Rap music makes its very first appearance in the US record chart. *Rapper's Delight* by the Sugarhill Gang features a spoken rap over the rhythm track of *Good Times* by Chic.

Video killing

20th October 1979 With perfect timing comes *Video Killed the Radio Star* by Buggles, otherwise known as Trevor Horn and Geoff Downes. It's a comment on the growing importance of video exposure over radio airplay. After a spell with progressive rockers Yes, Horn goes into full-time record production for Frankie Goes to Hollywood and Downes joins the supergroup Asia.

SPORT

Ice dream
Bristol-born figure skater Robin Cousins has the year of his sporting life when he takes the gold medal at the Winter Olympics at Lake Placid, New York, on 23rd February, skating a routine of artistic brilliance.

Gold rush for GB
With many countries, including the USA, boycotting the Olympic Games in Moscow in protest at the USSR's invasion of Afghanistan, there are claims that British athletes have greater opportunities in track and field events. Speedy Scot, Allan Wells scoops gold in the 100 metres final, with a time of 10:25, but proves any doubters wrong at a meeting in Cologne less than a fortnight later, where he beats the Americans Carl Lewis and Harvey Glance in the 100 metres with a time of 10:19 seconds. Elsewhere, Daley Thompson wins gold in the decathlon, a medal indicative of his dominance in the event during this period, regardless of who else is competing.

Clash of the tennis titans
The atmosphere on Centre Court is electric at Wimbledon on 5th July as Swedish ice man Bjorn Borg hopes to achieve a fifth, record-breaking men's singles title in a meeting with American 'Superbrat' John McEnroe. The confrontation, between two polar opposites, lasts for five nail-biting sets, including a fourth set tie-break that goes to 16-17, but Borg eventually triumphs and falls to his knees in his now familiar champion's ritual. The match feels like the apogee of tennis's golden era; two genius players with their wooden racquets and their headbands, playing at the height of their powers.

Brute force
British boxer Alan Minter faces Vito Antuofermo in a boxing match for the World Middleweight title, at Caesar's Palace, Las Vegas on 16th March. The pair go the full fifteen rounds, with a split decision result, in Minter's favour. Minter proves his supremacy on 28th June in a bloody rematch from which he emerges undisputed World Middleweight Champion but loses the title to Marvin Hagler later in the year.

---

18 JAN 1980

Sir Cecil Beaton, photographer, illustrator, and diarist, dies at the age of 76.

25 FEB 1980

Political comedy, *Yes, Minister* with Paul Eddington and Nigel Hawthorne, begins on BBC1.

19 MAR 1980

MV *Mi Amigo*, the ship from which pirate station, Radio Caroline broadcasts, runs aground and sinks in the Thames estuary.

1980

Middle-distance duels

Great Britain's prowess in middle-distance running during this period is embodied by the legendary rivalry of Sebastian Coe and Steve Ovett, two runners who break and counter-break each other's records, but whose actual meetings on the track are few and far between; until, that is, the Olympic final of the 800 metres in the Lenin Stadium in Moscow on 26th July. In a race Coe is widely expected to win, Ovett barges to the front of the pack to power down the final 100 metres and win gold (photo). Coe, suffering from what he later describes as a tactical disaster, settles for silver, but four days later, finds the form of his life to win gold in the 1500 metres. Ovett finishes with a bronze.

DOMESTIC
NEWS

British Steel strike

2nd January 1980 The Iron and Steel Trades Confederation call their 90,000 members at British Steel out on strike. The action ends in April with an agreed 16% pay rise, but not before the industry is rocked by the announcement that the Corby plant will close with the loss of over 11,000 jobs. This was in addition to the already advertised 4,500 job closure at Consett in September.

Naturist beaches

1st April 1980 Britain gets its first official naturist beach in Brighton. Despite shocking some, the idea proves popular, and soon others open across the country.

Iranian Embassy siege

5th May 1980 A horrified nation watches live on television as the SAS storm the Iranian Embassy in London, ending a six-day occupation of the building by the Democratic Revolutionary Front for the Liberation of Arabistan. Television captures the moment the SAS enter through an upper-storey window to attempt a rescue. Two hostages and five of the six terrorists are killed, the rest of the captives are rescued safely.

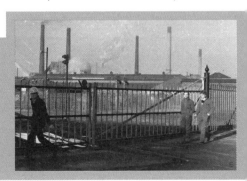

29 APR 1980

Death of Alfred Hitchcock, aged 88, British director with a string of suspenseful movies to his name.

21 MAY 1980

Star Wars Episode V - The Empire Strikes Back opens at cinemas.

13 JUN 1980

he UN calls for South Africa to free Nelson Mandela.

Sixpence withdrawn

30th June 1980 The pre-decimal sixpence, or 'tanner', is withdrawn from circulation. It had survived the initial decimalisation process, with a value equivalent to 2.5 new pennies, but is now set to be withdrawn as the country has adapted to the new currency.

Denmark Place fire

16th August 1980 Tragedy strikes London's Denmark Place, as petty criminal John Thompson seeks revenge for a disagreement with a barman in the Spanish Rooms. Thompson pours two gallons of petrol into the establishment and sets it on fire, killing 37 people in the bar and its neighbouring salsa club Rodo's. Thompson is sentenced to life imprisonment.

Unemployment highs

28th August 1980 Figures released throughout the year show that unemployment is rising quickly across the country. By August unemployment is at 2 million, the highest since 1935, with estimates that it will reach 2.5 million by the end of the year. Inflation also rises to 21.8%.

Hercules the bear

20th August 1980 Hercules the bear goes missing on the island of Benbecula in the Outer Hebrides. The bear, owned by wrestler Andy Robin, is there to shoot a Kleenex commercial when he manages to escape. Missing for 24 days, when he is recaptured, it is discovered that he has almost starved rather than kill any animals on the island, leading to Kleenex's 'Big Softie' campaign.

Alexandra Palace fire

10th July 1980 Alexandra Palace, or 'Ally Pally', is gutted by fire. The fire destroys half the building and only the outer walls and parts of the former BBC studios are preserved.

Third-gen Escort

1st September 1980 Ford launch the third generation of their ever-popular Ford Escort, a model which goes on to become the country's best-selling car of the decade.

Right to buy scheme

3rd October 1980 The new Housing Act becomes law, meaning that tenants of council-owned houses, who have lived there for three or more years, now have the right to buy their homes. These homes are sold at a large discount on market rates and are part of an aspirational policy hoping to see a rise in home ownership across the UK.

27 JUL 1980

England fans riot during England's opening European Championship match in Turin leading police to use tear gas.

1 AUG 1980

Buttevant rail disaster kills 18 and injures dozens of train passengers in Ireland.

3 SEP 1980

Jill Barklem's delightful, illustrated books about country mice, *Spring*, *Summer*, *Autumn* and *Winter Story* are published this month.

1980

Marlborough diamond stolen
11th September 1980
The Graff jewellery shop in Knightsbridge is robbed by thieves who take the £400,000 'Marlborough' diamond and several other jewels from the window display. A brave shop assistant follows them to their car and notes the registration, and the following day the thieves are arrested in Chicago. The diamond is never recovered.

Rendlesham Forest Incident
26th & 28th December 1980 Servicemen at RAF Woodbridge are puzzled by the sight of unexplained lights descending into the nearby Rendlesham Forest. These lights, along with rumours of higher-than-average radiation readings and the panic of local farm animals, become one of the most well-known UFO events in Britain.

Foot comes first for Labour
James Callaghan resigns as Labour leader, and despite the British media believing Dennis Healey will become next leader, it is instead Michael Foot (illustration) following a vote on 10th November. Despite his far-left views, Foot is a leader who many believe can unite the party.

The Queen Mum at 80
The Queen Mother celebrates her 80th birthday this year and on 15th July sets off with Prince Charles in the 1902 State Landau to attend a service of thanksgiving at St. Paul's Cathedral. On 4th August, her actual birthday, she greets crowds who gather outside the gates of her home in Clarence House.

ROYALTY & POLITICS

Shy Di
The relationship between Prince Charles and Lady Diana Spencer becomes public knowledge in September, after Diana is spotted watching the Prince fish on the Balmoral estate. An invite to the Queen's Highland retreat is widely known to be a signifier of something more serious and the following months see press intrusion reach new heights as 'shy Di', who works at a kindergarten, is pursued relentlessly by photographers.

3 OCT 1980
The Housing Act allows council housing tenants to buy their own home.

12 NOV 1980
Voyager 1 space probe reaches Saturn and sends back photographs of its rings of orange and yellow clouds.

14 DEC 1980
Thousands hold a vigil for Jo Lennon in Liverpool following his murder in New York.

No U-turn for the Iron Lady

Margaret Thatcher makes one of the defining speeches of her career at the Conservative Party conference on 10th October, standing firm against calls from others within her party to make a U-turn on her policy of economic liberalisation in the face of rising unemployment and recession. 'You can turn if you want to,' she says, 'The lady's not for turning.' The powerful phrase is one of Thatcher's most memorable.

Note this

1st April 1980 American Art Fry has had enough: his bookmark keeps falling out of his choir book. He comes up with a way to stick the bookmark to the page with a self-adhesive strip and experiments with the yellow pieces of paper on the notepad at the 3M office. Ultimately, 3M successfully markets the Post-it note.

FOREIGN NEWS

Tito is dead

4th May 1980 Three days before his 88th birthday, Josip Broz, alias Tito, dies. The founder and President of Yugoslavia, who has long advocated a 'Third Way' between the bickering East and West, will receive the largest state funeral the world has ever seen.

Solidarity recognised

14th August 1980 The protest against layoffs and inflation at the Lenin Shipyard in Gdańsk, Poland, marks the end of communism in the region. The strikers no longer demand 'a bigger sandwich' but solidarity and the recognition of trade unions. On 31st August, the anti-communist trade union Solidarność of Lech Wałęsa is recognised as the first independent trade union in the Eastern Bloc. One year after its founding, one in four Poles is a member, and the political consequences of this breakthrough are immense.

Street art

Art is for everyone and not just for the elite, is Keith Haring's motto. In New York he discovered graffiti, which he developed into his very own style. He makes chalk drawings on empty billboards in the subway, draws on the street and becomes known far beyond the national borders. Haring makes paintings, sculptures, paints pieces of canvas, applies decorations to vases and t-shirts. In 1985 he decorated the body of singer Grace Jones and contributed to her video *I'm Not Perfect*.

DO YOU REMEMBER THIS?

Ghetto blaster

Reagan is President
4th November 1980 In the US presidential election, Americans send the incumbent President Jimmy Carter back home to Georgia. The Republican candidate, former Hollywood film actor Ronald Reagan, will become the next President.

ENTERTAINMENT

Morning campers!
Hi-de-Hi, set in a 1950s holiday camp, begins on 1st January on BBC1. Written by *Dad's Army* creators Jimmy Perry and David Croft, the staff at Maplins are Yellowcoats (inspired by Butlin's real-life Redcoats) and it is a yellow coat that scatterbrained chambermaid Peggy (Su Pollard) covets, but she never seems to quite make it. Instead, she is Cinderella to the entertainment staff (led by Paul Shane's Ted), kept in her place by self-important senior Yellowcoat Gladys (Ruth Madoc) whose xylophone tannoy announcements keep Maplins running like clockwork and whose seductive wiles make manager Jeffrey Fairbrother (Simon Cadell) hot under the collar.

Walkies!
Barbara Woodhouse has been training dogs and horses for decades, with occasional spots on television and radio, but the ten-part series, *Training Dogs the Woodhouse Way*, which begins on BBC1 on 7th January, makes her a household name at the age of 70. Woodhouse has a natural confidence on-screen, bossing around dog owners and teaching the dogs how to 'Si-T' and how to go for 'Walkies!' nicely. A true original, Barbara Woodhouse becomes a television sensation.

Higher or lower?
ITV launches two new game shows to bring cheer to the winter months. *Family Fortunes* hosted by the smooth-talking Bob Monkhouse (photo) begins on ITV on 6th January, while Bruce Forsyth fronts *Play Your Card Right* from 6th February. *Play Your Cards Right* is another winner for Brucie (even though actually winning is more to do with luck than any skill).

Metal Mickey

Metal Mickey, a cute, five-foot-tall, eager to please robot, first appears on *The Saturday Banana* in 1978 before becoming the title character in a new kids' comedy show on ITV, starting 6th September. The versatile Mickey, whose favourite phrase is, 'Boogie, boogie' goes on to release several hit singles in addition to his TV success.

Game to geek out on

Seasoned BBC producer Patrick Dowling devises *The Adventure Game*, and the first of twenty-two episodes airs on 24th May. It's a melting pot of Dowling's interests in early computer adventure games, Dungeons and Dragons and Douglas Adams's *Hitchhiker's Guide to the Galaxy*.

The Elephant Man

David Lynch directs this heart-wrenching story of Joseph Merrick, whose life-limiting deformities made him an object of ridicule and curiosity in Victorian England. John Hurt plays Merrick and Anthony Hopkins is Sir Frederick Treves, the doctor who takes him in at the London Hospital and introduces him to high society.

Diff'rent Strokes

The American sitcom *Diff'rent Strokes* begins on ITV on 24th November. A wealthy New York widower adopts two Harlem boys after the death of their mother.

Pac-Man premieres

22nd May 1980 Launching today is a Japanese-originated video game destined to become one of the best loved and biggest selling in history. Developed by Namco with a design inspired by a pizza with a slice removed, Pac-Man is the first successful attempt to create a video game with to appeal to children and women as well as young adult males. Within two years, Pac-Man attracts over more than 50 million players across the world and inspires a whole new genre of chase-in-a-maze games.

Airplane!

If the 1970s was the decade of disaster movies, then the 1980s is the decade to parody them, and *Airplane!* starring Leslie Nielsen, Peter Graves and Lloyd Bridges is among the first and the best, inspired by films such as *Airport* and *Airport '75* and in particular 1957's *Zero Hour!* It's non-stop jokes and slapstick all the way.

It's a fair cop

Police dramas have been seriously lacking strong female characters, until this year when, like buses, two come along at once. On 11th April, Jill Gascoine is Detective Inspector Maggie Forbes in ITV's *The Gentle Touch* (photo). And on 30th August, BBC1 launch *Juliet Bravo*, with Stephanie Turner as Chief Inspector Jean Darblay, who must fight the prejudice of a male-dominated police force as well as criminals. Both series become hugely popular.

1980

Who Shot J.R.?
On 22nd November, 21.5 million UK viewers tune in to *Dallas* on BBC1 to discover the answer to the whodunnit of the decade. 'Who Shot J.R?' becomes the question on everybody's lips. Four episodes into season 4, the culprit is finally revealed. It's Kristin Shepard, J.R.'s sister-in-law and mistress, who gunned him down in a fit of pique.

Button Moon
Button Moon, which begins on ITV on 8th December, encourages its pre-school audience to follow Mr and Mrs Spoon as they travel to the big yellow button in the sky every episode. Everything on *Button Moon* is created from household objects including the Spoon family's space rocket, which is a converted washing-up liquid bottle.

Flash Gordon
Flash Gordon captures the comic-strip camp of the science-fiction adventure, and is turbo charged by a rollicking soundtrack from rock band Queen thumping along in the background as Flash only has 'fourteen hours to save the Earth' from Max von Sydow's Ming the Merciless. Eminently quotable lines include Brian Blessed's Prince Vultan roaring, 'Gordon's alive!'

Pennysavers
Fine Fare, the UK's third largest supermarket, launches a no-frills economy range, with plain white packaging stamped with tea chest-style font.

 MUSIC

World Police
20th January 1980 After conquering the UK in 1979 with a masterly fusion of power pop and reggae epitomised by the Sting compositions *Message in a Bottle* and *Walking on the Moon*, the Police take off on their first world tour of 37 cities in nineteen countries.

Sheer Madness
January 1980 Having taken their porkpie-hatted nuttiness from 2-Tone to the Stiff label, Camden Town band Madness begin a decade of chart dominance with *My Girl*, the first of a long stream of comic but faintly melancholy observations of North London life. *Baggy Trousers* follows, a look back at schooldays, while *Embarrassment* dissects the impact of a mixed-race relationship on a close family and their fear of what the neighbours will say.

AC/DC death
19th February 1980 Bon Scott, singer with Australian band AC/DC, dies in London aged 33. Cause of death is given as acute alcohol poisoning. Brian Johnson is named lead singer in his place in April.

Led Zeppelin disband
25th September 1980 Led Zeppelin drummer John Bonham is found dead by bandmate John Paul Jones at Robert Plant's house near Windsor. He was 32 and had choked in his sleep after a drinking session. The band decide not to continue and make the announcement in December.

Ireland wins Eurovision
19th April 1980 Johnny Logan wins the Eurovision Song Contest for Ireland with the song *What's Another Year*.

Ian Curtis suicide
18th May 1980 On the eve of Joy Division's first tour of the US, singer Ian Curtis commits suicide. Rather than disband, the rest of the group elect to re-form as New Order with new member Gillian Gilbert on keyboards. The new line-up plays its first gig in Manchester in October.

Northern echoes
Echoing the early 1960s, the north west of England is once again a hive of music making. Out of Liverpool's club scene - notably Eric's on Matthew Street - come the Teardrop Explodes and the Mighty Wah! while Manchester's Factory record label is a nursery for the likes of the Fall, Joy Division and A Certain Ratio. Another Factory band, Orchestral Manoeuvres in the Dark (photo), quickly sign with Virgin and make an immediate impression with *Enola Gay*, titled after the plane that dropped the atomic bomb on Hiroshima in 1945.

Super troupers
15th November 1980 Abba's seventh album, *Super Trouper*, sets a record for the most pre-orders (one million) ever received for a UK LP. Fans notice a darker tone to their songs, notably the break-up song The Winner Takes it All. Bjorn and Agnetha are now divorced and Benny and Anni-Frid's separation is not yet announced.

Sheena hits the big time
2nd July 1980 Scottish teacher and would-be performer Sheena Easton takes part in BBC TV show *The Big Time*, in which she is groomed for a pop career. The exposure boosts the resulting single, *Modern Girl*, and gives her a first hit. US success and a James Bond theme, *For Your Eyes Only*, follow in 1981.

John Lennon shot dead

8th December 1980 John Lennon is shot four times by a smiling fan, Mark Chapman, as he arrives home at Dakota Flats, Manhattan, from a recording session at the Hit Factory. He dies in hospital half an hour later. He had recently released his first album for four years, *Double Fantasy*, and had been undertaking press interviews to promote it. Lennon had celebrated his 40th birthday in October. The shock felt around the world is palpable. Exactly a week after his death, Yoko Ono asks people all over the world to join in a silent vigil in his memory.

MY FIRST 18 YEARS
TOP10   1980

1. **Brass in Pocket** *The Pretenders*
2. **Private Life** *Grace Jones*
3. **One Day I'll Fly Away** *Randy Crawford*
4. **To Cut a Long Story Short** *Spandau Ballet*
5. **Don't Stand So Close to Me** *The Police*
6. **Games Without Fronters** *Peter Gabriel*
7. **Three Minute Hero** *Selecter*
8. **It's Different for Girls** *Joe Jackson*
9. **Let's Get Serious** *Jermaine Jackson*
10. **On the Radio** *Donna Summer*

Open | Search | Scan

The other Elvis

Despite a chip-on-the-shoulder stroppiness that made him enemies in the US during 1979, Elvis Costello is proving one of the most influential artists of the post-punk period. His albums *Armed Forces* and *Get Happy!* are classic angry young man fare with accusing lyrics and rapid-fire delivery, while his production work for the Specials and Squeeze has helped both bands get established.

Industry troubles

The pointers are not great for music as the 1980s begin. Two of the biggest names in global music fall victim to takeover, EMI merging with Thorn Electronics and Decca joining the Polygram roster. Rising oil prices increase the cost of vinyl and prompt record companies to cut back on investment. Blank cassette sales soar while record sales drop, leading the music industry to launch a 'home taping is killing music' campaign.

SPORT

A

You cannot be serious?
Living up to his nickname of Superbrat, John McEnroe's furious outburst at umpire Edward James during a first-round match at Wimbledon on 22nd June makes headlines around the world. McEnroe disputes James's call that his serve was out and in full meltdown screams, 'You cannot be serious!?'. It's an incident that confirms McEnroe's hot-tempered notoriety and goes down in the annals of sporting history. Despite the tantrum, McEnroe's genius takes him all the way to the final where he finally unseats five-times champion Bjorn Borg. Borg, despite winning at the French Open this year, acknowledges there is a new king of centre court and announces his retirement early in 1983 at the age of 26.

Marathon men
The first London Marathon takes place on 29th March. 6,747 Runners take

THE **GILLETTE LONDON MARATHON**
29th MARCH 1981

part with 6,255 crossing the finish line on Constitution Hill.

Botham's Ashes
During the 51st Ashes series of Test matches between Australia and England, the talismanic all-rounder Ian Botham scores a breathtaking 149 not out during the 3rd Test at Headingley on 16th July, setting Australia a target of 130. Bob Willis then bowls a fearsome spell of 8 for 43 to dismiss Australia for 111. Botham also takes 5-11 in the 4th Test and hits 118 from 102 balls in the 5th. England retain the Ashes 3-1 in what becomes known, quite rightly, as 'Botham's Ashes'.

Rowing revolution
22-year-old Susan Brown, a biochemistry student, becomes the first woman cox in the history of the Oxford-Cambridge boat race when she steers her crew to victory on 4th April.

Davis pots to the top
Steve Davis wins his first World Snooker Championship title at the Crucible Theatre in Sheffield, beating the defending champion Cliff Thorburn in the semi-final and Doug Mountjoy in the final on 20th April by 18 frames to 12. It is the first of eight world championships Davis will win during a decade in which he dominates the sport.

B

---

27 JAN 1981

Rupert Murdoch is permitted to buy The Times without the usual investigation by the Monopolies Commission.

10 FEB 1981

The Coal Board announces plans to close 50 pits employing 30,000 miners.

1 MAR 1981

IRA prisoner, Bobby Sands begins a hunger strike at the Maze prison. He dies on 5th May.

1981

DOMESTIC
NEWS

Yorkshire ripper arrested
5th January 1981 Police arrest 34-year-old lorry driver Peter Sutcliffe on suspicion of being the serial killer known as the Yorkshire Ripper. Sutcliffe has killed thirteen women and attacked seven more. He is found guilty and sentenced to life imprisonment.

The Troubles
1981 sees a continuation of violence associated with the Troubles in Northern Ireland. In the UK there are two major bombings, one at RAF Uxbridge, which is successfully evacuated, and one at the Chelsea Barracks in London which kills two people. A parcel bomb addressed to the Prime Minister is intercepted and defused, and a coal ship, the *Nellie M,* is bombed and sunk by the Provisional IRA. January sees the murders of former MP Sir Norman Stronge and his son James, and an attack on civil rights campaigner MP Bernadette McAliskey who is shot nine time in her home.'

ZX81 computer launches
5th March 1981 The ZX81 is launched by Sinclair Research, intended to provide an affordable at-home computer to the public. It is small and simple and connects to a television set rather than coming with its own screen, with a cheaper cost for those who are prepared to assemble it themselves. 1.5 million devices are sold.

March for jobs
30th May 1981 London plays host to over 100,000 people from across the country as they come together to protest unemployment and economic deprivation in the 'March for Jobs', organised by the Trade Union Congress.

New Cross house fire
18th January 1981 A party at a house in New Cross ends in tragedy as a fire claims the lives of thirteen young people aged 14-22. The victims are black, and many believe the fire to be a case of arson. Moved by the tragedy, 20,000 people take to the streets.

Humber Bridge opens
17th July 1981 Her Majesty Queen Elizabeth II arrives in Hessle for the opening of the Humber Bridge. The longest of its type in the world, the bridge connects Barton-upon-Humber in the south, with Hessle in the north, allowing traffic to flow across the Humber estuary.

27 APR 1981
Paul McCartney's band Wings breaks-up.

8 MAY 1981
Ken Livingstone is elected leader of the Greater London Council (GLC).

11 JUN 1981
The Queen opens Europe's tallest building - the Natwest Tower in the City of London.

Penlee lifeboat disaster

19th December 1981 A rescue mission off the coast of Cornwall goes badly wrong when the lifeboat RNLB *Solomon Browne* is dispatched to rescue the crew of the MV *Union Star*. Despite reaching the vessel and evacuating some of the men, both ships are soon overcome by the Force 12 gales, and the sixteen men on board are lost. The volunteers aboard the lifeboat all receive posthumous medals for bravery and a devastated community raises £3 million for their village.

A year of riots

1981 sees a wave of riots sweep the country, mostly associated with rising racial tensions. In April the Brixton riots see clashes between the police and black youths which injure 300 people and cause serious damage to property, with riots following in Finsbury Park and Ealing. June sees clashes in Coventry at a National Front march and riots in Peckham, before rioting in Southall follows the deaths of an Asian Muslim family killed by arson in Walthamstow. Riots in Toxteth, Liverpool, and Moss Side, Manchester, are the most prominent across fifteen days of violence that sweep the country.

Moira reads the news

The BBC's Moira Stuart becomes the first black woman newsreader on television this year. Born in London to Caribbean parents, Stuart is known for her calm, poise, and silken voice.

ROYALTY & POLITICS

End of an era

Princess Alice, Countess of Athlone, the last surviving grandchild of Queen Victoria, dies on 3rd January at Kensington Palace at the age of 97 years and 313 days.

Shots fired at Queen

On 13th June, the Queen is riding her horse, Burmese, at the annual Trooping of the Colour ceremony, when Marcus Sarjeant fires six blank shots at her. The Queen calmly settles Burmese who is momentarily startled while Serjeant is apprehended and later charged under the 1842 Treason Act. He is sentenced to five years in prison.

Charles pops the question

After months of intense speculation, Buckingham Palace announces the engagement of Prince Charles and Lady Diana Spencer on February 24th. The couple pose for the press with Diana wearing a blue skirt suit from Harrods to set off her sapphire engagement ring.

13 JUL 1981

Martin Hurson is the sixth IRA hunger striker to die.

5 AUG 1981

After touring depressed areas of Merseyside, Michael Heseltine announces a series of measures to help alleviate problems.

10 SEP 1981

Start of Day of the Triffids on BBC1, based on the 1951 science-fiction novel by John Wyndham.

Charles and Di say 'I do'
After six months of frenzied anticipation with the nation in the grip of royal wedding fever, Prince Charles and Lady Diana Spencer marry at St. Paul's Cathedral on 29th July. The 750 million viewers who tune in to watch the wedding finally get their first glimpse of the much-discussed wedding dress, a style which launches a thousand meringue gowns and appears to need a good iron. Nevertheless, it is a glorious spectacle, with all the pomp and pageantry expected and when during the vows a radiant but understandably nervous Diana stumbles over the order of her husband's Christian names, it makes the world love her even more.

Gang of Four
William Rodgers, David Owen, Roy Jenkins and Shirley Williams announce a break from the Labour party with their formation of the Council for Social Democracy on 25th January, the prototype of a new party intended to fight for social justice. The so-called Gang of Four form the SDP and on 16th June announce an alliance with David Steel's Liberal party to fight the next general election as a single organisation.

**FOREIGN
NEWS**

Anne Frank's diary
1st January 1981 Five months after the death of Anne's father Otto Frank, Anne Frank's original diary is released.

Hostages returned
11h January 1981 The day after Ronald Reagan is sworn in as the 40th President of the US, Iran releases the 52 hostages it has been holding since the storming of the US embassy in 1979. They are set free in return for nearly eight billion dollars of Iranian assets frozen in American banks.

Reagan shot
30th March 1981 Ronald Reagan and four others are shot outside the Hilton Hotel in Washington DC by John Hinckley Jr. A bullet punctures the President's lung and he is close to death on arrival at hospital. Prompt action saves his life.

DO YOU REMEMBER THIS?

Kenner Star Wars figures

12 OCT 1981

A report finds that the traditional nuclear family is beginning to fragment as one in eight children live in a single-parent family.

26 NOV 1981

Shirley Williams wins the by-election at Crosby, Merseyside, overturning a Conservative majority of 19,272.

8 DEC 1981

Arthur Scargill is elected president of the National Union of Mineworkers.

Space shuttle
12th April 1981 Six years after the famous handshake between the US and the Soviet Union in space and twenty years to the day since Yuri Gagarin became the first human in space, NASA launches the first space shuttle. This is a reusable space-craft designed to efficiently transport people and cargo into space. Columbia flies 36 laps around the Earth and lands in California 54.5 hours later.

Attempt on the Pope
13th May 1981 Pope John Paul II is shot twice as he enters St Peter's Square in Vatican City. He survives the assassination attempt by a Turkish gunman, Mehmet Ali Agca, who Pope John Paul II will meet two years later in jail.

AIDS identified
5th June 1981 General practitioner Joel Weisman encounters a number of homosexual young men in his practice, all of whom suffer from a reduced number of white blood cells. A few months later, Weisman publishes a report for the US Centers for Disease Control with immunologist Michael Gottlieb concerning a disease which will soon be known by the acronym AIDS (acquired immunodeficiency syndrome).

Fast and invisible
18th June 1981 The F-117 Nighthawk, the newest American fighter aircraft, is a precision bomber with a remarkably futuristic, angular appearance designed to be difficult to detect with radar. This first aircraft with so-called stealth properties is almost invisible to the enemy.

Sadat assassinated
6th October 1981 Egyptian President Anwar Sadat is assassinated in an attack by the Islamic Jihad during a military parade. It follows a failed coup in June after which he ordered a mass round-up of his Islamist opponents. Vice-President Hosni Mubarak is wounded but takes office as Sadat's successor.

TGV in service
27th September 1981 The first paying passengers board the brand new TGV at Gare de Lyon station in Paris. This *train à grande vitesse* takes travellers at top speeds of around 300 km/h.

ENTERTAINMENT

Nanny
The series *Nanny* starts on BBC1 on 10th January with Wendy Craig as Barbara Gray, a divorcee and new nanny whose itinerant career sees her moving around, taking positions with a succession of dysfunctional upper-class families where she works her Mary Poppins magic on her charges.

De Niro is a knockout

Robert de Niro fully commits to his leading role in Martin Scorsese's master-piece, *Raging Bull*, the story of the rise and fall of boxer Jake LaMotta. He takes up boxing, becoming a serious contend-er, and in order to authentically portray LaMotta's post-boxing descent into a bloated has-been, goes on a gastronomic tour of France and Italy to gain weight. His efforts are not in vain, and he wins the Academy Award for best actor this year.

Thinking aloud

Think Again, presented by Johnny Ball, begins on 16th January and is billed in the *Radio Times* as 'an entertaining excur-sion into an aspect of everyday life that you might be taking for granted'. *Think Again* tackles a wide range of subjects, explaining how everything works from the publishing industry and financial markets to the national grid with Ball managing to be both upbeat and jokey, but also clear and concise; a true leading light of factual entertainment.

Raiders of the Lost Ark

Harrison Ford, his stock high following two stints as Han Solo in *Star Wars*, takes on the role of archaeologist-adventurer Indiana Jones in *Raiders of the Lost Ark* which opens in UK cinemas on 30th July. Armed with his fedora and bullwhip, Indy is on a quest to find the Lost Ark of the Covenant before the Nazis do and has to negotiate various obstacles on the way: a pit of vipers, unfriendly bandits and a rumbling boulder relentlessly pursuing him through a cavern.

Time Bandits

Terry Gilliam invites fellow Pythons, John Cleese and Michael Palin, to join him as he directs this time travel fantasy, in which a boy finds himself slipping through time and space in the company of a gang of dwarfs who are using a stolen map to steal treasures. They bump into Robin Hood, Agamemnon, and Napoleon along the way.

The Art of Darts

Darts game show Bullseye begins on ITV on 28th September, with Jim Bowen as host. With audiences of 20 million *Bullseye* serves up many a head-in-hands moment.

Postman Pat

Everyone's favourite postman makes his screen debut on 16th September. As well as delivering mail to the residents of Greendale, the community-minded *Postman Pat* helps to solve their daily dilemmas and problems, ably assisted by his faithful black and white cat, Jess.

Language, Timothy!

The BBC1 sitcom *Sorry!*, first broadcasts on 12th March, with diminutive Ronnie Corbett as Timothy Lumsden, a mild-mannered librarian in his forties, browbeaten by his domineering mother (Barbara Lott) into permanently living at home. Timothy's attempts to find a girlfriend and make a life for himself are repeatedly thwarted by mummy while his father, equally under the thumb, occasionally issues a stern, 'Language, Timothy!' from behind his newspaper, usually as a result of mis-hearing his son. *Sorry!* continues for seven series and by the final episode in 1988, when Timothy finally finds happiness with girlfriend Pippa, Corbett is fifty-seven years old!

Donkey Kong

Nintendo release the arcade game *Donkey Kong* in July. After Nintendo's *Radar Scope* (their answer to Space Invaders) failed, it is the firm's first global success and rescues them from financial ruin.

Chariots of Fire

'The British are coming' announces Colin Welland in his acceptance speech after winning the best screenplay Oscar for *Chariots of Fire*. The film wins four Academy Awards in total, including best picture and best soundtrack for Vangelis's unforgettable, swelling electronic theme song. A true story of two remarkable men and their rivalry at the 1924 Paris Olympics, this uplifting piece of period perfection is guaranteed to bring a lump to your throat.

Impulse buy

Impulse body spray, available in five different fragrances including 'Gipsy' and 'Hint of Musk', launches a memorable UK TV commercial this year, with a woman pursued through the streets by a man desperate to present her with a hastily purchased bunch of flowers, having caught a whiff of her magnetic scent, it's all because 'Men can't help acting on impulse.'

Ken and Deirdre get spliced

Jumping on the royal wedding bandwagon, Ken Barlow and Deirdre Langton say 'I do' on *Coronation Street*, on 27th July, two days before Charles and Di. Viewers, all 21 million of them, are amazed to see Deirdre without her trademark saucer-sized specs for once.

Cats opens in West End

Andrew Lloyd Webber's (photo) musical, *Cats*, based on T. S. Eliot's *Old Possum's Book of Practical Cats*, opens at the New London Theatre on 11th May. The musical is revolutionary; it's sung-through, and performed partly in the round with a hidden orchestra so the audience are part of an immersive experience. Lloyd Webber mortgages his house to help fund the venture, a risk worth taking as *Cats* runs for 8,949 performances until 2002; a benchmark for a new brand of blockbuster musical.

The Fizz come first at Eurovision

The Eurovision Song Contest takes place in Dublin on 4th April with a win for the United Kingdom thanks to Bucks Fizz, and the song *Making Your Mind Up*.

Noele reaches a career crossroads
Noele Gordon has played Meg Richardson in ITV's *Crossroads* since it first began in 1964. When Central TV take over the franchise from ATV, they plan a revamp which includes ridding the show of Meg. When the announcement is made in June there is public outrage; Gordon has been voted favourite female personality by *TV Times* readers no fewer than eight times. She makes her final appearance on 12th November.

Stately homes and teddy bears
The adaptation of Evelyn Waugh's 1945 novel, *Brideshead Revisited* on 12th October is one of the year's television events. Jeremy Irons is Charles Ryder who while at Oxford befriends Lord Sebastian Flyte played by Anthony Andrews. Invited to stay at Sebastian's palatial family pile, Brideshead Castle, Charles is dazzled and seduced by the Flyte family and finds his life interwoven with theirs over the coming years. Filming the seven two-hour episodes took forty-two weeks in total.

MUSIC

Collins goes solo
9th February 1981 Genesis singer-drummer and all-round workaholic Phil Collins releases his first album, *Face Value*, so beginning a phenomenal solo career running parallel with the band. Intensely personal and melancholic in tone, most of the album's songs concern his recent divorce from his wife Andrea.

Lennon tribute
7th February 1981 The shock waves from John Lennon's murder continue. Written by John for his *Imagine* album in 1971, *Jealous Guy* is the song that the re-formed Roxy Music choose when asked to honour Lennon on a German TV show. Liking the result, they release the track and achieve Roxy's first and only UK No. 1 during March.

Antmusic
9th May 1981 Adam and the Ants confirm their status as the pop sensations of the moment with *Stand and Deliver*, a No. 1 for five weeks. Adam is art student Stuart Goddard who dresses in pirate gear and Native American face paint and has a signature sound combining tribal drums and Gary Glitter-like hollers. It's a potent mix adored by the colour-rich teen pop magazines like *Smash Hits* now starting to appear in newsagents.

MTV opens
1st August 1981 A media revolution begins in the US with the launch of cable channel Music Television (MTV), devoted to playing music. It's a whole new marketing medium for the music industry but the channel is at first almost wholly reliant on UK record companies for material, as US labels aren't yet attuned to the potential of the promo video. The result is a new 'British invasion' of acts who break through in the US on the basis of their videos.

Ross sets a record
14th May 1981 After saying goodbye to Motown Records by duetting with Lionel Richie on the film theme *Endless Love*, Diana Ross ends her 21-year association with the label by signing for RCA in a deal worth twenty million dollars - an industry record. The move pays an immediate dividend with a No. 4 UK placing for a revival of Frankie Lymon's *Why Do Fools Fall in Love*.

Ghost Town
11th July 1981 Never has a record been more chillingly timed than the Specials' *Ghost Town*, which reaches No. 1 just as widespread rioting adds to the all-round malaise that pervades early 1980s Britain. It's the last record that the Specials will make in the band's current form: Neville Staples, Lynval Golding and Terry Hall are poised to form the Fun Boy Three. In the chart at the same time is another Midlands band with a Jamaican sound and a sharp political message: Birmingham's UB40 with *One in Ten*, about the ten per cent who now make up the unemployed in the UK.

Marley is dead
11th May 1981 Bob Marley, the great creative force in contemporary reggae and a peacemaker between warring factions in his native Jamaica, dies of cancer aged 36. After being diagnosed with a melanoma in his right foot he refused to have it amputated because of his Rastafarian beliefs. The cancer spread to his brain, lungs and liver. He is given a state funeral in Jamaica on 21st May.

Ballet spruce
16th August 1981 Out of the Blitz club in Covent Garden come Spandau Ballet, formed by brothers Gary and Martin Kemp. A feature on TV's *20th Century Box* launches them as a 'new romantic' band, as important for the styles they wear - anything from kilts to loin cloths - as the synth-led dance music they play. With Tony Hadley's trained voice giving them real distinction, the Spandaus reject punk gloom and embrace the lure of fantasy and dressing up. The funky *Chant No. 1* cements the band's rise.

Whole lotta Shakin' goin' on

28th March 1981 For many years Shakin' Stevens and his band the Sunsets were the hottest draw on the UK's rock'n'roll revival circuit playing Elvis. Now the Cardiff-born singer is at No. 1 with a brilliant rockabilly-style re-creation of the 1950s Rosemary Clooney hit *This Ole House*.

MY FIRST 18 YEARS
TOP10 **1981**

1. **Labelled with Love** *Squeeze*
2. **New Life** *Depeche Mode*
3. **Don't You Want Me** *Human League*
4. **In the Air Tonight** *Phil Collins*
5. **Being with You** *Smokey Robinson*
6. **Celebration** *Kool and the Gang*
7. **Bette Davis Eyes** *Kim Carnes*
8. **Kids in America** *Kim Wilde*
9. **I Go to Sleep** *The Pretenders*
10. **Once in a Lifetime** *Talking Heads*

Open 🟢 | Search 🔍 | Scan 📷

Electro magnets

For a long time synthesisers were just a prog rock thing, but cheaper technology and the advent of the Roland drum machine in particular have changed the game. Allied to a showy 'new romantic' look, the electro sound is everywhere in the early 80s, whether in the hands of singer-plus-synth duos like Soft Cell (*Tainted Love*), Tears for Fears (*Mad World*) and Yazoo (*Only You*) or bands with a more art school bent like Sheffield's Heaven 17 and Human League. Some like ABC and Depeche Mode (photo) embrace the whole pop experience while others like Ultravox remain a bit aloof. The failure of the latter's somewhat pompous *Vienna* to shift Joe Dolce's novelty hit *Shaddup Your Face* from No. 1 is treated in some quarters like a national scandal.

Julio on the ball

5th December 1981 Once a promising young goalkeeper for Real Madrid, Julio Iglesias turned to singing when a car accident ended his football career. He now brings a whiff of old style tuxedo-and-bow-tie glamour to the UK chart with an ice-cream smooth chart-topping version of *Begin the Beguine*, written by Cole Porter in 1935.

League of their own

11th December 1981 Human League score the year's top-selling single and a Christmas No. 1 with *Don't You Want Me*, a really clever combination of a great pop break-up pop song, a synth-led soundtrack and a film noir-style video.

SPORT

Streaking for England

On 2nd January, during an international rugby match between England and Australia at Twickenham, Erika Roe runs onto the pitch and strips off her top and bra, much to the appreciation of the half-time crowd. Hustled off by police who cover her assets with a flag and helmet, the incident - described by the BBC as 'perhaps the most famous of all streaks' - makes front-page news.

Rebels suffer cricket ban

Fifteen English cricket players are banned from international cricket for three years, as a penalty for a 'rebel' tour of South Africa currently in progress.

Feel the burn

Jane Fonda's Workout video sparks a new craze for aerobics, women's fitness - and legwarmers - as Jane takes a rapidly growing fan base of keep fit devotees through routines to tone and hone, telling us to 'Feel the burn' and 'No pain, no gain'.

Disappearance of Mark Thatcher

12th January 1982 Mark Thatcher, son of Prime Minster Margaret Thatcher, is officially declared missing after a four-day loss of contact during the Paris-Dakar Rally. Missing somewhere in the Sahara alongside his driver and mechanic, a large search is launched by the Algerian military who finally locate him two days later, 31 miles off course.

ESPAÑA 82

'The Best England Team That Never Won'?

England arrive at the World Cup in Spain with a line-up that includes Bryan Robson, Ray Wilkins, Kevin Keegan, Terry Butcher and Trevor Francis. England look like the team to watch during the group stages, beating France 3-1 in an inspired first match. They win the group but are next drawn against title holders West Germany and then Spain. Both matches are a draw; a missed header from Keegan against Spain is blamed on his perm softening the power of his attack. Despite scoring six goals in the tournament, conceding just one and not losing a match, England are knocked out and head home.

---

26 JAN 1982

UK unemployment figures reach 3,000,000 for the first time since the 1930s.

12 FEB 1982

George Davis opens the first Next clothing store. By the end of July, there are 70 branches around the country.

4 MAR 1982

The Barbican Centre is opened by the Queen after 11 years of construction and budget-blowing £153 million.

Watson wins Open double

American golfer Tom Watson becomes only the fifth man to win both the US and British Opens in the same year amongst the challenging bunkers at Royal Troon on 19th July.

A golden Commonwealth Games

The Commonwealth Games take place in Brisbane from 30th September to 9th October. Great Britain's gold medal tally is 38, one behind Australia.

First papal visit to UK

28th May 1982 Pope John Paul II becomes the first reigning Pope to visit the UK. Drawing crowds of thousands, his 'Pope-mobile' transports him around nine cities where he delivers speeches and open-air Masses.

DOMESTIC
NEWS

DO YOU REMEMBER THIS?

VHS video recorder

Collapse of Laker Airways

5th February 1982 Laker Airways succumbs to increased competition and strategic behaviour in the aviation industry when it collapses leaving 6,000 passengers stranded. The airline's owner, Freddie Laker, sues 12 airlines for conspiracy, reaching an out of court settlement of $50 million.

Israeli ambassador shot

3rd June 1982 The 1982 Lebanon War breaks out after the attempted assassination of Israel's ambassador to the UK, Shlomo Argov. Attending a banquet at the Dorchester Hotel, Argov is seriously injured. He never fully recovers, remaining in hospital until his death in 2003.

Falklands War

2nd April 1982 War breaks out after the invasion of the Falkland Islands by Argentine forces. The British Falkland Islands government surrenders and the British surprise many from around the world by immediately dispatching a Royal Navy task force to recover the islands. Over the next the three months the public are gripped by events such as the sinking of the *General Belgrano*, HMS *Sheffield,* and HMS *Coventry,* and the *Battle of Goose Green*. The war lasts 74 days and ends with the surrender of Argentine forces at Port Stanley. 255 British and 649 Argentine lives are lost in the conflict.

2 APR 1982

Britain breaks off diplomatic relations with Argentina.

12 MAY 1982

The *QE2* leaves for the Falkland Islands

30 JUN 1982

Crimewatch begins on BBC1, aiming to highlight unsolved crimes and enlist the help of the public by asking for information.

20 pence coin introduced

9th June 1982
Further changes to the currency are made when the new 20 pence coin is introduced with 740 million minted in the first issue. The new coin is a heptagon, and features a crowned Tudor rose on the reverse.

Hyde and Regent's Park bombs

20th July 1982 Two bombs planted by the Provisional IRA explode in central London. One bomb, in Hyde Park, targets mounted soldiers of the Household Cavalry regiment the 'Blues and Royals'. Four soldiers and seven horses are killed when a car bomb explodes as the soldiers ride past. Two hours later, a second bomb in Regent's Park explodes beneath a bandstand where the band of the Royal Green Jackets are performing to a large crowd. Seven bandsmen are killed, and across both attacks a further 51 people are injured.

Last telegrams sent

30th September 1982 The closure of the UK Inland Telegram Service means the UK says goodbye to the telegram, a mode of communication in use for over 100 years.

Mary Rose raised

11th October 1982 The wreck of Henry VIII's flagship, the *Mary Rose*, is raised from the Solent after its discovery in 1971. The wreck is moved to a dry dock at the Portsmouth Historic Dockyard; a special museum opens to display the extraordinary artefacts discovered with it.

Droppin Well bombing

6th December 1982 A bomb planted by the Irish National Liberation Army explodes at a disco known as Droppin Well in Ballykelly. Many people are wounded and seventeen are killed, eleven of them British soldiers from the nearby barracks who were known to frequent the disco.

ROYALTY & POLITICS

Riding with Reagan

The Queen invites US President Ronald Reagan and First Lady Nancy Reagan to stay at Windsor Castle. Reagan and Her Majesty go riding together in Windsor Home Park on the morning of 8th June; it is clear they have bonded over their shared love of horses.

Stranger danger

Early in the morning of 9th July, an unemployed North London labourer manages to break into Buckingham Palace and find his way to the Queen's bedroom undetected, where he appears with a bottle of wine found in the royal cellar. The Queen keeps calm and talks to the intruder until a maid and her page discover the situation and are able to raise the alarm.

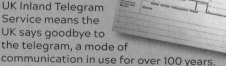

19 JUL 1982

After admitting to a homosexual affair, the Queen's bodyguard, Michael Trestrail, resigns.

30 AUG 1982

St. David's Hall opens in the heart of Cardiff as a national concert hall for Wales.

22 SEP 1982

Prime Minister Margaret Thatcher arrives in China for talks over the future of Hong Kong.

G

A midsummer prince is born

On 21st June, Prince Charles drives his wife to the Lindo Wing of St. Mary's Hospital where at 9:30pm she gives birth to a 7lb 1 ½ oz baby boy. Emerging from the hospital, Charles is greeted by chants of 'For He's a Jolly Good Fellow' and tells waiting reporters that he and Diana were still discussing names. Prince William Arthur Philip Louis, who is second in line to the throne, is christened at Buckingham Palace on 4th August.

FOREIGN
NEWS

Climate change

1st January 1982 An alarming report by US researchers Atkins and Epstein shows that sea levels have risen by eleven centimetres since 1940. The reason: in the same time, 50,000 cubic kilometres of ice have melted at the North and South Poles. Sea level rise provides hard evidence that the Earth is warming.

Pope stabbed

12th May 1982 Less than a year since the last attempt on his life, Pope John Paul II is the intended victim of another attack. At the shrine at Fatima, a Spanish priest opposed to the Pope's reforms stabs him with a bayonet and is overcome by guards. The Pope is slightly injured but not in mortal danger. The priest is jailed for three years and excommunicated.

A new music medium

17th August 1982 Soon after the first commercially available compact disc player, the Sony CDP-101, is launched, the first CD goes on sale. It is a 1979 recording of Chopin waltzes played by the Chilean pianist Claudio Arrau.

Commodore 64

With more than ten million copies sold, the Commodore 64 is the best-selling personal computer in history. The computer consists of a thick keyboard with 64 kilobytes of RAM underneath and a cassette port for loading games and professional software. It surpasses many more expensive competitors with its flexible hardware and great sound.

H

Computer virus

30th January 1982 The first computer virus is found on a private PC. The Elk Cloner Virus is written during a winter vacation by fifteen-year-old student Richard Skrenta. It embeds itself via the floppy into the operating system, from where it copies itself onto every floppy inserted in the floppy drive.

2 OCT 1982

Popular Birmingham comic, Jasper Carrott, moves to the BBC with a new, live show called *Carrott's Lib*.

NOV 1982

The government announce that 400,000 houses have been purchased under its right-to-buy scheme.

15 DEC 1982

Gibraltar's border with Spain is opened after thirteen years.

Diet Coke

According to Coca-Cola, women drink too little of its brand, so the soft drink giant devises an attractive variant for those who are thinking about dieting: Diet Coke. The light version comes a full eighteen years after rival Pepsi launched Diet Pepsi and contains the sweetener aspartame instead of sugar, good for only thirteen instead of 142 kilocalories per can.

Princess Grace dies

13th September 1982 Princess Grace of Monaco, the former movie actress Grace Kelly, suffers a stroke while driving near her home. She dies in hospital the next day, aged 52. Over 400 dignitaries attend her funeral including Diana, Princess of Wales.

:-)

19th September 1982 At Carnegie Mellon University in Pittsburgh, a student prank prompts discussion about the limits of jokes. Computer scientist Scott Fahlman proposes labelling all messages on the digital notice board. If something is intended as a joke, you mark your message with :-). If the remark is meant to be serious, you add :-(to your message. The first emoticons are born.

Andropov replaces Brezhnev

10th November 1982 The death of Soviet leader Leonid Brezhnev is announced. His successor is KGB head Yuri Andropov who remains in post for fifteen months before his own death paves the way for Mikhail Gorbachev to take over.

ENTERTAINMENT

Bling *Dynasty*

Shoulder pads at the ready. *Dynasty* first airs on BBC1 on 1st May. The super-rich Carringtons of Denver, Colorado, headed by patriarch Blake Carrington (John Forsythe) have made their money in oil. Sound familiar? ABC creates the Aaron Spelling-produced *Dynasty* as a direct response to the success of CBS's *Dallas*, serving up supersize helpings of glitz, glamour, feuding, cat fights, bed hopping and preposterous storylines. The soap has moderate success in its first season, but the dramatic entrance of Joan Collins as Blake's first wife, Alexis, gives Dynasty a boost and by the mid-80s, it's a ratings winner. Despite the camp and melodrama, this is a show that puts older women centre stage, all while dressed to the nines by Nolan Miller. Quite simply, *Dynasty* is the show that defines the excess of the 1980s.

Bladerunner - beautiful dystopia

Widely recognised as a masterpiece of science-fiction cinema, *Blade Runner*, directed by Ridley Scott, is first shown in the UK at the Edinburgh International Film Festival in August. Set in a dystopian Los Angeles of 2019, Harrison Ford is detective Rick Deckard, searching out 'replicants' - androids masquerading as humans - while unwittingly falling for one (Sean Young). Scott's jaw-dropping sets show a future that is bleak but also beautiful.

Dear Diary

The Secret Diary of Adrian Mole aged 13 and ¾ by Sue Townsend is published on 7th October. Adrian's daily ruminations not only reveal his innermost thoughts about his love for posh Pandora, his parents' marriage breakdown or the pain of trying to cover his Noddy wallpaper with black paint, but also act as an amusing guide to the early 1980s as he shares his views on the royal wedding, the Falklands War, Margaret Thatcher and Selina Scott.

Rambo

Vietnam veteran John J. Rambo is on the run from the law and fighting his demons in *Rambo: First Blood*. Sylvester Stallone, pumped up and oiled, co-writes and stars in this box office smash, which inspires one of the easiest fancy dress outfits of the 1980s. Headband, check. Sweaty vest, check, A toy machine gun and round of ammo check. *Rambo* opens at UK cinemas on 16th December.

Feeling blue

The Smurfs, the little blue people in Phyrgian caps created by Belgian artist Pierre 'Peyo' Culliford, have become a global phenomenon, with the film, *Smurfs and the Magic Flute* released in the UK in 1979, a hit song with Father Abraham in 1977 and 32 million collectible figures sold in 1981 alone.

Fame

'Fame costs, and right here's where you start paying - with sweat.' So goes the stern warning from Debbie Allan in the opening credits of *Fame*, the TV series based on the 1980 film in which Allan played dance teacher Lydia Grant. First broadcast on BBC1 on 17th June, for several years in the 1980s, thousands of UK teenagers wish they were students at the New York School of Performing Arts alongside Leroy, Doris, Bruno et al, where spontaneously breaking out into dance routines or belting out a heart-rending ballad at the piano seem a natural part of the daily timetable.

Gizza job

At the time *Boys from the Black Stuff* is shown on BBC2 between 10th October and 12th November, there are three million unemployed in Britain, making Alan Bleasdale's powerful drama a timely parable on the human cost of economic policy under Margaret Thatcher. A group of men, once part of a tarmac crew ('the black stuff') return to a Liverpool in the grip of industrial decline, to find the only jobs available are illegal and cash in hand.

Channel 4 launches

On 2nd November Channel 4 launches, with an ambitious menu of programmes. Quiz show *Countdown* (photo) has the honour of opening proceedings and continues as a mainstay of the channel for the next 40 years. A new soap, *Brookside*, set in a cul-de-sac of a modern housing estate in Liverpool, promises juicy, issue-led storylines considering it's the creation of Phil Redmond, best-known for *Grange Hill*, and on 5th November, a young bunch of comedians star in an Enid Blyton spoof, *Five Go Mad In Dorset*, under the name, *The Comic Strip Presents...*, among them Dawn French and Jennifer Saunders.

The Tube

Anarchic music programme *The Tube* broadcasts live from Tyne Tees studio in Newcastle for the first time on 5th November. Jools Holland, who is lead presenter with Paula Yates, later recalls of their audition, 'The TV people said we were hopeless but they couldn't stop watching us.' It's chaotic but cool, with an eclectic line-up every week from big names to new acts.

Scumbag students

Alternative comedy explodes onto screens on 9th November on BBC2 with *The Young Ones*. Written by Ben Elton, Rik Mayall and Lise Mayer, the action is set in the squalid flat of four Scumbag College students, violent punk Vyvyan, downtrodden hippy Neil, a self-important Rik (who worships Cliff Richard) and cool, calm Mike. It's a sitcom in the most anarchic, surreal and often puerile sense of the word.

Gandhi

Richard Attenborough's twenty-year quest to tell the on-screen story of Mohandas Kharamchand Gandhi finally comes to fruition with the release of *Gandhi* in cinemas on 3rd December. Ben Kingsley went full method in taking on the lead role; losing weight, and even learning to spin cotton. Attenborough too cut no corners in this epic, three-hour long film that uses authentic historical locations and hundreds of thousands of extras. *Gandhi* wins eight Academy Awards including Best Picture, Best Director for Attenborough and Best Actor for Kingsley.

The Sloane Ranger Handbook

The Official Sloane Ranger Handbook by Peter York and Ann Barr of *Harper's & Queen* magazine becomes a bestseller this year. Mildly self-deprecating but hugely amusing, the manual offers rules for wannabe and established Sloanes,

an upper-class species found roaming around Chelsea and Fulham or at home counties shooting parties. They're the types that wear pie crust collars, pearls, and Hunter wellies; who consider a crash in the Land Rover to be a mere prang, but the wrong shade of blue on a Tuesday to be an utter disaster. High priestess of this cult is Princess Diana, who features front and centre on the cover of this arch observation on a peculiarly British phenomenon.

Quatro

Fruity canned fizzy drink Quatro is launched this year claiming its place as a soft drink to define the decade with a TV advert where the tropical beverage is formulated in an arcade game-style vending machine, operated by a dude with a mullet. Quatro's fizz goes flat eventually, and it is discontinued in the UK in 1989.

A Touch of Glass

In the 2nd December episode of *Only Fools & Horses*, Delboy and Rodney take on a job in a country house cleaning chandeliers. Nothing ever goes smoothly where the Trotters are concerned, and this is no exception. The smashing climax becomes one of the sitcom's best-loved moments.

Walking in the Air

A Christmas tradition is born on Boxing Day this year when Raymond Briggs's 1978 illustrated book *The Snowman* is brought to life in an animation directed by Dianne Jackson for Channel 4. The

combination of Briggs' illustrations together with a score by Howard Blake (including *Walking in the Air* sung by St. Paul's Cathedral choir boy Peter Auty) makes *The Snowman* one of television's most timeless and magical festive treats. The following year, *The Snowman* has the added cachet of an introduction by none other than David Bowie.

E.T. phone home

E.T.'s strange but appealing appearance was apparently created by superimposing the eyes and forehead of Einstein onto a baby's face. Steven Spielberg's sweet extra-terrestrial proves not all aliens are out to get us in this charming film, released 13th August, which has the world repeating E.T.'s plaintive request, 'E.T. phone home.'

MUSIC

Ozzy's year
20th January 1982 Assuming it's made of rubber, Ozzy Osbourne bites into a live bat thrown from the audience at a gig in Des Moines, Iowa. But it's not the worst thing to happen to him this year: in March, a light aircraft in which his lead guitarist Randy Rhoads is a passenger, clips Ozzy's tour bus and crashes. Rhoads, his pilot and another passenger are killed. More happily, Ozzy marries Sharon Arden in Hawaii on 4th July.

Olivia gets *Physical*
23rd January 1982
Olivia Newton-John's *Physical* spends the last of ten weeks at No. 1 in the US - the longest chart-topping run since Elvis Pres-

ley's *Hound Dog* in 1956. It's a big switch of pace for the singer whose fame went up another level with the film *Grease* in 1978. A change of image sees her dressed in Jane Fonda-type aerobics gear (dig those legwarmers) in a curve-accentuating video and singing of, well, physical pleasures.

Goodbye to the Monk
17th February 1982 Jazz piano legend Thelonious Monk, known as the High Priest of Bebop, dies in New Jersey aged 64. His compositions included *Round Midnight* and *Straight, No Chaser*. His most famous saying was 'The piano ain't got no wrong notes.'

Doobies disband
31st March 1982 The Doobie Brothers, America's leading west coast band after the Eagles, announce their break-up. Formed in 1970, their *Listen to the Music* and *What a Fool Believes* remain all-time radio classics.

Rocking the Casbah
24th May 1982 One of the few original punk bands still espousing radical politics, the Clash release *Combat Rock* just as Topper Headon leaves the band and Joe Strummer returns from a mystery disappearance. It includes Clash classics *Rock the Casbah* and *Should I Stay or Should I Go*.

Get the Message
1st July 1982 Released today, *The Message* by Grandmaster Flash and the Furious Five is a genuine milestone. One of the first true hip hop records from a genius of the turntables, it breaks new ground with a portrait of inner-city life that's full of tension and fury.

Celtic soul
7th August 1982 Dexy's Midnight Runners lead man Kevin Rowland fashions a complete change of image - all dungarees and sandals - for the band to tie in with the release of new album *Too-Rye-Ay*. The single *Come On Eileen* harks back to Rowland's Belfast roots while the music is a hybrid that he calls 'Celtic soul', mixing blues rhythms and highly non-trendy folk instrumentation. Can anyone remember the last time an old-fashioned fiddle was heard on a No. 1 single?

Mad about the Boy

23rd September 1982 For UK parents, the sight of Boy George singing *Do You Really Want to Hurt Me* with Culture Club on *Top of the Pops* is one of those classic 'Is it a girl or a boy?' moments. Playing in

a reggae-cum-soul style, Culture Club is another band to emerge from the Blitz club, the cradle of London's 'new romantic' scene. George explains that the band's name reflects its mixture of cultures - a gay Irishman on lead vocals, a black Londoner on bass, a white Englishman on keyboards and a Jewish drummer.

Pass the... what?

2nd October 1982 How did a song about passing round a marijuana joint make it to No. 1 - and in the hands of Musical Youth, a five-piece band from Birmingham whose members are all under eighteen years old? The answer is that they changed the letter 'k' in *Pass the Kutchie* to 'd' and explained to the press that a 'dutchie' was a Jamaican serving dish.

Marvin reborn

20th November 1982 After leaving Motown and moving to Belgium for tax reasons, Marvin Gaye emerges rejuvenated with *Sexual Healing* from the album *Midnight Love*. Returning to the erotic themes of his *Let's Get it On* period, he jump starts his career and wins his first Grammy award.

MY FIRST 18 YEARS
TOP10   1982

1. **I Don't Wanna Dance** *Eddy Grant*
2. **Fame** *Irene Cara*
3. **House of Fun** *Madness*
4. **A Town Called Malice** *The Jam*
5. **Love Plus One** *Haircut 100*
6. **Planet Rock** *Afrika Bambaataa*
7. **Poison Arrow** *ABC*
8. **Centerfold** *J. Geils Band*
9. **Save a Prayer** *Duran Duran*
10. **The Model** *Kraftwerk*

Open 🟢 | Search 🔍 | Scan 📷

Jackson heights

1st December 1982 Michael Jackson's *Thriller* hits the stores. Continuing his collaboration with producer Quincy Jones and songwriter Rod Temperton, it is set to

top the chart in every country of the world and will become the biggest selling album of all time - 45 million copies and counting by 2024. No fewer than seven singles will be extracted from it including the title track, which is supported by a thirteen minute video directed by John Landis and featuring a red jacketed Michael dancing with a horde of zombies.

Weller splits the Jam

11th December 1982 The Jam play their final gig at Brighton Conference Centre, then disband. It is Paul Weller's decision and bassist Bruce Foxton will not speak to him for twenty years. The band bow out with a last No. 1, *Beat Surrender*.